MW00883640

LYING WONDERS

OF THE

RED PLANET

EXPOSING THE LIE OF
ANCIENT ALIENS

S. DOUGLAS WOODWARD

FOREWORD BY L.A. MARZULLI

Other Books by S. Douglas Woodward

Are We Living in the Last Days?

Decoding Doomsday

Black Sun, Blood Mood

Power Quest, Book One

Power Quest, Book Two

Co-authored with Douglas W. Krieger and Dene McGriff

The Final Babylon

LYING WONDERS

OF THE RED PLANET

Exposing the Lie of Ancient Aliens

S. Douglas Woodward

FAITH HAPPENS

OKLAHOMA CITY

LYING WONDERS
OF THE RED PLANET:
EXPOSING THE LIE OF ANCIENT ALIENS

By S. Douglas Woodward

Published by Faith Happens
Oklahoma City 73142

www.faith-happens.com

Please contact the author at: doug@faith-happens.com

All pictures are public domain unless noted. Images of books, movies, and other media are considered fair use.

Photographs of Mars are considered public domain and used for educational purposes.

Scripture is cited from the King James Version of the Bible unless otherwise noted.

Printed in the United States of America

ISBN-13: 978-1494762360

ISBN-10: 1494762366

Table of Contents

i

Table of Figures

To our friends
Patricia, Rain, and Kristofer Miljain

Your constant love, prayers, and hard work
in our ministry are indispensable
to its many accomplishments

Acknowledgements

This book was greatly helped by so many friends who have encouraged its creation and cheered me on to its completion.

It came together very differently from anything that I have written. Half of the book was written concurrently with the previous book, *The Final Babylon*. My partners in that effort, Douglas W. Krieger and Dene McGriff were patient with me, allowing time to work on this effort even while we labored together in researching, writing, and continue to promote *The Final Babylon* right up to this day. Both gentlemen have been great partners.

Additionally, thanks to my friend L.A. Marzulli who facilitated writing much of *Lying Wonders of the Red Planet* as a "serial" release of sorts, printing it within his monthly online magazine. The discipline of creating monthly articles, all with a connection to how Mars has contributed to Ancient Alien theory, made it easier to produce this volume. He also graciously agreed to write a thoughtful foreword to this new book. His friendship and interaction have meant much to me and added a valued perspective on the material presented here.

My friends at Prophecy in the News have offered many constructive insights. I was blessed to have an audience with Gary Stearman and Bob Ulrich on numerous occasions during the past year to discuss many aspects of Ancient Alien theory, eschatology, transhumanism, and the perilous direction of our culture. Of course, Bob always contributes great ideas on how to structure an appealing book, cover suggestions, and marketing.

I continue to receive support from various friends who serve the family of God by the conduct of interviews. These events yield new insights, ideas, and encouragement. Here I'll just mention first names since some folks have "stage names" and I don't want to smoke anyone out: Derek, Stan, Gonzo, Basil, Natalina, Kristen, Stacy, Daniel, Doug, Rob, Josh, and others that I have overlooked, thanks to you too, though you remain nameless.

Thanks go out also to many of my well-spoken "fans" and eschatological buddies who took the time to look at draft covers and read the introductory material to supply much needed input.

Thanks to Denis Burgess for volunteering to proofread. You caught a lot of typos and wrong words. Still, given my numerous proclivities to torture the King's English, I take full responsibility for anything that slipped through your capable correction. It was a big price you paid just to get to read the book before everyone else! Still, I hope you found the time spent worthwhile. Stay warm there in Alaska.

A special thank you to my anonymous science friend who read an early draft of the book and caught a number of scientific inaccuracies. Your knowledge of rocket science, many of the characters mentioned in the world of interplanetary travel, and common sense (more erudite than common), all played a constructive part in this book's presentation. Once again, no doubt there are a number of other scientific misstatements still present. I wrote a good part of the book after your review. All blame lies with me.

A written shout out to my new friends in New Zealand, Mike Goodman and his contingent there. Let me know what you think of the book! I will be watching my email for your feedback.

Finally, a heartfelt thanks to my family, especially my wife, for putting up with my flights of fancy on this topic, listening to me talk about Mars much too often, and believing that there are people out there who care enough about this subject to buy a book devoted to its many far-reaching issues for humankind.

Foreword
by L.A. Marzulli

S. Douglas Woodward's new book, *Lying Wonders of the Red Planet,* is a must read and here's why. Woodward manages to cram an incredible amount of vital information between the covers of this book. He hits key aspects of most every important topic regarding the burgeoning UFO phenomena in what may become a researcher's go-to guide for UFOs, ET and whether intelligent life ever existed (or exists today!) on Mars.

You'll be intrigued and informed as Woodward weaves a spellbinding web touching subjects like Wernher von Braun's link to Walt Disney, the connection between the great pyramids of Giza and the pyramids on Mars, an ongoing cover-up by NASA regarding ET, and how Darwinian evolution jumps to hyperspace in an atheistic, naturalistic attempt to explain life's origin! Woodward posits that if ET travelled millions of miles to get here, "Why doesn't he give us the cure to cancer instead of telling us Jesus really wasn't God?" His arguments stand out in the same ballpark with famed UFO researcher Jacques Vallée, that these entities—wherever they are from and whoever they are— seem to be aligned more closely with demonic entities we encounter throughout the Bible than anything from outer space.

Lying Wonders will also take you into the dark world of the occult workings of Jack Parsons and the satanic rituals he performed in order to open a gateway or portal for the people of earth into what I call the second heaven (the dwelling place of the Fallen Angels). Did "opening" this demonic gateway act as a springboard for UFO phenomena? Likewise, are people entering into altered states of consciousness to make contact with so-called ET entities? If so, then does this shatter the myth that these entities are from somewhere else in the universe? Or does it just reinforce the concept that they are, in fact, inter-dimensional and not really from the stars and planets nearby?

Lying Wonders reveals the fascination of our forebears with the possibility of life on Mars, going back to before the twentieth century, and how this captured the public's imagination, even though the so-called "canals" (first discovered by Pietro Secchi in the 1870s) were barely more than lines on a sketchpad. He reintroduces us to astronomers Percival Lowell and Camille Flammarion and their penchant for the paranormal. Woodward reminds us of the forgotten radio chatter between Tesla, Marconi and "the Martians" in 1901 leading up to the irrational panic of listeners to Orson Welles' broadcast of *War of the Worlds* in 1938.

He then leaps forward to present day and reveals what Vatican astronomers like Jose Funes have been up to as they seemingly embrace ET as "our space brother!" Next, he updates the ongoing fight between the experts concerning what NASA's Mars photographs tell us about supposed "artifacts" on the Red Planet. He explores the meaning of ancient megalithic structures from across the globe like Peru's *Puma Punku*, and Turkey's *Göbekli Tepe* questioning whether they bespeak advanced technologies in the same vein as what researcher Richard C. Hoagland conjectures exist with the "monuments of Mars" at Cydonia. And then he recaps the amazing biblical assessment of the late David Flynn.

So what lies at the bottom of this dark well of Orwellian drama? The idea that ET created intelligent life on this planet— that the human race was genetically manipulated by extraterrestrials for their purposes, and that we owe civilization itself to ET's initiative. And now, at this critical juncture, they stand ready to return, to usher in a time of peace, prosperity and enlightenment—a new golden age for humankind—what Woodward and I unashamedly declare constitutes *The Coming Great Deception!*

You're in for quite a ride, so dig in. And after you've finished the final page, I'm sure you'll want to keep your night light on!

L. A. Marzulli
Author, Lecturer, and Host of The Watchers!

Preface

The Ragged Genesis of Ancient Alien Theory

The era of pulp fiction predates most of us. From before the turn of the nineteenth century (1896) to the emergence of television in the 1950s, pulp magazines were the rage of popular culture. Science fiction got its start within this widespread medium, although at first the genre wasn't known by that label.

Instead, it was initially tagged *scientific-tion, an awkward name coined* by pulp publisher Hugo Gernsback. Gernsback founded and edited a particular pulp magazine that survived the era and helped define it—*Amazing Stories*. As the adjacent cover of the April, 1926 edition of *Amazing Stories* highlights, *this pulp fiction magazine* featured stories from the likes of H.G. Wells, Jules Verne, and Edgar Allen Poe—names of which no doubt the reader is most familiar.

Figure 1 –Cover of *Amazing Stories* April, 1926

Pulps' preferred publishing formats were "novellas"—long short-stories or short-novels, *you pick*—and serialized versions of longer works. Good examples would be H.G. Wells' *The Time Machine* and Isaac Asimovs' *Nightfall*.

These raggedy but remarkable periodicals were nicknamed *pulps* since publishers employed cheap wood pulp paper in their production, released them without trimmed edges, and sported no interior pictures or any other "eye-candy." Just plain ol' pulp. All they had in common with "the slicks"—the traditional polished periodical—was the glossy color cover. Back in the Twenties and Thirties, pulps sold for ten to twenty-five cents. Quite a bargain for entertainment in those days.

Many starving authors, in particular one thinks of the brilliant H.P. Lovecraft, made a thin-living by writing for "the pulps." The periodicals *Amazing Stories*, *Argosy*, *Detective Stories*, and *Weird Tales* (for whom Lovecraft wrote) were among 400 other pulps published monthly at the height of the craze. Without "the pulps", short stories might not have flourished to the extent they did and science fiction might not have gotten off the launching pad. A great pulp edition could sell a million copies. No wonder fabulous writers like Lovecraft were attracted to this pop media format.

Parodies of Martian Literature

Lying Wonders of the Red Planet, is my seventh book (sixth writing solo). My cover (I do them all myself—I'm a frustrated artist!) recalls the provocative cover art of pulp magazines—a style meant to grab attention and compel the customer to plop down a quarter of a dollar without giving a second thought.

Additionally, as with the works by great science fiction authors (Lovecraft, Asimov, Ray Bradbury and even earlier adventure authors like Edgar Rice Burroughs—one thinks of his popular series on civil-war-hero-cum-Martian explorer, John Carter), the lion's share of this book was published in serial form. Spanning the last twelve months, I wrote most of the chapters initially as articles for LA Marzulli's "eMagazine:" *Politics, Prophecy and the Supernatural.* You will see some traces of the serial nature of this writing as there is a bit of duplication from time to time.

I hope that will not be a distraction but rather will allow you, the reader, to jump to the subjects of most interest without worry you will lose the flow of the book. My only caution would be the save the final four chapters until the end. These chapters were written after completing the serialization effort and created especially for this book. However, whether appearing in original form in the Marzulli Magazine or here for the first time, all deal with the "amazing stories" of Mars and its relationship to today's burgeoning cult of Ancient Aliens Theory, promoted so favorably and in my opinion, unfortunately (because there is no counterpoint) by Prometheus Entertainment and the History Channel.

With each article, I explain how fantastic claims about extraterrestrial influence has been the stock and trade of Mars' enthusiasts for more than a century. In fact, the Red Planet has been the subject for all kinds of sensational assertions—for almost 150 years—shaping popular thought and breeding all manner of cultic expression. I chronicle these incredible accounts which blend science, spiritualism, space exploration, and the paranormal.

Now understand *I believe only a few, if any, of the contentions within any specific subject taken up here.* I do not intend to convince you these amazing stories are true—just that countless people have believed them to be so—and what they believed *adds to what is so amazing about them.* The fact that some of what I describe *is* true, only heightens the mystery and suspense.

Why Christians Must Address Ancient Alien Theory

On the other hand, I am not a full-on skeptic either. Nor do I dismiss today's Ancient Alien Theory with a disparaging sigh or shrug like a disinterested historian. No, I take seriously the challenge of "space cults," "extraterrestrial visitation," and the belief that "life originated first on other worlds" (known today as The *Panspermia Theory*—a sort of outer space pollination process)—that dates back to Anaxagoras (Aristotle's teacher) in the fifth century BC, and in modern times to Swedish chemist Svante Arrhenius circa 1903.

Along with many other Christian authors today, I share the perspective that Ancient Aliens Theory stands as the primary candidate destined to compose a mesmerizing mess—an unwholesome concoction of you-know-what, about which Christian eschatologists have long warned civilization. For almost 2,000 years, Bible prophecy pundits have admonished disciples of Jesus Christ that there will be a final great deception promulgated by the man of sin, the Antichrist, along with the help of his False Prophet. Informed students of Bible prophecy know this deception as "The Lie." It will be so illusive, so distorted, but nonetheless so compelling the whole world will be led astray.

Furthermore, there comes a time when the Lord God of heaven and earth allows all humankind to be "given over" to THE LIE. In effect, the Spirit of Christ stops striving with our species to restrict the work of The Adversary who seeks to capture the hearts and minds of humanity. What will happen when this restraint is taken away? The Apostle Paul gave us an earful about this frightening and imminent moment. With a "full disclosure" of a biblical sort, he sternly warned us to beware:

> *7 For the mystery of lawlessness (that hidden principle of rebellion against constituted authority) is already at work in the world, [but it is] restrained only until he who restrains is taken out of the way.*

> *8 And then the lawless one (the antichrist) will be revealed and the Lord Jesus will slay him with the breath of His mouth and bring him to an end by His appearing at His coming.*

> *9 The coming [of the lawless one, the antichrist] is through the activity and working of Satan and will be attended by great power and with all sorts of [pretended] miracles and signs and delusive marvels—[all of them] **lying wonders**—*

> *10 And by unlimited seduction to evil and with all wicked deception for those who are perishing (going to perdition) because they did not welcome the Truth but refused to love it that they might be saved.*

*¹¹ Therefore God sends upon them a misleading influence, a working of error and a **strong delusion** to make them believe what is false,*

¹² In order that all may be judged and condemned who did not believe in [who refused to adhere to, trust in, and rely on] the Truth, but [instead] took pleasure in unrighteousness. [(2 Thessalonians 2:7-12 (shared here from *The Amplified Version*). Note: parenthetical comments in the original of *The Amplified Version*]

Finally, these "signs and lying wonders" (a phrase used more than a dozen times in the New Testament), will be so astounding that, if it were possible, even Christ's disciples—His elect—would be utterly deceived (see Matthew 24:24, Mark 13:22). If we who espouse this hypothesis are correct, that Ancient Alien Theory comprises "THE LIE' of the Last Days" (and we're quite sure it does), it constitutes nothing less than a doctrine of demons coming straight from "The Pit." In other words: since the stakes couldn't be higher for humanity, we had better understand what trouble is brewing right here, right now, in River City.

Mars Mythology and Ancient Alien Theory

But there is more.

I advance the thesis that Mars stands as a dominant bright red thread woven throughout a bizarre tapestry leading to this climactic moment in which we live. Indeed, I venture that Mars will play a key part in the deception (indeed, as will be chronicled here, it already has). For more than a century, millions have been led astray. Like lemmings, millions more are ready to follow.

In the "grand scheme of things," what is the meaning of Red Planet? *Mars stands as an icon of humanity's desire for godhood and immortality apart from the God of Jews and Christians.* I propose what may yet be uncovered on Mars will provoke an even greater apostasy, a total falling away or departure, from the truth as told in scripture, what my friend L.A. Marzulli calls the "cosmic chess match" that characterizes the underlying story arc, if you will, of the entire Bible.

Because I affirm the infallible inspiration of the Bible, I contend that humankind seeks an explanation for its origin and purpose other than what the God of the Bible declares. In effect, Mars represents humanity's rebellious creed, an affirmation that we weren't created in the image of Yahweh—but in the image of that challenger who has and still seeks our worship.

At this very moment the contest has reached a fever pitch. The anointed cherub Lucifer, who once *"walked amidst the stones of fire"* (Ezekiel 28:14)—those brightly burning wandering stars we know as the planets—contends with Yahweh over the eternal destiny of all men and women. In context of the human species (at least since the time of Adam forward), given its brilliant red color, Mars has created the greatest curiosity, apprehension, and mythology among ancient humanity of all heavenly bodies (save perhaps the Sun). However, such myth-making thrives even today among both the scientifically enlightened and those less so, but all of whom should know better.

We saw this with the effusive language of cheerleader for all-things-astronomical, the late but still noteworthy Carl Sagan, who recognized that the meaning of Mars to humanity goes far behind the mere quest to explore. In his 1980 best-seller *Cosmos*, he opined: *"Mars has become a kind of mythic arena onto which we have projected our earthly hopes and fears."* True enough. But keep in mind: when you dismiss God from the arena we call Life, mysteries like the mythology of Mars rush to fill the void.

Indeed, the "whole truth" transcends Sagan's sanguine assessment. By providing the incredible history before you—so chock full of those amazing stories about the secrets of Mars (stories which their advocates ardently believed)—I hope to help you "read between the lines" to discern humanity's most earnest yet misguided motive. For beneath our fascination with the Red Planet lurks the quest for divine enlightenment that will initiate the apotheosis of humanity, a "transformation into gods" that humankind's religions have sought since time immemorial.

Finally, a Personal Note

On a personal note, writing this book has been a delight. I have enjoyed the research and I hope that you, the reader, can sense the enthusiasm I feel for the subject. I anticipate you will discover value on many fronts as well as pure reading pleasure, even while you learn about the *most amazing stories*—our apprehensions, our accomplishments, and our future hopes—that the Red Planet has inspired.

S. Douglas Woodward
Oklahoma City
January, 2014

Lying Wonders of the Red Planet

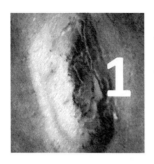

Ancient Aliens, Antichrist, and the One World Religion

The Paucity of Hope in America

As the twentieth century came to a close, America was flexing its fiscal muscles. For the private sector, times were good. Economically, America enjoyed budget surpluses and low levels of unemployment. Wall Street was soaring. America's corporations were hitting on all cylinders.

On the other hand, the Public Sector could have been better. Hillary and Bill left the White House downcast after the Monica Lewinsky affair, making uncertain the lasting legacy of President Clinton. America inaugurated a new Republican President (Bush the Younger) only after it had been determined he had a few less "hanging chads" than Democrat Al Gore. The lack of a decisive vote in the 2000 election created a constitutional crisis that a Supreme Court decision and a gracious Al Gore finally settled.

Likewise, the prognosis of America's spiritual health was not particularly encouraging. Mainline churches were losing members left and right while altruistic faith-based institutions (George H.W. Bush's "thousand points of light") sputtered along too, often hampered by scandal. By any stretch, faith in the Society's institutions was hardly hitting the high water mark.

Bucking the trend, however, were numerous non-traditional evangelical "mega-churches." Buttressed by their "gospel of prosperity" (a good believer is a *wealthy* believer), promoting a positive message (bad things happen because of *bad attitudes*— so be upbeat!), and recasting the gospel so it would be "seeker friendly" (preaching *agin'* sinning hurts attendance after all), many Americans' notion of God grew more loving as their view of evil's reality dissipated. A "neo-evangelical" faith was born.

3

Cynical talk-show hosts and opinionated media moguls combined efforts to reset values about right and wrong, passed judgment on good and bad religion, and challenged the old-fashioned view of God (who reserved the right to punish the guilty and hold all humanity accountable to His rules). Since the horrific terrorist strikes were quickly judged an aberration of fanatical monotheists (not a symptom of humanity's fallen state), the spiritually inclined sought a more placid and accommodating sense of divine presence. No, the God of Abraham, Isaac, Jacob, (and even Jesus) should be purged of any vestiges of extreme ideological predispositions or unappealing, apparently dour, and surely ungracious behavior. Religious belief should spur us to good deeds, not fear or guilt. Never mind that this was an age old heresy Christianity weathered in the second and third centuries.[1] Americans, especially "new-agers" and mega-church evangelicals had found this moralistic, vindictive God of the Old Testament most lacking in our day too. The transcendent "god without" was replaced with the less accusatory and usually mollifying "god within."

Of course, who in their right mind (except those obscurantist fundamentalists) would argue otherwise? At least not in public. Clearly, our progressive culture and its need for an alternative god-concept mandated this deity makeover.

In 2008, an enchanting new President emerged who had the audacity to hope government would solve societal problems. His enthusiasm enlivened politics as a potential savior and caused many to hope that this well-spoken and handsome young lad would revitalize America. With his spirited leadership, he would

---

[1] Known as the *Marcionite* heresy, named after *Marcion*, its teaching proposed there were two gods... an evil God of the Old Testament—a most irascible , grumpy old chap—and the good God of the New Testament, portrayed by Jesus. Professor at both Oxford and Cambridge, Henry Chadwick called Marcion "the most radical and to the church the most formidable of heretics." See-http://alexklimchuk.wordpress.com/2010/09/16/famous-heretics/.

help us forget the inarticulate George "W," bank failures, economic crisis, quashed retirement funds, high unemployment, and the downside of runaway debt caused by quantitative easing. Wall Street was fingered as Public Enemy #1, deserving stiff penalties and demanding stronger regulations. If it couldn't be fixed, perhaps it should be "occupied" until it was shut down. Health care for everyone would surely make things right in our nation. Visions of government grandeur twinkled in the eyes of socially-minded up-and-comers convinced that publically funded programs would fix what ailed us.

Alas, six years later, this optimism has been all but dashed. As we move into 2014, the capacity of politics to make things better and the charming ways of our latest president have both proven unworthy as a certain place to pin our hopes. Like all other Federal regimes, this one has hardly proven immune to scandals, decisions made behind closed doors, and attacks on its enemies with unlawful use of power. Despite derision and threatened action targeting the excesses of investment banks, no one went to jail, demonstrating who really held all the cards. In the summer of 2013, an unfortunate series of events for the Administration snow-balled. IRS scandals broke, the Edward Snowden affair disclosed we were spying on our allies, and proof became undeniable that Big Brother really was watching. Indeed, given the revelations of the National Security Agency's (NSA) "blanket eavesdropping" on our cell phones and web queries, many concluded this edition of the Federal Government sought to restrict personal liberties even more than its Republican predecessor.

Who could have predicted that? And yet, never has the emergence of the police state seemed more probable than it does now. Critics had labeled the Administration *socialist*. But recent disclosures suggest it should be more accurately termed "national socialist." Whether true or not, the ranks of the disheartened and disillusioned swelled during 2013. Yes, the audacity of hope was too bold to come true. So now where should we place our hope?

On Our Own

Given this state of events, it seems reasonable to ask, reluctantly I might add, "Does America stand at the same crossroads as Europe was one hundred years ago?" Then, a battle weary and downtrodden Europe looked for new leadership, no longer trusting in monarchies. Instead, it elected a new regime who heeded the German philosopher king from four decades earlier, Friedrich Nietzsche, an iconoclastic author who boasted that "God is dead" and man must make his own way. Old mores and values must be discarded. Humanity must choose its own principles by which to guide its individual and social behaviors. God is irrelevant—only humanity answers the roll call. What Nietzsche meant by his notion of the *Übermensch* was precisely this: Mankind stands alone. Therefore, we must shoulder all responsibility. *We shall overcome*—but without the help of God. Better to leave Him entirely out of the picture. The lesson for us lest we forget: this was the philosophy behind Adolf Hitler—this perspective manifested the spirit of Antichrist in its ugliest incarnation.

Has America adopted the same *weltanschauung* as Germany did in 1923? It is understandable why we might conjecture the only way to carve a path through the jungle—to chart a new course—amounts to bald self-reliance. And if our "selves" are not up to the task, maybe it is time we improve upon our circumstances with the knowledge of how to make our race stronger, better, and more resilient to the existential limitations we face. Maybe the only answer for human nature is to transcend our nature altogether. This was part of the plan of the Third Reich. Science and technology stood apart as THE source of hope. The pending promise of transhumanism, to alter our DNA that is, might just be the best and only real answer to our dilemmas. We do not know what the future holds—*but only we hold the future.*

From this authors' perspective, should we come to that conclusion, we best beware for we have forsaken the Bible's teaching regarding our sacred identity as image bearers of God. We forsake our birthright. By concluding we were NOT created in God's image, we choose to be transformed into the image of God's enemy. In a biblical cosmology, these are the only two choices. If we reject that cosmology, that worldview, that weltanschauung, we proclaim there exists no ontological necessity for good and evil.[2] That is, we deny good and evil are *realities* in our universe. And therein lies the greatest peril: *Any society that denies evil stands ready to enthrone it.*

Nietzsche's call for humanity to remake God into man's image, to dismiss the notion of real good and evil, may appeal to the intellectual who overrates his or her place in the world, but it lacks appeal for the common man. Despite the skeptic's enduring challenge to question God's existence, humanity cannot quench its innate thirst for its maker: humankind will not accept the finality of an atheistic, materialist (i.e, *naturalist*) answer. There has to be a reason why we are here—there has to be someone out there who cares what happens to us. There must be someone mightier than we who made us what we are. Even if humanity ardently argues it has outgrown the need for God, it never stops looking for someone bigger than itself to explain why it exists. Such a quest comprises one of its most primal and persistent urges. We may alter our DNA, but the lesson learned from the Frankenstein monster still holds true: we will strive for our maker's affirmation.

Indeed, we persevere in our belief that God exists, although it does now appear humanity has been conditioned to dramatically alter its creed regarding the identity of this deity and how we relate to him (or, as it were, "THEM"). This affirmation—that our Creator and Nurturer *comes* from the stars rather than being *the One who made them*—is the Great Deception of the time in which we live, a time this author believes constitutes "the last days" before Jesus Christ returns to this earth. It is the final world religion.

---

[2] Ontology is the study of existence or the nature of being. An ontological necessity would mean that a "thing must exist by the nature of its definition."

A New Spin on Religious Programming

Despite being a bit disheveled, belief in spiritual realities remains alive and well. The casual observer might not recognize the nature of spiritual yearning in today's world since it appears disguised in all manner of technology-enhanced video, high-definition multi-media graphics, and über-visual production values. Nonetheless, if we delve into the meaning of the burgeoning social phenomena associated with the highly strange and paranormal, we uncover that humanity still seeks the divine—albeit in odd places. To be specific, affirmations of faith show vivid signs of life in unexpected quarters. We see these creeds embedded in a few, formerly odd, but now successful television shows which captivate the masses. In this respect, no drama spellbinds us more than the TV quasi-documentary, *Ancient Aliens*.

Produced by Prometheus Entertainment, *Ancient Aliens* has contributed mightily to the success of Cable TV's History Channel. From its website we read:

> Established in 1999, Prometheus Entertainment has been a leader in supplying critically acclaimed, highly-rated programming to the cable marketplace. The company has produced nearly 500 hours of dynamic and diverse television for clients such as History, A&E, E!, WEtv, Travel Channel, Bravo, Animal Planet, Lucasfilm Ltd., National Geographic Channel, AMC, Warner Bros—and more.

Just how successful has *Ancient Aliens* been? Quite successful. It just completed its fifth season and its producers have created a spinoff series. Debuting in 2014, *In Search of Aliens* will feature the usual crew of *Ancient Aliens* with Giorgio A. Tsoukalos (that guy with the crazy hairdo—formerly publisher of the now defunct *Legendary Times Magazine*), and Erich von Däniken—the infamous although mildly charming author of the cultural phenomenon, *Chariots of the Gods?* (1968). Due to its popularity, *Ancient Aliens* and Prometheus Entertainment are arguably the primary reasons the History Channel created a second cable channel, called simply "H2". *Ancient Aliens* was moved to H2 a couple of years ago (and *In Search of Aliens* will follow it there), no doubt to form the nucleus of its programming strategy as well as guarantee high ratings to attract advertisers.

So it is that sensational television has a new golden child. Cosmic wonders, UFOs, and the mysteries of ancient civilizations combine to advance extraordinary extraterrestrial credos. Not only does it make for great television, the programming provides fascinating answers to ultimate questions.

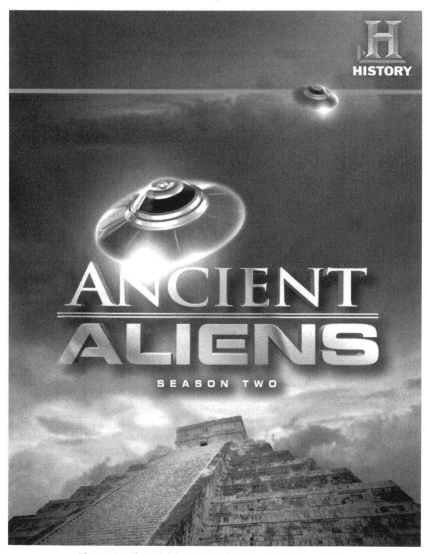

Figure 2 - The Highly Successful *Ancient Aliens* Series

Thanks to *The History Channel* and Prometheus Entertainment, spiritual themes have been reintroduced to the public, pandering to our covert quest to understand where we come from. These techno-affirmations of faith ring true to many, thanks to both state-of-the-art media magic and a thorough baptism of pseudoscience. Who says we don't like to watch religious programming on television?

As if their affront to traditional faith was not flagrant already, these same producers just recently (late 2013) brought forth *Bible Secrets Revealed*, an intentionally misnamed and ultra-misleading assault on orthodox perspectives of Bible truth. Oy vey. Based upon its name alone (*Prometheus* was the mythic Greek god who, with Aphrodite, fashioned humankind from the clay), we should have known where its producers were taking us.

Ancient Alien Programming Not All That New

However, today's popular preoccupation with alien astronauts and unexplained archeology revisits the same phenomenon from the 1970s (we will later see, even from 100 years prior).

Figure 3 - The 1973 Television Series, *In Search of Ancient Astronauts*

Not long after Erich von Däniken published *Chariots of the Gods?* a German movie was made in 1970 with the same name. Then an American version followed in 1973, retitled *In Search of Alien Astronauts*. The US movie was so successful that in 1975, Alan Landsburg created a three-part TV documentary, also named the same, which ran on NBC hosted by his friend Rod Serling.

Like the current craze, the story featured inexplicable archeological artifacts from around the world. This documentary was so popular it spawned a series *"In Search of..."* that ran from 1977-1982. Before the successor series launched, unfortunately, Serling would pass away. Leonard Nimoy, no longer trekking about, took over the helm as narrator. Von Däniken went on to write over 25 books and the Cult of Ancient Astronauts had been thoroughly seeded in the modern American audience. [3]

Certainly contributing to the cultivation of the notion were the books of Graham Hancock. Hancock proposed that there was no need to bring extraterrestrials into the equation. Instead, Earth once gave rise to ancient civilizations with advanced technologies that were lost after a series of cataclysms. His 1995 book, *Fingerprints of the Gods*, echoed the concepts of nineteenth-century author Ignatius Donnelly, who claimed that the artifacts of Egypt bespoke the connection to a not-so-mythical Atlantis, which was the progenitor of all ancient civilizations. The so-called Lost Continent bequeathed to humanity advanced technologies in architecture, astronomy, and mathematics. The Pyramids of Giza were the prime example. The purpose and capability of the mysterious pyramids far exceeded mere tombs for dead Pharaohs or monuments to their celestial gods.

Perhaps it was nine seasons of the very popular X-Files series (1993—2001) on FOX Television that catalyzed interest in UFOs, alien abduction, and the highly strange. At its peak, X-Files built an audience of over 18 million viewers.

Then there are the discussion forums that also contributed to the hunger for paranormal programming. In particular, we should make mention of the call-in talk radio show *Coast to Coast AM* which frequently featured supernatural themes and

---

[3] In the mid-nineties, the show was rebroadcast on A&E and garnered a number of fans. But other fiction programming and new names were to burst on the scene expanding the research and increasing the speculation of Alien Astronaut theorists.

experts (both real and self-described) drawing over three million listeners every day before the crack of dawn.

Figure 4 - Talk show of the Paranormal, Coast to Coast AM

Beginning in 1984, the program was hosted by the outspoken Art Bell and years later by the more soft-spoken George Noory. Bell argued *Coast to Coast AM* peaked as his time with the program came to a close. Furthermore, according to Bell, Noory ruined the program because he refuses to challenge the positions and views taken by his guests—many of which are beyond the pale, or as we say today, "over the top." Noory counters that the program serves as a forum for the eccentric, a forum that would otherwise not exist, as these voices would otherwise not be heard. Apparently, his listeners agree since the program continues undaunted. But regardless of who was hosting, *Coast to Coast AM* played no small part in catapulting Ancient Astronaut Theory back into the public's consciousness once again. [4]

Where Did the Theory Get Its Start?

Nevertheless, by definition the "Ancient Alien Theory" links *extraterrestrials* with *pre-history*. Generally speaking, ancient alien theorists distinguish and keep separate modern-day sightings of UFOs from discussions of ancient artifacts they claim prove the visitation of alien astronauts in yesteryear. However,

---

[4] Moreover, the program continues to offer up the opinions of fringe authors as well as genuine explicators of the extraordinary. One thinks of theoretical physicist Michio Kaku as a prime example of the genuine expert. Frequent guest, Richard C. Hoagland (about whom we will say much) represents "the fringe."

when it is time to give credit to where credit is due, ETs—not humans—must be regarded as the originators of inexplicable achievements from Giza to Baalbek to Chichen Itza. After all, we surely know ancient humanity was not clever enough to accomplish such marvels. At least that is what our history teachers said.

Figure 5 - Ignatius Donnelly

Anthropologist, writer, and researcher Jason Colavito has written a series of books exploring this subject matter. In his book, *The Cult of the Alien Gods*, he provides a history of how the theory was first advanced in the nineteenth century. He cites the work of Ignatius Donnelly (1831-1901, a Minnesota congressman with diverse interests to say the least), and his book on Atlantis as the genesis of modern day Ancient Alien Theory:

> *Atlantis: The Antediluvian World* set the tone and tenor for all subsequent books on alternative histories. It was all here: the ancient mysteries, the cross-cultural comparisons, and the outrageous claims that similarities across cultures were the work of those from the Outside, since the natives were never believed to be intellectually capable of advanced culture.[5]

Colavito continues:

> Though he seems to think little of Greek religion, Donnelly provided the seed for an important aspect of the ancient-astronaut hypothesis: that the gods were not mental creations but were once flesh-and-blood creatures, moreover, flesh-and-blood creatures who represented a lost civilization, one of enormous technological development.[6]

---

[5] Jason Colavito, *The Cult of Alien Gods: H.P. Lovecraft and Extraterrestrial Pop Culture* (Kindle Locations 325-327). Kindle Edition
[6] Ibid., Kindle Locations 306-308.

Based upon their nineteenth-century "field work," Colavito points out that the archeologist Heinrich Schliemann (who excavated the ruins of Troy) and German biologist Ernst Haeckel (whose studies in the South Pacific led him to theorize the first humans were Polynesian),[7] contributed significantly to the view that our forebears were unnaturally advanced ancestors. They did much to prove that such epic cities as Troy were not just myths made up in the minds of folk historians like Homer, but were based on actual places and real people.

However, it was Madame Helena Petrovna Blavatsky (HPB) that generated the most interest in Atlantis and Lemuria as civilization's true origin. According to Colavito, it was the extravagant claims of HPB in her occultic magnum opus, *The Secret Doctrine* (purportedly channeled as a reprise of an ancient *Book of Dzyan*), which so upset one particular science fiction writer in America, H.P. Lovecraft, that he was motivated to compose a series of stories loosely based on mythical Atlantis (and its extraterrestrial connection). Colavito takes the position that Lovecraft's work hardly sought to endorse Ancient Alien Theory. He more or less meant to mock it. Lovecraft considered himself a "scientific materialist." Colavito states:

> Even after skeptics debunked her [HPB's] *Book of Dzyan* as a fraud, her followers continued to assert its reality. One modern author wrote as late as 1970 that *The Book of Dzyan* was filled "with its sacred symbolic signs. No one in the world knows its real age.... For thousands of years this esoteric doctrine was guarded as top secret in Tibetan crypts." Even if the lost continent of Lemuria was disproved, the Secret Doctrine lived on. H. P. Lovecraft held pseudoscience in disdain, but he was happy to use Theosophy [HBP's subsequent creation] as a prop if it would help make his fiction deeper and more meaningful. That the society embraced the concept of a lost sunken continent could only bolster interest in Lovecraft's own sunken world.[8]

---

[7] However, more to the point: from the mythical land of Lemuria.
[8] Ibid., Kindle Locations 372-376.

Colavito's thesis asserts that Ancient Alien Theory begins with the science fiction of H.P. Lovecraft and its haunting, supposedly madness inducing ideas. Noted occult historian, Peter Levenda, in his newly released book *The Dark Lord* (devoted to Lovecraft and the connections to author Kenneth Grant and black magician Aleister Crowley) challenges Colavito's interpretation of Lovecraft in some respects as we will discuss toward the end of this book. However, in this instance Levenda essentially agrees with Colavito: "Lovecraft has his own idea about Aeons: that they represented enormous lengths of time, and that the contemplation of them (and what life-forms may have evolved during them) would

Figure 6 - Jason Colavito's *The Cult of Alien Gods*

drive a normal person insane, as would the contemplation of the vast distance of space between the Earth and the stars." [9] Lovecraft's principal work, *The Mountains of Madness*, hits upon themes that modern-day Ancient Alien theorists continue to echo—hieroglyphs at the South Pole, extraterrestrial beings living beneath the sea, and humans as pawns caught in the midst of cosmic wars. Lovecraft portrays humanity as an incidental organic substance that was cultivated, not as slaves to mine gold for the Anunnaki (those proposed other-worldly gods of the Sumerians as explicated by late Zecharia Sitchin[10]), but merely as foodstuffs for extraterrestrials.

---

[9] Peter Levenda, *The Dark Lord*, Lake Worth FL, Ibis Press, 2013, pp. 25.

[10] Sitchin's books (*The 12th Planet* leads the list) also contributed to Ancient Alien Theory. He has passed on but he left his imprint in such conspicuous places

Lovecraft was heavily influenced by H.G. Wells and Edgar Allan Poe. Colavito informs us that in his spare time—for pleasure—he read mysticism and pseudo-science. Eventually, he became a renowned master of horror—but not until well after his death in 1937. Otherwise, he was a starving artist of sorts. Colavito recaps Lovecraft's sad biography with these words:

> Born into a wealthy [Providence] family in 1890, Lovecraft's life was a series of reverses and declines as his family lost their fortune and his parents succumbed to madness...
>
> When he set about writing his own works, he began to blend the modern world of science fiction with his favorite tales of Gothic gloom. Lovecraft tried to bring the Gothic tale into the twentieth century, modernizing the trappings of ancient horror for a new century of science. Lovecraft published his work in pulp fiction magazines, notably *Weird Tales*, though some of his works were not published until after his death in 1937. Throughout the 1940s and 1950s, science fiction and horror magazines reprinted Lovecraft's tales numerous times, and he became one of the most popular pulp authors. Lovecraft's works banished the supernatural by recasting it in materialist terms. He took the idea of a pantheon of ancient gods and made them a group of aliens who descended to earth in the distant past.[11]

Colavito notes it was Lovecraft's work as well as the writings of Louis Pauwels and Jacques Bergier, that most influenced the books of Erich von Däniken. Pauwels and Bergier wrote their 1960 classic (one of this author's favorite books), *The Morning of the Magicians*, in which Pauwels and Bergier promulgated their theory of advanced but lost civilizations and their preference

---

as the movie, *Cowboys and Aliens (2011*—starring Daniel Craig and Harrison Ford*)*, as its plotline borrowed heavily from Sitchin's notion that the Anunnaki sought gold from our planet to supplement the depleted store on their home Niburu aka Planet X. Gold was needed to shore up their atmosphere (I cannot explain, so don't ask). Sitchin translated (more accurately interpreted) the many extant clay Sumerian tablets which tell tales of Earth's first civilization, and indicated that humanity was a slave race whose DNA was altered by the Anunnaki tens of thousands of years ago to make us capable of being better miners for their purposes. Sitchin is mentioned often in Ancient Aliens.

[11] Colavito, Jason (2013-03-21). *Faking History* (Kindle Locations 297-310). JasonColavito.com Books. Kindle Edition

for a preternatural alternative worldview (which sought to overcome the limitations of the "positivist"[12] nineteenth century perspective). In the book, they expressed their admiration of Lovecraft and another author of similar ilk, Englishman Arthur Machen (1863-1947).

For Colavito, who admits to being smitten in his youth by Ancient Alien Theory, following the thread from present-day Ancient Alien Theory back to the fiction of Lovecraft was an essential step to satisfy his eventual bewilderment over the matter of human origins and ultimate questions. Colavito references the analysis of Robert M. Price and Charles Garofalo from their 1982 book which speculated on the link between Lovecraft and von Däniken:

> They [Price and Garofalo] concluded that despite the high degree of correlation between von Däniken's evidence and claims and Lovecraft's fictional conceits, direct influence was impossible because von Däniken denied ever having read or heard of Lovecraft. As we have seen, though, the influence need not be direct. The connections between those who propose ancient astronauts as fact and those who write of them as (science) fiction are myriad, and the web of influence runs in many directions. Perhaps someday the Great Race will swap minds with some of us and tell the world how aliens once ruled the past, but until that happens, Cthulhu [Lovecraft's octopus-headed god with dragon's wings, the "boss" of the underwater world he depicted in *The Mountains of Madness*] will have to rest in his tomb and the ancient astronauts will have to stay in their fictional chariots.[13]

What is the best evidence von Däniken plagiarized his hypothesis from Lovecraft and later, Pauwels and Bergier? According to Colavito, it rests in the fact von Däniken paid a settlement that terminated a law suit initiated against him by author Bergier.

---

[12] Positivism dismisses questions of ultimate origins and focuses on observation only as a basis for truth.

[13] Robert M. Price and Charles Garofalo, "Chariots of the Old Ones?", in Robert M. Price (ed.), *Black, Forbidden Things: Cryptical Secrets from the "Crypt of Cthulhu"* (Mercer Island, WA: Starmont House, 1992), 86-87. Cited by Colavito in his book 2013 book, *Faking History* (Kindle Locations 545-552). JasonColavito.com Books. Kindle Edition.

In recapping, Blavatsky influenced Lovecraft. Lovecraft influenced Pauwels and Bergier. Pauwels and Bergier influenced von Däniken. And it was von Däniken's *Chariots of the Gods?* which set in motion Ancient Alien Theory from the 1970s to our present day. According to Colavito, however, without the fiction/horror writer Lovecraft, we might not enjoy the clandestine religion that masquerades as science we know as *Ancient Aliens*.

In summary, although he comes from the perspective of an atheistic naturalist, Colavito recognizes what this author does. *Ancient Aliens* conceals a powerful pseudo-religion. Colavito recaps his disdain for this grandiose deception and its proponents with this colorful but understandably disparaging assessment:

> The twentieth century version of the theory had argued that ancient gods were really aliens; its modern religious version [the twenty-first century variety] told Ancient Aliens' 1.5 million weekly viewers that the aliens were in fact their true gods. At least the Raëlians and Scientologists[14] had the courtesy to admit upfront that their ancient astronaut theories were alternative religions. Ancient Aliens' slipshod pseudo-scholars wrap their faux-religion in the borrowed raiment of science and appear to pray for a future when they will be granted their rightful place as prophets, or kings.[15]

So Where is Mars in Ancient Alien Theory?

However, Colavito's thesis actually overlooks a huge point—the primary reason this book has been written—that humanity's

---

[14] Readers will likely be familiar with L. Ron Hubbard, the one-time contributor (and possible spy for the U.S. Navy) who worked with Jack Parsons at JPL in Pasadena, who founded the controversial religion we know as Scientology. However, it is less likely readers are aware of Raëlism. Raëlism is a religion founded in the 1970s by Claude Vorilhon, a one-time French auto racing journalist. Vorilhon changed his name to Raël after an encounter with a deity traveling in a flying saucer. Raëlism extols Ancient Alien Theory as the true interpretation of Jewish and Christian religions. The story: Raël met a 25,000 year-old ancient astronaut named Yahweh who taught him about beings called Elohim. Especially novel: Jesus was resurrected through a cloning process (including the bringing forward of one's memory)—a means by which we all may seek immortality.

[15] Colavito, *Faking History*, op. cit., Kindle Locations 268-282.

views on the planet Mars have contributed in no small way to the development of Ancient Alien Theory, and will, in my estimation continue to drive the advancement of a final one-world religion.

My thesis is this: For almost 150 years, *Mars has been the primary catalyst within popular culture spawning false religions fabricated on the basis of belief in extraterrestrials.* Today other factors influence the theory, such as the burgeoning awareness of UFOs and countless dramatic sightings. *Nevertheless, I predict Mars will soon impact this phenomenon in a big way yet again.*

As the reader will notice in the chapters ahead, there is an entire genre of literary work, scientific investigation via space exploration, and popular commentary on said efforts, which contribute to the theory ancient aliens founded our civilization and nurtured humankind as their personal, high-priority project.

This material dovetails from several sources. First, there is literature penned from the 1870s forward by dozens of authors lured by the mysteries of Mars. This comprises a mountain of material—sometimes intended as fiction and sometimes not, as numerous authors claimed to be channeling the words of extraterrestrials or unashamedly supernatural beings. In other words, purporting to be fully factual, these writings contend they were paranormally communicated to the medium-cum-transcriber for our edification and posterity—not merely to publish for mammon's sake.

In his outstanding tour of two centuries of "Martian" literature, Robert Crossley confirms that the channeling of Martian material (de facto *travelogues* as he sarcastically notes) was taken seriously by many (both scientists and mystics), "back in the day:"

> Théodore Flour-noy, professor of psychology at the University of Geneva and a psychical researcher, published Des Indes à la Planète Mars (1899), his extensive case study of a Swiss medium who called herself Hélène Smith. Smith's supposed visionary experiences, manifested in her paintings of the Martian landscape, inhabitants, and artifacts and, centrally, in the Martian language that she

spoke and wrote, attracted the attention of linguists and psycho-pathologists, dream analysts and surrealists.[16]

Literature devoted to the Red Planet, whether intended as fiction or not, contributed significantly to the wonderment and speculation concerning extraterrestrial beings and their real or potential impact on our Earth. The best Mars' fiction books—H.G. Wells' *War of the Worlds* (1898), Edgar Rice Burroughs' *The Princess of Mars* (1917), C. S Lewis' *Out of the Silent Planet* (1938), and Ray Bradbury's *Martian Chronicles* (1950)—must be reckoned noteworthy along with important non-fiction books that, in their time, sought to educate the public on what was known and ventured about the

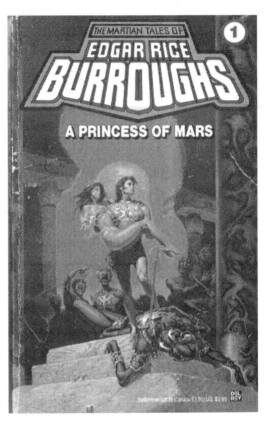

Figure 7 - Burroughs' *A Princess of Mars*

planet Mars. In this respect, a number of non-fiction titles come to mind: Percival Lowell's *Mars* (1895), Camille Flammarion's *The Planet Mars* (1892) and *Popular Astronomy* (1907), and even the much more

---

[16] Crossley, Robert (2011). *Imagining Mars (Early Classics of Science Fiction)* (Kindle Locations 3001-3005). Wesleyan University Press. Kindle Edition.

recent *Cosmos* (1980), by Carl Sagan, a book made to accompany the most-watched public television program of the 1980s.

When the twentieth century began—and for the next four decades—Mars captured the public's imagination. Mars was even the subject of various object lessons, be they personal for little children or political for society in general, to teach earthlings how to achieve utopia and why making war should be stopped. One could even write a chapter (although I didn't dare as it might estrange certain readers not as conservative as I), on

Figure 8 - Mariner 4 photos, a moon-like Mars?

Mars and Marxism, as many socialist authors shamelessly exploited the fascination most people held regarding Mars for an ulterior motive—to advance the cause of Marx and Lenin not long after the 1917 revolution in Russia.

It must be remembered that until Mariner 4 zipped past Mars in July, 1965 (providing pictures of a surprisingly "moon-like" surface peppered with craters both small and large), the general populace believed (as did many scientists), that Mars boasted life of no minor kind.[17]   Thus, combined with the afore-mentioned noteworthy literature generally pre-dating World War II, stands the remarkable (if not romantic) pursuit of post-1960s' photographic evidence from NASA's robotic Martian picture takers, fulfilling an insight by Ray Bradbury that "humans begin with the romantic and move to the realistic." Once scientists overcame the initial shock of a highly cratered surface (dashing the romance), closer inspection yielded optimism that life might have existed there. These images eventually led to a virtual consensus that Mars was inundated with water at some time in its past. Consequently, this developed into a more hopeful perspective that Mars once hosted life, ranging from the merely microbial to the mathematically-astute (although the latter club had a much smaller membership!)

A quick and admittedly over-simplified taxonomy of these spacecraft explorers follows:

- *Mariner* satellites from the 1960s (Mariner 4 being the first photo contributor with 22 close up pictures transmitted digitally back to Earth);

- *Viking* interplanetary travelers of the 1970s (the first Martian "rovers" that soft-landed, then meandered about albeit slowly,

---

[17] Much of this optimism owes to the fact Mars shares various intriguing planetary features with our Earth: almost the same tilt on its axis (around 22 degrees) and a Martian day that is barely shorter than an Earth day (a smidge under 24 hours). The fact it also had polar ice caps and green markings that changed with the seasons only made it more obvious for the optimists that Mars must be teeming with life! And then, there were those canals...

and ultimately overachieved their mission, as they lingered on the surface operationally sound for over six years);

- More recent orbiting cartographers (picture taking map-makers) like *Odyssey*; and finally...

- *Curiosity* (aka the much-larger *Mars Roving Laboratory*) that landed on Mars in August of 2012.

These marvels of modern science have generated tens of thousands of pictures over five decades—spawning no end of heated discussion and wild speculation as we will soon cover. In fact, the conversation addressing these fascinating photographs comprises a substantial portion of our study.

But our love affair with Mars isn't just from afar. There are those persons who claim first-hand perspectives. This features expert testimony of former astronauts (such as Buzz Aldrin, Edgar Mitchell, Gordon Cooper, et al) who, while not walking on Mars, have experience traveling into space, walking on our moon, and witnessing *UFOs* first-hand, as so many say. For it is not just what the Apollo astronauts have stated publicly, but what second-hand accounts purport they once said behind closed doors.

Then there are those who explore space through another very different means, what we now term *remote viewing*.[18] These personalities—Ingo Swann, Joe McMoneagle, Pat Price, and especially Ed Dames—represent a half-dozen or so names that pop up in books on the subject of "supernatural spying" and whose lectures on its history and usage are frequently featured in Internet videos. Although discounted by the scientific community, their accounts also amaze if not alarm, given their assertion about what they have seen with their "mind's eye." We will evaluate their contributions in short order.

---

[18] Remote viewers are mediums or channelers (though they may claim otherwise), that have proven themselves most useful to military intelligence since they were first put in place in the 1970s. The men and their techniques will be taken up later in this book.

Then there is the controversial matter of "contact." Remote viewers certainly have something to say about directly encountering extraterrestrials. But even famous scientists at the turn of the twentieth century, in particular Nikola Tesla and Guglielmo Marconi, were regarded as significant contributors to the evidence for intelligent life on Mars, thanks to their wireless inventions, the *radio*. Through periodicals, both daily and monthly, they publicly announced they had encountered intelligence from Mars using their wireless devices—although it is not clear which was regarded as more unexpected, intelligent life on Mars or wireless communications. As we shall see, their accounts, and the folklore that surrounded them, are most remarkable additions to our story.

However, the popular history of Mars is inextricably linked to the paranormal. The founder of Martian speculation in America, Percival Lowell, began his study of Mars in the 1890s while he was completing a trip to Japan where he researched and then published a study on the occult in the orient. Lowell eventually distanced himself from the combination, although many of his fans continued to intermix the subjects in their questions to him and comments on his work. (We must recall that *spiritualism*[19] amounted to no small segment of religious belief as the nineteenth century came to a close). Camille Flammarion, arguably the famous Frenchman before World War I (but after Napoleon Bonaparte's time), uncritically combined the subject of Mars with investigation into the paranormal. Although there is no evidence that he took a psychic excursion to the Red Planet, in Flammarion's day, "soul travel"—another name for "out-of-body experience" (OBE) or astral projection was considered by many to be a viable and even a proper pathway for pursuit of knowledge, despite its acquisition through unconventional means. Indeed, while many fiction authors worried about how to get their heroes

---

[19] *Spiritualism* is also known as *spiritism*—the belief in ghosts, crystal balls, and contacting the dead through mediums.

to Mars and back, fans of Edgar Rice Burroughs'[20] books (devoted to John Carter's Martian exploits), will recall that Carter more or less "willed" himself to Mars through psychic means, coming and going as he did from a most mysterious cave suffused with the artifacts of Indian shamans in the "Old West" (i.e., Arizona territory). The rigors of spaceflight were easier in those good old days.

Conclusion: Mars and the Meaning of Man

With the rationale for the book explained and a brief overview of selected highlights introduced, we now move on to the tell the colorful history of the Red Planet and its intoxicating effect on our culture; its many mysteries which have intrigued some of our best minds from the century just past; along with its *lying wonders*—which in the years ahead, both promise to enthrall and threaten to mislead once more.

This deception is not so much that intelligent life existed on Mars aeons ago—for this remarkable possibility may yet be proven true. No, the deception looms in misunderstanding what Mars ultimately teaches us about ourselves and moreover, who actually watches our world, and if you will, continues to "watch out" for humanity.

Figure 9 - Life and "Death" on Mars?

Dr. John Brandenburg, author of a daring study on ancient Mars, *Life and Death on Mars: The New Mars Synthesis*, presents the case for why life

---

[20] Burroughs would be remembered more for his works employing Tarzan.

once flourished there and why it vanished suddenly and cata-strophically. In closing his book, Brandenburg made this predic-tion: "Mars is close to yielding its great secret, and with it the se-cret of humanity's place in the cosmos."[21] Exactly so. Whether we discover the truth about Mars, however, or conclude something entirely false about the Red Planet, it will likely impact the human race in more ways than we can enumerate. Why is this so? *It will dramatically change what we believe about ourselves.*

In other words, the meaning of Mars squarely rests in what humanity decides about what *humanity's meaning is*, not just in relation to Mars but to the entire cosmos.

To draw out the implications of that assessment is the follow-ing series of pivotal questions to consider in the course of our study:

- Do we stand at the edge of a dark chasm facing an apocalyptic destruction of this world? Or are we on the cusp of experiencing an entirely new universe?

- Will we decide that ancient aliens were our forebears? Or that the presence of these supposed actors on the stage of human his-tory was just mythical, or worse—that their true nature was ac-tually darkly supernatural, i.e., *demonic and deceptive*?

- Will we liken Mars to a symbolic *stargate* which portends to transport us to a destiny apart from the God of the Bible? Or will we understand the cosmos as a reality in which a transcendent deity exists beyond it, who created it *ex nihilo*—out of nothing?

- Will humanity venture forth without regard for this God? Or will we accept the destiny for which the Bible says God created us—to one day enjoy a "new heavens and a new earth" remade without corruption and minus all effects of entropy[22], in which *"Eye hath not seen, nor ear heard, neither hath it entered into*

---

[21] John Brandenburg, *Life and Death On Mars: The New Mars Synthesis*, Kin-dle Locations 2258-2259), SCB Distributors, Kindle Edition. (2013)

[22] A law of thermodynamics which asserts that systems become more ran-dom, that energy is depleted, and perhaps that the universe is, to so speak, in a state of "winding down" or "running out of steam."

the heart of man, what things God hath prepared for them that love him." (I Corinthians 2:9)

Regardless of finding answers to these ultimate questions, Mars' contribution to the inexorable fabrication of worldwide religion comprises a fascinating tale in its own right. In stark contrast to the perspective of Lovecraft, humanity is not trapped hopelessly in the middle of a cosmic war—but is the very subject of that battle.

Hence, my goal here transcends creating an apologetic for the veracity of the Judeo-Christian cosmology and the spiritual reality from which it is drawn. The work before you celebrates the incredible imagination and creative genius of humanity. For as the late Christian intellectual Francis Schaeffer taught, even in our fallen state, there resides in us immense dignity and value. This ingenuity and imagination deserves a festive bit of prose to demonstrate that God was not unwise in creating this cosmos and placing within it intelligences capable of marveling at its design. Hopefully, this author is up to such a worthy task.

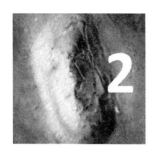

Mars and the Final Great Deception

Are the Pyramids of Mars and Egypt Linked?

O N JULY 25, 1976, *VIKING I* PHOTOGRAPHED THE MARTIAN RE-GION KNOWN AS THE *CYDONIA MENSAE* FROM AN ALTITUDE OF 1,162 MILES. LYING AT ROUGHLY 40° NORTH LATITUDE, AN image seemed to appear of what could be likened to a human face looking skyward. Known as photo F035A72 (the 35th image on the 72nd orbit—see the photo below), it was one of over 51,000 other photos taken during Viking's mission. Eventually other images

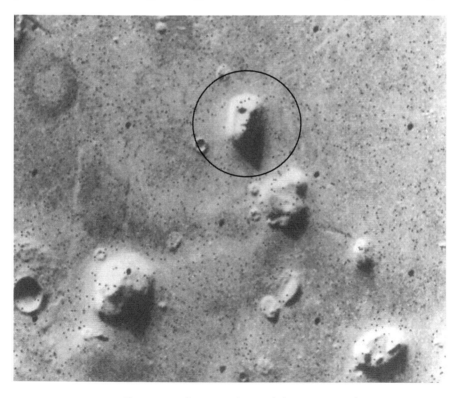

Figure 10 - The Face of Mars (Photo F035A72)

29

were found in NASA's stash which reaffirmed the facial likeness was not a simple "trick of light and shadows" (although NASA claimed it to be nothing more than that), resulting from a single angle of the sun's light.

By 1980, it was publicly admitted the images existed, but without confirmation that they were "artificial" (i.e., made by intelligent beings rather than natural processes). Richard Hoagland, a former consultant to CBS News and NASA, who with Mike Bara wrote a provocative tome entitled *Dark Mission: The Secret History of NASA*, stumbled across this issue in 1983 when working on a project related to Saturn's rings at Stanford Research Institute (SRI). Authors Lynn Picknett and Clive Prince commented in

Figure 11 - *Dark Mission* by Richard C. Hoagland and Mike Bara

their important book, *The Stargate Conspiracy: The Truth about Extraterrestrials and the Mysteries of Ancient Egypt* (1999):

> To Hoagland's eye there seemed to be a whole complex of pyramidal and other structures, covering an area of about 12 square miles. He excitedly termed it the "City". This appeared to be made up of several massive, and some smaller pyramids, plus some much smaller conical "buildings" grouped around an open space that he called the "City Square". In the north-east corner of the City was an enormous structure that appears to be made up of three huge walls, which Hoagland dubbed the "Fortress."

Figure 12 - Richard C. Hoagland

Perhaps the most significant assumption Hoagland made—and surely the one with the least justification on such slight knowledge—was his association of these features with Egypt. As soon as he discovered the City, Hoagland wrote: "I was reminded overwhelmingly of Egypt." He then went on to identify various other features in Cydonia: the "Cliff", a 2-mile-long wall-like feature near a crater 14 miles directly east of the Face; and several small (250—400-foot) objects dotted about the Cydonia plain that he called "mounds".[1]

Excited about the possibilities, Hoagland received a $50,000 grant in 1983 from SRI (Note: SRI has been a mainstay of federal government research on the paranormal) after a meeting conducted at the Study of Consciousness in Berkeley, California. Attending was former intelligence officer Paul Shay who was then SRI's president of corporate affairs. Importantly, a member of the team for the study included Lambert Dolphin Jr., the physicist who

---

[1] Lynn Picknett and Clive Prince, *The Stargate Conspiracy*, New York: Berkley Books, 1999, p. 122.

led SRI research teams at Giza, Egypt from 1973 to 1982. While not the first such incident, the members of this extraterrestrial search party connected "The Face" (soon to be declared by proponents of intelligent life on Mars, a sphinxlike monument with human and "lionesque" features) and the pyramidal complex in Egypt.

Picknett and Prince quote Tom Rautenberg, a social scientist who eventually joined the project team.

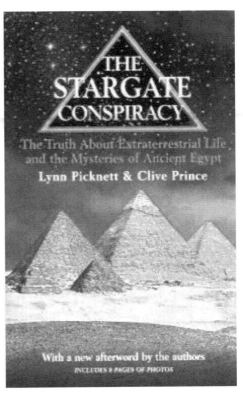

> "At first I thought it was some kind of a joke, or *maybe a complex social experiment being conducted by the CIA*—to study psychological reactions to such a hypothetical discovery. I mean—SRI involvement, "Faces" on Mars...? What would *you* think...? Was this an elaborate psychological experiment, sponsored by the defense community?" [Emphasis mine][2]

Figure 13 - The Stargate Conspiracy

What It Means When the CIA Gets Involved

Picknett and Prince assert the involvement of SRI in anything should set off the alarms, but when you combine this with CIA and Defense Department experiments (notably, the practice known as remote viewing), it is high time to wake up and discover what game is afoot.

---

[2] Ibid., p. 123, quoting Hoagland's *The Monuments of Mars*, p. 160.

First, there was their puzzling interest in Giza [to investigate new theories about the meaning and purpose of the great pyramids], "and now they were funding Hoagland's Mars Mission, after having sent Dolphin to Giza in the 1970s..."[3] After all was said and done, what did the study conclude? *That the structures were most likely artificial!* In other words, intelligent beings were behind the construction of these "buildings". Consequently, the study recommended efforts should be expended to return to Mars and evaluate the likelihood intelligent life once existed there. By its overt actions, the U.S. government was at the very least passively asserting an anti-biblical cosmology by inferring past alien existence on our neighbor Mars.

The consequences could hardly be more crucial. Quoting Hoagland from his book, *The Monuments of Mars*: "For it is now clear... that, if appropriately researched and then applied to many current global problems, the potential 'radical technologies' that might be developed from the 'Message of Cydonia' could significantly assist the world in a dramatic transition to a real 'new world order'... if not a literal New World."[4] Picknett and Prince observe, "In other words, Hoagland is implying that these putative [reputed] extraterrestrials actually created the human race, and this idea, odd though it may appear, is rapidly gaining currency throughout the world."

In 2011, the third season of *Ancient Aliens* on the History Channel is sure to please advocates of this theory and stands as proof that this new take on "where we came from" is endeavoring to provide an alternative worldview (or better yet, a cosmological view) opposed to the biblical depiction of humankind's origins. If ET were to phone home, would he be placing a call to Mars? Moreover, if humanity were to go looking for the bones of Adam and Eve, should they plan a space flight to the Red Planet?

---

[3] Ibid., p. 125.
[4] Ibid., p. 128, quoting Hoagland from The Monuments of Mars, p. 373.

The Evidence for Intelligent Life Now Extinct

Richard Hoagland and coauthor Mike Bara, in *Dark Mission*, attempt to prove that intelligent life once existed on Mars. In this assertion, like so many others involving the incredible, the devil is in the details—mathematic details that is. According to these authors, the "City" on the Cydonian plain shows all sorts of meaningful angles and tetrahedral shapes.[5] We should consider how probable their assertion that mathematics was employed in the way the various structures were "laid out" at Cydonia. For mathematics, once confirmed extant (existing), is an objective witness that intelligence was work.

Another popular "alternative history" author Graham Hancock, interprets the arithmetic inference with these words:

> Still, we cannot deny that the act of placing a tetrahedral object[6] on Mars at latitude 19.5° contains all the necessary numbers and symbolism to qualify as a "message received" signal in response to the geometry of Cydonia. Moreover, such a game of mathematics and symbolism is precisely what we would expect if NASA were being influenced by the type of occult conspiracy that Hoagland, for one, is always trying to espouse.[7]

However, Hancock actually reverses course in his book *The Mars Mystery* (1998) surmising that Hoagland's contention regarding an ancient civilization and its connection to Egypt has substance. He accepts both the reality of Cydonia's intelligent origin as well as its encoded mathematical message. Furthermore, he likewise agrees Cydonia is linked with the civilizations of ancient Egypt. Picknett and Prince critique this fanciful view asserting it is a case

---

[5] We will discuss the importance of this particular angle later. For now, it signifies a key geometry that hints at a gateway to "worm holes" and an alternative physics.

[6] Known as the simplest of the so-called Platonic "solids", this object consists of four equilateral triangles forming a four-sided pyramid—counting the "bottom" of the shape as a side. In a three-dimensional universe, such solids would be regarded as a universal language and a verification of intelligence

[7] Ibid., p. 325, quoting Graham Hancock from *The Mars Mystery*.

of circular argumentation (setting out to prove what you have already assumed to be true):

> The basic argument is that, because there are pyramids and a Sphinx in both Giza and Cydonia, the two are connected. But of course that depends on the Face on Mars being a Sphinx. The Cydonia clique describes it as being Sphinx-like; indeed, James Hurtak[8] was using such emotive language even before it was officially discovered... [Hoagland claims, that one] is "simian" in appearance, the other "leonine"—an anthropoid and a lion. The great Sphinx at Giza is a man's head on a lion's body. Conclusion: we have two Sphinxes—in close proximity with pyramids—on both worlds!"[9]

According to Picknett and Prince, acting in the spirit of the CNN's Anderson Cooper ("keeping them honest"), Hancock and frequent co-author Robert Bauval talk as if Hoagland's conjecture is scientifically proven. Indeed, looking at the face of Cydonia, it is easy for the imagination to get the best of one's faculty of sight and recognition, composing a fanciful portrait of something (or someone) that *really is not there.* This author wonders if it is not the case of one authority lending credibility to another by merely citing the same far-fetched view; and that akin to members of a cult reinforcing one another's beliefs—a form of fallacious reassurance—in which their absurdly held beliefs "must be true" because the group members all find it comforting to reassure one another they hold their most unusual perspective in common. When contrary evidence conflicts with their beliefs (aka Festinger's "cognitive dissonance"[10]), they disregard it out of hand. Subsequently, the "cause

---

[8] James Hurtak, an assistant to Andrija Puharich when The Nine was getting revved up in the 1950s, has become a leading authority on the connections between Mars and Egypt. Prior to the photographic evidence for a face on Mars, Hurtak remote viewed the face, declaring its presence and evidence for intelligent life on the Red Planet.

[9] Picknett and Prince, op. cit., pp. 134-135.

[10] "Cognitive dissonance refers to a situation involving conflicting attitudes, beliefs or behaviors. This produces a feeling of discomfort leading to an alteration in one of the attitudes, beliefs or behaviors to reduce the discomfort and restore balance etc." See http://www.simplypsychology.org/cognitive-dissonance.html.

of truth" succumbs to the enthusiasm of cult proponents, an enthusiasm energized by subconscious "reasons to believe" having little to do with objective facts. Additionally, in the case of Hancock, Bauval, and even Hoagland, the pecuniary motive is also a matter hard to dismiss—for conspiracy theories sell a lot of books.

Joseph P. Farrell, yet another important alternative historian who has written much in the same spirit as these authors, considers Hoagland a friend and is sympathetic to his cause. However, although Farrell seems to consider the conspiracy true and the "hyper-dimensional" insight revelatory (regarding vortices at 19.5° latitude on massive bodies), the author has not found evidence that Farrell specifically confirms Hoagland's view that Cydonia contains "artificial" structures.[11] Indeed, while there are strengths in Hoagland's NASA conspiracy theory that many find persuasive if not conclusive (including this author), his supposition "the Face" evincing life on Mars begins to stretch the credulity of even the most enthusiastic believer in intelligent life on other planets. Indeed, perhaps the greatest support for the ancient existence of Martian intelligence comes from the military's remote viewers who frequently "visit" Mars, confounded by what they "see". If the reader regards their witness as worthy evidence, Hoagland's Martian theory remains compelling. We will examine their contribution later in this book.

Is There a Cosmic Conspiracy at NASA?

On the other hand, although Hoagland's Martian theory may be extreme (in this author's opinion it falls far short of proven), his conspiracy theory (that NASA has since inception chosen arcane flight times and landing locations on the moon and Mars—an agenda influenced by Nazi and Freemason connections within NASA) aka his "ritual alignment model", appears substantiated by

---

[11] I reached out to Farrell via email to confirm this fact (having not read all of his books), but Dr. Farrell has supplied no response.

many repeating "coincidences." In other words, a pattern of repeating synchronicities seen in many historical events strongly suggests we are dealing with intention and not coincidence.

One example to confirm this point: the landing site of NASA's return to Mars on July 4, 1997, *Pathfinder*, was centered at a designated "landing ellipse" precisely at "19.5° North x 33.3° West" which is exactly where the tetrahedral-shaped landing craft put down its three legs in perfect triangular fashion—as if the design of the spacecraft itself and its touchdown spot was a communiqué to any attentive Martian that noticed: "Tetrahedral Message received."

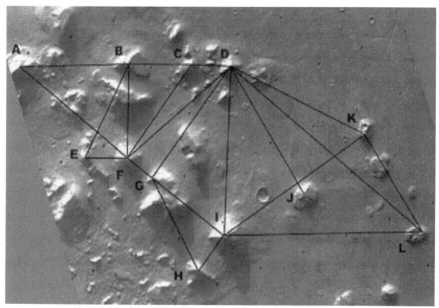

Figure 14 - The "City"? Hoagland's Mathematics on Mars

Nick Redfern, author of the book, *The NASA Conspiracies*, provides the following summary that cited the research done by the late Mac Tonnies published in 2003, regarding "The Face" which clearly gives Hoagland and his theory "the benefit of the doubt:"

> When it comes to the still thriving controversy surrounding the Face on Mars, the late Mac Tonnies made a very strong, logical case to the effect that dismissing the face as a mere trick of the light could prove to be a major disaster, scientifically, historically, and culturally. It remains to be seen whether NASA is actually guilty of hiding hard

evidence that the face is an artificial construct, or merely prefers to play down the whole matter because it has become tired of dealing with accusations that it is sitting on top of secret proof that intelligent, long-extinct Martians constructed the face countless millennia ago. [12]

Certainly, the fact NASA remains relatively quiet on the issue appears to be the equivalent of "no comment"—suggesting they do have knowledge of matters they do not wish to disclose. That reluctance to engage openly in the dialogue strongly hints there is much more to the story than John Q. Public may be allowed to learn.

For further elaboration on Hoagland's point of view, please delve into *Dark Mission*.[13] However, plan to burn some midnight oil. It is a lengthy, intriguing, but somewhat arduous read.

What if Intelligent Beings Once Inhabited Mars?

A personal and recent experience to further compound the mystery: My brother's son-in-law works currently as a project manager (i.e., a genuine rocket-scientist) at JPL in Pasadena on the successful Mars Rover project *Curiosity* which landed safely in August of 2012 (in no small part due to the work of his team). Before launch, he was a bit baffled by the request from the "higher ups" who requested he outfit the Rover with a microphone. A microphone? Who, he wondered, were Government officials (outside of his team)

---

[12] Nick Redfern, *The NASA Conspiracies,* Pompton Plains, New Jersey: New Page Books, 2011, p. 204.

[13] I don't touch here on the immense amount of data Hoagland and Bara cover concerning artificial structures on the surface of the moon and their belief that the Apollo astronauts were hypnotized to forget what they saw when there. Specifically, he contends there are residual but highly fractured glass domes, massive in scope and covering a number of the largest craters, creating a living space for intelligent creatures who originated them. He includes numerous photos taken by the astronauts and minute interpretive details to prove his point. However, in regards to the moon, I simply don't see what they seek to expose—even though I've spent considerable time studying the photos included in the book. Perhaps I need to have my reading glasses improved. Furthermore, from my perspective, their interpretation of the data on this subject only serves to diminish their other assertions that I do find somewhat compelling.

planning to talk with? My "nephew-in-law" might have considered what was really in store for this spacecraft, and who it might meet up with when completing its mission to Mars. If the U.S. military's remote viewers are right, *Curiosity* would need to sound an alarm clock since the ancient race that once thrived there resides beneath the surface in specially prepared caverns for safe keeping—in a state of suspended animation!

At stake for those who hold to the Biblical worldview is identity, the reason for our being here, in a word, our *genesis*. If intelligent life could be discovered on Mars, what would it infer about how life originated on earth? Was life here seeded by Martians? Or is the reverse true? Did an ancient race (perhaps a civilization destroyed at least 12,000 years ago as some speculate) achieve vast knowledge of the cosmos, travel to Mars, and seed life there? Is this the connection to the Egyptian pyramids and the "City" on Mars? Would the Bible allow that a pre-Adamic race once existed prior to Genesis 1:2 and was responsible for the signs of ancient civilization on earth and Mars?

It should be pointed out that the late David Flynn, an evangelical researcher and writer who held to the biblical worldview, did an extensive study on this Martian controversy in his book, *Cydonia: The Chronicles of Mars* (2002—and recently republished by Defender Books as part of an anthology of his works). Later in this book we will discuss his views which delve into the origin of humankind and its possible connection to civilization that may have, according to Flynn, first blossomed on Mars.

For those who hold to the hypothesis that ancient astronauts nurtured humanity and may have genetically altered our DNA to enhance our intelligence (e.g., Erich Von Däniken, the late Zecharia Sitchin), finding artifacts that substantiate intelligence (albeit extinct) elsewhere in our solar system, would certainly be a windfall proving their theory at least partially true. If "the great deception" to introduce "the last days" connects to this theory of human origins (as opposed to the Biblical account of the creation of humanity in Genesis 1 and 2), the *Red Planet and what is discovered there will be an indispensable element in propagating this myth.* The Apostle Paul predicted that a grand delusion would accompany the revelation of the Antichrist in the events leading up to the return of Jesus Christ:

> *8 And then shall that Wicked be revealed, whom the Lord shall consume with the spirit of his mouth, and shall destroy with the brightness of his coming:*
>
> *9 Even him, whose coming is after the working of Satan with all power and signs and **lying wonders**,*
>
> *10 And with all deceivableness of unrighteousness in them that perish; because they received not the love of the truth, that they might be saved.*
>
> *11 And for this cause God shall send them strong delusion, that they should believe a lie* (2 Thessalonians 2:8-11).

Conclusion: Mars and the Mythology of Humankind

The fact that Mars has been a source of speculation about the origin of humanity for hundreds if not thousands of years, suggests that today's research and speculation about *the origin of humanity on the Red Planet* may be a catalyst for a dramatic alteration of the average person's view of the universe. Indeed, this threat is the challenge posed to the Judeo-Christian worldview; in other words, the cosmology assumed true in the Bible. Mars has, and may become again, a key to understand spiritual, not just technological or astronomical deception.

Exploring the recent past (the last 150 years) will prove most instructive in demonstrating the power of the Red Planet to shape the mythologies and belief systems of humankind. This book is dedicated to that task in hopes that the reader will become aware that strange notions regarding our origin as a species, currently lurking in the background of discourse, *may become the prevailing view*—with the impact felt in the personal lives of billions and re-weaving the fabric of most of our social institutions.

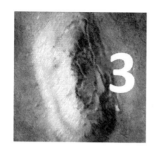

The Role of Mind in UFO Manifestations

A Different Explanation for Why UFOs Manifest

I F THE RESEARCH OF AUTHOR NICK REDFERN IS CORRECT, THERE MAY BE AN UNEXPLAINED CORRELATION BETWEEN THE MARKED INCREASE IN UFOS IN THE LATTER HALF OF THE 20TH CENTURY AND SCIENCE fiction authors who began to flourish at about the same time. Red-fern has studied and written about the UFO phenomenon for years. One of his recent and most important books, *Final Events* (subtitled: *The Secret Government Group on Demonic UFOs and the Afterlife*) touches on the association between science fiction writers, rocket scientists, and the advent of apparent "extraterrestrial" spacecraft in our skies. His data begs the question why this could be so. Redfern's book provides a provocative explanation for why UFOs became so commonplace in the years after World War II. It also comprises essential reading for Christians

Figure 15 - Nick Redfern's Book, *Final Events*

tuned in to the subject of "alien" intrusion in the empirical world and its implications for humankind in the years just ahead.

The plot's central element revolves around the noted rocket scientist, Jack Parsons. Arguably, Parsons stands as one of America's

41

more important home-grown rocket scientists[1]. But without question, he is its most controversial. For starters, Parsons devised the formula for solid rocket fuel (based on the ancient secret weapon of Greek fire) which made launching rockets relatively safe.[2] Furthermore, along with German Theodore von Karman, Parson founded NASA's Jet Propulsion Laboratory (JPL). Among those "in the know", JPL is satirically referred to as "Jack Parson's Laboratory." While it continues to be a crucial element of NASA even today, nonetheless, JPL is not Parson's most incredible claim to fame.

A Rocket Scientist and an Occult Priest

In addition to his scientific exploits, Parsons was an extraordinary occultist, leading the Pasadena chapter of *Ordo Templi Orientis* (OTO) in the 1940s. The OTO was a black magic fraternity associated with the even more infamous and sinister English magician Aleister Crowley who originated the OTO as the 20th century began. Forty years later, during the final years of his life,[3] Crowley mentored Parsons in the dark arts, particularly specific rites of *sexual magick*, the ceremonious magic Crowley perfected.[4]

Figure 16 - Jack Parsons, Rocket Scientist and *OTO High Priest*

---

[1] Robert H. Goddard is generally regarded as much more noteworthy.

[2] The actual composition is asphalt and potassium perchlorate.

[3] Perhaps it is not coincidental that Crowley died in 1947.

[4] Crowley famously conjured an ultra-dimensional being he called LAM in 1918 almost 30 years before Parsons performed the famous Babalon Working ritual to be discussed later. Crowley's drawing of LAM clearly resembles the gray alien of UFO folklore, although his eyes were not big and black, but slitted and 'shifty'. Think Richard Nixon with a giant bald head.

Casual UFOlogists may not know of Parson's many fascinating connections directly tied to the sudden and inexplicable appearance of UFOs in American skies. Foremost among these links: Parsons was an acquaintance of Kenneth Arnold, the pilot who famously described nine curved-winged aircraft that flew his direction when he was airborne near Mt. Rainer on a June day in 1947. According to one researcher, Parsons and Arnold were actually pilot partners.[5] The fact that Arnold was a known friend of Jack Parsons AND the first highly public UFO witness at the dawn of the UFO era, adds considerable intrigue to the mysterious meaning of UFOs. Their association seems to imply they were indeed "birds of a feather" in more ways than aeronautical.

Yet another fascinating connection concerns the most famous of science fiction writers who conjectured about space travel and beings from alien worlds—authors who were also good friends of Parsons. Moreover, this club met often at Parson's House. They jokingly called his home, *The Parsonage*.[6]

Redfern lists Robert Heinlein, Jack Williamson, Anthony Boucher, and Ray Bradbury as members of Parson's science fiction clique. As they say, "To be a fly on that wall!" But the most profound of science fiction writers known to Parson—and who worked beside him—was the ill-reputed L. Ron Hubbard. Hubbard not only founded the cult of *Scientology*, but wrote *Battlefield Earth*, a 1982 science fiction book made into a "critically *disclaimed*" movie (in 2000) starring John Travolta. The saga of Hubbard and Parsons constitutes a scintillating subject on its own demerits. Suffice it to say, Hubbard ran off with Parson's wife after a series of sexual exploits stemming from the perverse sexual rituals conducted by

---

[5] Redfern cites John Judge and a comment he made during a radio interview on channel KPFK, Los Angeles, on August 12, 1989, that Parsons and Arnold were flying partners. This is a connection seldom mentioned in UFO folklore.

[6] Churchgoers may recognize this term which refers to the house typically supplied by the church for its pastor or "parson."

these scandalous actors in what remains one of the most bizarre accounts seldom told about America's rich and infamous.[7]

Another Rocket Scientist Calling Roswell Home

Perhaps it is not surprising that other equally astounding coincidences orbit about one Robert Hutchings Goddard. As a noteworthy rocket scientist in his own right, Goddard's story predates Parsons by two decades. And like Parsons, Goddard's rocketry is linked to science fiction: for who should have inspired Goddard but the most famous of all science fiction writers, indeed the founder of the genre, H.G. Wells? According to Redfern, it was Well's science fiction thriller depicting the Martian invasion, *War of the Worlds*, that Goddard "devoured" eventually leading to his interest in rocket science and his ground-breaking Smithsonian-published whitepaper on high altitude flight (1919) and later the first launch of a rocket in America (1926). We should also note that Goddard moved his laboratory in 1930–ominously–to Roswell, New Mexico. From there, launching his progressively bigger and more powerful rockets, he began punching a hole in the sky through which other more "notorious" disk-shaped craft would purportedly pass.

However, the pivotal event for Redfern's book remains Parson's *Babalon Working* ritual. Parsons sought to conjure the "Whore of Babylon" and a new type of humanity through his monumental ceremony. Parsons completed his "conjurings" sometime before the landmark Roswell event of 1947. What was the import of this ritual? Redfern quotes another researcher—Adam Gorightly—who observed: "After Babalon Working, UFO sightings began to be reported en masse, as if a Devil's Floodgate had been opened, and into the earth realm flew powers and demons from beyond, much like

---

[7] According to Redfern, Hubbard began writing science fiction as early as 1940, publishing a novella in the July issue that year of *Unknown Fantasy Fiction*. He was also an acquaintance of Raymond Palmer, the then editor of the science-fiction magazine *Amazing Stories*. Palmer even helped Kenneth Arnold write his book, *The Coming of the Saucers*. It is a small world after all.

an H.P. Lovecraft tale[8], unleashed upon an unsuspecting human populace."[9] This ritual was a watershed for UFO sightings in the modern world.[10]

Redfern introduces us to a secret Defense Department group, the so-called Collins Elite[11], who investigated Crowley, Parsons, and the whole issue of UFOs–including demonic intrusion into our world. From his account, we learn the group soon concluded UFOs weren't extraterrestrial spacecraft at all–they were satanic agents seeking to deceive humankind and replace earth's human inhabitants with hybrid beings! According to Redfern, the Collins Elite, despite its connection to the U.S. Government, has struggled to make their findings public while feuding with other agents within our government that seek to manipulate the powers of the "alien intruders," amassing them into strategic advantage for world domination by the U.S. Military-Industrial Complex.

---

[8] H.P. Lovecraft was another American writer living in the first half of the twentieth century, whose genre was partly science fiction and partly horror. His writings possess a very strong sense of foreboding and present the 'highly strange'. See Jason Colavito, *The Cult of Alien Gods*, for an academic examination of Lovecraft's impact on Ancient Alien theorists. We take up Lovecraft later in this book.

[9] Redfern, Nick, *Final Events*, San Antonio: Anomalist Books, Kindle Edition, p.24.

[10] UFOs have been reported throughout history. But in modern times, the Arnold sighting and only weeks later, the Roswell event, were the distinguishing occurrences sparking a cosmological revolution with vast spiritual implications. That it occurred immediately after Babalon Working and the coming together of other "signs of the apocalypse" have made UFOs and Bible prophecy subjects often discussed in the same setting.

[11] The Collins Elite was named after a small community in New York State. This group of more than a dozen persons from the defense community were formed into a group and financed off the books by the CIA just weeks before Parson's death in 1952. The catalyst for their formation was Parson's stealing government secrets right after his top secret clearance had been revoked. His actions apparently stemmed from a job offer to Parsons by the young nation of Israel. The sequence of events is stunning: Parsons died in late June, the Collins Elite were formed around July 4, 1952, and then UFOs buzzed the nation's capital over two successive weekends, July 20 and July 27. This incident was known as the Washington "Flap". As they say, timing is everything. With "the Flap", the UFO era was off and running along with the birth of myriad UFO movies. Thus began a cavalcade of flying saucer incidents and entertainment which grew progressively in frequency and in spectacle.

Confirming the Views of Some Christian Authors

While the story is disquieting if not shocking, it confirms what many Christian authors have been conveying for more than a decade. Plus, the reader should make note: Redfern is not a professed believer in "Christian cosmology." Consequently, his account delivers unbiased corroboration for Christian researchers and authors (such as L.A. Marzulli, Chuck Missler, this author, and a host of others), that what our world has encountered in the UFO phenomenon constitutes the diabolical and not just the technological.

The conclusion one reaches when discerning these breathtaking connections between science fiction writers, rocket scientists, and UFOs is that the whole affair blurs the distinction between reality and fantasy. What is true and what is fiction? Why are there so many unexpected connections between the folkloric figures when one peers beneath the surface? What does it mean that science fiction seems to have conjured up UFOs and spurred real-life alien encounters? No doubt the interplay of these factors both befuddles true believers and encourages reluctant skeptics. It demands careful assessment and an informed response.

Nevertheless, the fan of science fiction recognizes this very fact: the best examples of the genre foreshadow phenomenal facts hidden "beyond the veil." Indeed, it seems only moments after we contemplate these far-fetched fantasies in our best fictional stories, that merely *focusing upon them in our imagination causes them to be transformed, like magic, into irrefutable realities before our very eyes.*

So we should take this matter one step further: What is the relationship between the "imaginings" of these science fiction writers and the surreal if not paranormal activities that began to be witnessed not only surrounding them but in our skies overhead, starting in 1947 and especially beginning in 1952 with the "Washington Flap" (when the national capitol was buzzed by UFOs for two consecutive weekends in July of that year)? Was there any relationship between these noted authors conjuring up imaginary spaceships (through their literary works as well as—in the case of Parsons and Hubbard—*ritual* magic), with the reality UFOs were becoming more commonplace everywhere? Was there a cause-and-effect connection with flying saucer sightings, alien abductions, and a general interest among the population regarding such subjects? Was the massive cultural enthusiasm beginning in the 1950s somehow giving rise to the realities that were appearing on our radar scopes? Did belief help manifest spaceships?

How Key is Belief in Making UFOs Materialize?

This line of reasoning might suggest my theory regarding the appearance of UFOs has nothing to do with whether they really exist and everything to do with whether we believe in them. In other words, perhaps the reader infers this author believes skeptics never see UFOs while true believers almost always do. If that were so, would it not be the case that flying saucers, aliens, and messages from outer space—supplied through their compliant, if not adoring channelers—are all merely a psychological phenomenon? Would not this be the outer space equivalent of a physical illness (a psychosomatic condition) brought about by a mental matter on a societal scale, i.e., a social pathology akin to groupthink? Are not UFO witnesses just seeing things because they wish them to be so? Are these disc-shaped vehicles (which defy the known laws of aerodynamics) simply mental tricks caused by earnest believers who want them to be real, perhaps because they prove "transcendence" (i.e., there is some meaning to life") for those who believe? Are aliens a surrogate for God?

The answers to all these questions appear to be, at least from this author's perspective, partially "Yes". But it is not because our minds trick us into seeing what is not there. That explanation is much too simple. Based upon the most recent witness of how physics works in the space-time world, such spaceships may materialize,

47

literally, because our minds contribute something to their appearing. In other words, our minds play a definite role in making them materialize in the physical world. How can this be so?

Throughout the study of alien appearances, their anti-gravity propelled transportation, and their messages of warning for the human race (that we had better mend our ways or we will wake up one morning and find our world a roasted cinder), favorable researchers typically assume they are only reporting "just the facts mam" as Jack Friday from the old TV show, *Dragnet* would instruct his witness. However, there may be more to "the facts" than the common-

Figure 17 - Memory Metal from Roswell Crash

place worldview allows. Furthermore, it is not just how our minds shape the data that comes our way (as the famous philosopher begetting the science of epistemology[12] Immanuel Kant, might explain). It has more to do with the recent discovery that our minds

---

[12] *Epistemology* is the science of "knowing". It examines how we know and even *how we know we know*. Faith, reason, knowledge, the mechanisms of how our minds work (not just how our physical brains function) are all part of this science. Kant was not the first to take up the subject, but he was the most important. He attempted to build a case for human knowledge based upon "how we think"—that while not proving our thinking corresponds to reality "as it is"—he believed categorizing how we think and how our minds structure the data coming to us through

help create physical reality—at least a little—but to a scientifically measurable extent. Additionally, when one gathers enough intelligent persons together thinking about topics about which they feel earnest, the "power of the combined minds" may alter the space-time world and thus, reform reality. It even seems this alteration of reality which we witness today could be based in part upon what we will be thinking about tomorrow. Experiments done during the past two decades regarding random number generators and how they are influenced by mental processes (both local and global) seems to provide a scientific basis for this fact.[13] As far out as it seems, effects can influence causes in contradistinction to Newtonian and even Einsteinium physics. The universe is more mysterious than we thought. (Or maybe it is so mysterious because of "how we thought!")

Mind, Matter, and Aliens

In this brief treatment of the subject, we will not pursue the epistemological implications of these newly argued views proffered by various physicists and cosmologists, some of which believe in intelligent design and others who even believe in the God of the Bible. Instead, we will open the door to a powerfully related example of the interplay between "mind, matter, and aliens." This issue actually suggests a number of intriguing things about the increasing

---

our senses, was a legitimate basis for science and ultimately for faith. To go on just a little, although for Kant faith relied more upon a notion of "ought" and not just a *categorical imperative*—akin to dismissing something as true only if when it corresponds to the way our minds work. How ironic his approach was developed to respond to the skepticism of David Hume. For when he was done defining the "categories of the mind" and distinguishing "transcendental truth" (how human's know things) from "transcendent truth" (a perfect knowledge only God could have) Kant had actually paved the way for *greater doubt* in the world of philosophy.

[13] This discussion is carried out in a helpful way by Lynn Picknett and Clive Prince in their recent book, *The Forbidden Universe* (2011), a story on how *Hermeticism* (the "high" occult teachings of the ages) influenced the formation of modern science. While not agreeing with the spiritual conclusions drawn by the authors, I can recommend the book for a lively discussion and readable explanation about these intriguing possibilities.

cases of UFOs, alien abductions, channeled messages from outer space, and ultimately the false gospel of nurturing aliens who created humankind (or at least altered our supposed "evolution" a million years ago—or as the late popular author and Sumerian scholar Zecharia Sitchin proposed—within the past 60,000 years).

Here is my thesis: our minds are not simply receptors of neutral data transmitted our way by outside entities (be they egalitarian extraterrestrials or much more likely, malfeasant spiritual beings who, if they had their way, would control us). We create the opportunity for receiving messages that usually go unheard, based upon what we choose to believe. We willfully open a "hailing frequency" as they used to say in *Star Trek*. We start searching for messages that may have been there all along, but to which we weren't "sensitized." Colloquially speaking, "We did not have our ears on." By dabbling with certain sorts of transmitters (drugs, rituals, Ouija boards) we establish contact. Once we do, a whole new reality begins to bleed into our everyday world. Again, this is not just a case of allowing our minds to trick us; the empirical world—reality itself—is altered. Space-time is no longer exactly the same. By our active receptivity, we allow spiritual beings to become interlopers (or more plainly, party crashers) in what happens in our world. It takes two to tango. Or saying it another way without mixing the metaphor: they want to dance but we have to turn on the music.

We may assume that what we think or believe has little to do with what happens in the world, but science proves otherwise. Just as the *Ghostbusters* learned when asked to "choose the form of the destroyer" even a hypothetically docile entity, such as a giant Stay Puft © Marshmallow Man, can really ruin your day.

We began our discussion in this chapter by referencing Nick Redfern's *Final Events*. Redfern brings a considerable amount of useful information to his readers. Indeed, this author deems it one of the more important books to read and study (carefully) on the subject of UFOlogy.

Parsons Opens a Portal and What Should We See?

Going back to Jack Parsons, the point of the so-called Jack Parsons "techniques" which the clandestine group, The Collins Elite purportedly studied was that the scraps of materials left in the desert near Roswell in 1947 (that may or may not have included bodies), were actually artifacts created as a result of the rituals Parsons and his occultic colleagues performed. His rituals apparently "opened a portal" which allowed entities (possibly from *another dimension*) to deposit highly strange and unique materials from "out of this world" in an attempt to prove visitors from interstellar space had been there. The famous "memory metal" that could not be permanently bent or damaged by earthly tools (hammers and such) was only one of these items that were intentionally spun like Rumpelstiltskin's gold by these dream weavers from another dimension. Therefore, their deception was purposeful. They wanted to give evidence in molecular form to prove aliens from the far reaches of outer space were visiting our world. And as the false gospel of Ancient Alien Theory proclaims, they weren't just light-hearted tourists out to see the sights. According to their admirers, their loitering around our planet was to look in on (supposedly) their creation and nudge us the right direction before we destroy ourselves.

Consequently, I argue that Roswell evinces a real connection between mind and matter—or between spiritual realities and physical realities, which is another way to say the same thing. The two dimensions can intersect. And the residue of their interconnection can leave physical evidence behind. Think of "Slimer" and the green gel-like ectoplasm he covered Bill Murray's character with, in the movie *Ghostbusters*. Going beyond "green slime," The Collins Elite came to see through the evidence and realized it was planted by not-so-distant provocateurs in a grand, cosmological deception. That is to say, they did not believe that flying saucers and space aliens were the real actors littering this elegant "space junk" around the Foster ranch at Roswell. They came to believe the entities were "local" albeit from a nearby dimension known as the spiritual realm.

51

It is astonishing a group of Federal intelligence personnel would come to this conclusion. However, after years of research that is exactly what happened. And yet, it is only part of their amazing story.

Research Connections to the Paranormal?

The mind/matter connection (we should say the mind/matter interaction) was made even more concrete by the fact that hooking up with the aliens was done mostly through altered states of mind. A former member of the Collins Elite, the informer to Redfern (one Richard Duke), related a pertinent anecdote regarding meetings between the Elite and the notorious *Andrija Puharich*. (Mentioned earlier in a footnote, he remains one of my most favorite colorful characters of the UFO and ESP worlds, coincidentally the uncle of one of my good friends, and a character I discuss in depth in a previous book, *Power Quest: The Ascendancy of Antichrist* in America).

Although officials denied that there was ever any research connection between the government and Puharich, meetings and discussions did take place (Puharich was a noted specialist in channeling, ESP, studies in LSD on behalf of the military, and the central authority in the appearance of the so-called "NINE" forces from outside our solar system claiming to also be the Egyptian Ennead or pantheon. These bodiless voices continually predicted their physical return although in case you have not noticed, so far they remain "no-

Figure 18 - Jacque Vallée, UFOlogist

shows"[14]). Redfern indicates the whole subject "went black because of the UFO thing and the Parsons theories.'" No one wanted to admit—let alone have Congress, the media, and the public know—that they were digging into controversies suggesting a link between UFOs, demonology, and altered-states of mind." [15]

Redfern goes on to provide a reference to a particular report shared between J. Allen Hynek, the noted UFO military consultant charged with obfuscating UFO accounts[16] and Jacques Vallée (the well-regarded UFO researcher, author, and undoubted prototype for the French UFOlogist in Spielberg's *Close Encounters of a Third Kind*) and related to a meeting held on July 9, 1959 at the CIA office in Washington:

> Under the direction of Arthur Lundahl of the CIA's National Photographic Interpretation Center. Present at the meeting was a representative of the Office of Naval Intelligence, and seven CIA officers—three of who [sic], Richard Duke maintained, were attached to the Collins Elite. Three days prior to the July 9 meeting, a Naval Intelligence officer, one Commander Larsen, discussed with Lundahl... [a failed experiment which involved a Naval intelligence contact, Francis Swan in the summer of 1954]... Larsen was encouraged to repeat the experiment, which involved him "going into a trance," [he] later told writer and filmmaker Robert Emenegger. This time it was successful: a flying saucer suddenly appeared on the scene." [17]

Redfern comments the Collins Elite were "bothered by the fact that some intelligence officials were now being influenced by the saucer people to such an extent that they, too, were being seduced *into entering altered states* to contact what might just as well have

---

[14] This is the story discussed in Picknett and Prince's *Stargate Conspiracy* (2000) and made famous in the pro-UFO book, *The Only Planet of Choice (1993)*, who's Foreword was written by James Hurtak, noted UFOlogist; and who earlier in his career, was the assistant to Andrija Puharich. It is a small world after all.

[15] Redfern, Nick, *Final Events,* Kindle Edition, location 993.

[16] But who ultimately came to believe in UFOs.

[17] Ibid., Kindle Edition, location 1025.

been demons as extraterrestrials."[18] [*Emphasis added*]   All deeds were purely performed in the interest of science of course.

Conclusion: How Could Our Minds Land the Ship?

The point of this chapter can be summarized as this: If real physical extraterrestrials were coming to earth, traveling to us from dozens (if not hundreds) of light years away, and therefore had mastered the physics of the universe, one would suppose that they needn't rely upon the human mind to give them a point of entry into our world. We are, after all, still waiting for their spaceship to land on the White House lawn despite the fact they've been feigning appearances, according to their many mediumistic adherents, for decades—if not several centuries. For instance, the Maya were waiting for their feathered serpent god, Kukulkan to reappear in 2012.   But why would

Figure 19 - Redfern and the Collins Elite

they (and many new-ager newcomers) have to prepare the way of his coming by performing religious rituals? If this is so, what does

---

[18] Ibid.

it say about the nature of extraterrestrials? *Could they be more psychic than physical?* Could they be "gods" (ultra-dimensional beings—angels, demons, or something "in-between") rather than ETs?

Furthermore, the facts also suggest alien appearances mimic apparitions (now you see them, now you don't—which also seems to imply phantasms require the cooperation of the mind); hence, their "pure" corporeal substance stands as highly questionable. Yes, these entities sometimes can "break on through to the other side" as singer Jim Morrison of *The Doors* advised in a song by the same title (in his case, his preferred door opener was mescaline—a substance-of-choice shared by Aldous Huxley—of whom Morrison's lyrics and the band's name itself were inspired). But these beings require some force or capacity of the human mind to make the magic happen.

Exactly what this suggests about the "final event", i.e., the outcome of the "gospel of Ancient Alien Astronauts," requires further discussion. Nevertheless, the spiritual dangers suggest that when someone opens a portal "to the other side" aka "the doors of perception"—about which Huxley and Morrison were champions—responsible spiritually attuned beings, namely Christians, best find a way to close the door as quickly as possible.

For as we've seen from the famous debris field created in the New Mexico desert circa July 1947, there really is no telling what type of matter the cat (or in our case, the mind-altered "mediums", ritual magicians, and their alien friends) might just drag into our world. For once they do, whatever they conjure into our world seems next-to-impossible to send back.

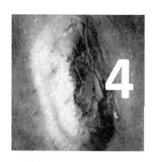

"Seeing Things" on the Planet Mars

Victorian Visions of the Red Planet

R EADERS MAY RECALL THE ASTRONOMER PERCIVAL LOWELL (1855-1916) WHO, WITH THE AID OF HIS TRUSTY TELESCOPE, FIRST WROTE ABOUT (AND DREW SO CREATIVELY) THE *CANALS* of Mars. Whatever he lacked in scientific precision he made up for with an astronomical imagination.

Indeed, Lowell was a giant in planetary astronomy. His most notable scientific achievement is associated not with Mars, but with another far more distant planetary body. He searched meticulously for what was labeled in his time, *Planet X*. Within two decades of his death, his Lowell Observatory in Arizona eventually discovered it (actually the find would be that of astronomer Clyde W. Tombaugh in 1930). Planet X was not *Nibiru* as the recent work of the late Zecharia Sitchin popularized—it was in fact the planet (now *dwarf* planet) *Pluto*.

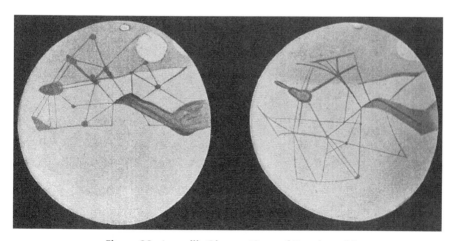

Figure 20 - Lowell's Observations of Canals on Mars

57

Lowell influenced his generation in a way similar to Carl Sagan's influence on ours. Lowell was one of the first scientists to actively advocate the possibility that life existed on Mars. Lowell's impact on public interest in Mars was enormous. Without Lowell's earlier work, Orson Welles' famous radio broadcast presented on October 30, 1938 (a tale of another Wells, H.G. Wells', *War of the Worlds—*

1898), would not have stirred much controversy. As it was, Lowell paved the way for both Wells (Welles) to be permanently etched in our culture. But it is worth noting the hysteria all began by *seeing things on Mars.*[1]

However, the observation of canals on the Martian surface did not begin with Percival Lowell. The *Encyclopedia of Science* provides this short anecdote of the history of seeing things on Mars.

Figure 21 - Percival Lowell at the Lowell Observatory

[Canals] the term [was] first used by Pietro Secchi, and later adopted by [Giovanni Virginio] Schiaparelli[2] and others, to describe certain features claimed to have been observed on the surface of Mars. *Canali* can be correctly translated from the Italian either as "channels" or "canals." Schiaparelli

---

[1] Because *The Mercury Theatre of the* Air was a radio broadcast without commercial interruption and was presented as a series of continuous news bulletins, thousands of listeners became convinced the Earth was under invasion by aliens. The fret over aliens attacking our planet has become a standing plotline for books and movies ever since.

[2] Schiaparelli, Giovanni Virginio (1835 – 1910) was the unintentional instigator of the debate regarding intelligent life on Mars by observing and documenting *canali* (not cannoli mind you, a favorite pastry dish) one of the most far-reaching cases of words whose intended meaning was lost in translation.

generally intended and preferred the former and, indeed, often used an alternative description, *fiumi* (rivers) for the same features. Almost inevitably, however, *canali* was usually translated into English as "canals," implying an artificial origin.

At an address to the Boston Scientific Society on May 22, 1894, Lowell shared his enthusiasm for approaching discoveries concerning life on Mars: "This may be put popularly as an investigation into the condition of life on other worlds, including last but not least their habitability by beings like [or] unlike man... there is strong reason to believe that we are on the eve of [a] pretty definite discovery in the matter." Lowell believed that the intelligence implied in the use of canal to translate *canali* was not amiss: "... in them we are looking upon the result of the work of some sort of intelligent beings ..." 3 Contemporaries to Lowell were as kind to him as are professional critics of our modern-day Martian enthusiast, Richard C. Hoagland. They challenged his belief in Martian life through their academic brouhaha. To their point of view, Lowell was merely caught up in the romance of conjecturing intelligent life on Mars. James Keeler, a contemporary of Lowell's provided this not-so-complementary summation of Lowell's responsibility for exciting interest in Mars during the dedication ceremony of Wisconsin's Yerkes Observatory in 1897:

> It is to be regretted that the habitability of the planets, a subject of which astronomers profess to know little, has been chosen as a theme for exploitation by the romancer, to whom the step from habitability to inhabitants is a very short one. The result of his ingenuity is that fact and fantasy become inextricably tangled in the mind of the layman, who learns to regard communication with inhabitants of Mars as a project deserving serious consideration...4

---

3 See www.daviddarling.info/encyclopedia/L/LowellP.html, an article in *The Encyclopedia of Science,* on Percival Lowell.
4 Ibid.

This particular notion of *romance* deserves some elaboration. To our ears, the word *romance* summons images of courtship, love affairs, and being amorous. But romance also conveys the notion of "a spirit of adventure" or a "fascination with something." The incurable romantic inclines toward believing in what reinforces his or her fascination, rather than "facing the facts" that might conflict with what he or she believes. Scientists generally feign dispassion in their quest for knowledge. Detachment makes the scientist appear more credible. However, the truth of the matter is that without a passionate connection, most scientists would be lousy at their work.

Consider the scientist referenced above who blazed the trail for Schiaparelli and Lowell, Pietro Secchi. *Secchi* (1818—1878) was a Jesuit priest and the director of *The Roman College Observatory* forerunner to today's *Vatican Observatory*. Secchi believed in *pluralism*, otherwise known as the doctrine of many worlds. In 1856 he said, "It is with sweet sentiment that man thinks of these worlds without number, where each star is a sun which, as minister of the divine bounty, distributes life and goodness to the other innumerable beings, blessed by the hand of the Omnipotent." Carl Sagan could not have said it more poetically himself (although he did try). Secchi would eventually teach in London and later at Georgetown University in the United States before returning to Rome where he directed the work at the observatory.

Today we marvel at the fact that members of the Vatican Observatory conjecture about extraterrestrials and their attempts to rationalize the possibility of intelligent life. It seems an interesting point to recognize, however, that today's Jesuit Vatican astronomers like José Gabriel Funes and Michael Heller follow in Secchi's path. For at least two centuries, the Vatican has construed extraterrestrial life a probable consequence of the vastness of space and the innumerable stars obvious to our eyes (both aided and unaided). Given the historic position of the Roman Catholic Church—one thinks of Galileo's trial for heresy (by endorsing the Copernican system—the sun, rather than the earth, placed at the center of God's universe). What has happened? A decided change in outlook to be sure.

Proximity of the Red Planet

Because of the differences in the shapes and diameters of the orbits of Earth and Mars, there are times when the planets are close together and times when they are very far apart. This ranges from approximately 35 million to 250 million miles. This relationship was crucial for astronomers armed with their newly more powerful telescopes to observe the Red Planet. In 1845 and in 1924 Mars was particularly near to earth. In 2003, it

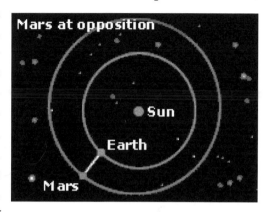

Figure 22 - Opposition of Earth and Mars

was the closest that it had been in almost 60,000 years. Thanks to modern rocket science that makes close up inspections commonplace, the proximity of Mars allowing a close inspection, makes what is called "the opposition of Mars" mostly irrelevant—at least as far as mere observation goes. On the other hand, timing the trip of the rocket from the Earth to Mars still makes the "opposition of Mars" a practical consideration for our rocket scientists today.

At the outset, I made the point, "Mars seemingly makes smart people see things that may not be there." In the first chapter, I raised the issue of Richard C. Hoagland's romanticism about Mars.

> This thought crossed the minds of [researchers and authors] Lynn Picknett and Clive Prince... when they examined Hoagland's iconoclastic contentions concerning Mars and the origin of life. While not eager to discredit Hoagland's arguments and certainly not intending to question his sincerity—nonetheless, they challenge his observations and especially the extent of his conclusions. They question

whether such momentous claims are reasonable, let alone justified, given the ramifications (of) humankind's beliefs about itself. Are not these speculations really just the enthusiastic assertions of an eager believer hot on the trail of evidence to prove his personal conspiracy theory and cosmology—specifically, his personal view regarding how humankind came to be?[5]

Citing the words of Picknett and Prince verbatim:

To Hoagland's eye there seemed to be a whole complex of pyramidal and other structures, covering an area of about 12 square miles. He excitedly termed it the 'City'. This appeared to be made up of several massive, and some smaller, pyramids, plus some much smaller conical 'buildings' grouped around an open space that he called the 'City Square'. In the northeast corner of the City was an enormous

Figure 23 - Mars on 08-23-2003, a mere 34.7 million miles from Earth, its closest approach in 60,000 years.

---

[5] See http://faith-happens.com/seeing-things-on-mars/.

structure that appears to be made up of three huge walls, which Hoagland dubbed the 'Fortress'.[6]

For the reader's convenience, I cite Picknett and Prince's critical comment here again:

> Perhaps the most significant assumption Hoagland made—and surely the one with the least justification on such slight knowledge—was his association of these features with Egypt. As soon as he discovered the City, Hoagland wrote: 'I was reminded overwhelmingly of Egypt.' He then went on to identify various other features in Cydonia: the 'Cliff', a 2-mile-long wall-like feature near a crater 14 miles directly east of the Face; and several small (250—400-foot) objects dotted about the Cydonia plain that he called 'mounds'.[7]

Quoting Hoagland from his book, *The Monuments of Mars*: "For it is now clear... that, if appropriately researched and then applied to many current global problems, the potential 'radical technologies' that might be developed from the 'Message of Cydonia' could significantly assist the world in a dramatic transition to a real 'new world order'... if not a literal New World."[8]

Picknett and Prince observe, "In other words, Hoagland is implying that these putative [reputed] extraterrestrials actually created the human race, and this idea, odd though it may appear, is rapidly gaining currency throughout the world." Just like Theists, Ancient Alien Theorists reject *unattended* evolution. Perhaps St. Thomas Aquinas was not all that wet when he proposed the notion of a "First Mover."

Whereas Lowell observed straight lines signifying intelligence in design, Hoagland has indicated clear indications of intelligence through mathematics implicit in the structures he sees on Mars. Graham Hancock, another alternative historian eager to make a

---

[6] Ibid.

[7] Picknett and Prince, *The Stargate Conspiracy*, New York, Berkeley Books, 1999 and 2001, p. 122.

[8] Ibid., p. 128, quoting Hoagland from *The Monuments of Mars*, p. 373.

plash with provocative comments, lends credibility to Hoagland with these words: "Still, we cannot deny that the act of placing a tetrahedral object on Mars at latitude 19.5° contains all the necessary numbers and symbolism to qualify as a "message received" signal in response to the geometry of Cydonia."[9] It bears repeating, so I will, noting Picknett and Prince's critique of Hoagland's (and Hancock's) romanticism, alleging a case of circular argument:

> The basic argument is that, because there are pyramids and a Sphinx in both Giza and Cydonia, the two are connected. But of course that depends on the Face on Mars being a Sphinx. The Cydonia clique describes it as being Sphinx-like; indeed, James Hurtak was using such emotive language even before it was officially discovered... [Hoagland claims, that one] is 'simian' in appearance, the other 'leonine'—an anthropoid and a lion. [However, the two are different since...] The great Sphinx at Giza is a man's head on a lion's body. Conclusion: we have two Sphinxes—in close proximity with pyramids—on both worlds![10]

Full Disclosure and the Planet Mars

Hoagland's *The Monuments of Mars (1987)* has become the modern day equivalent of Lowell's speculative books on the Red Planet published almost 100 years earlier. [11] The point of repeating these passages here is to underscore the following semi-provocative insight: Hoagland is romantic about Mars in the same vein as Percival Lowell, to wit, he also may be guilty of "seeing things on Mars" besides THE FACE on *Cydonia Mensae* (by the way, a *mensae* is the altar stone atop a religious place of worship). In other words, very recent observations of Richard Hoagland as demonstrated in his presentations featuring high resolution photographs from Mars' *Curiosity* (the Mars Science Laboratory) emphasizes that his knack

---

[9] Ibid., p. 325, quoting Graham Hancock from *The Mars Mystery*.

[10] Picknett and Prince, op. cit., pp. 134-135.

[11] Lowell published several books: Mars (1895), Mars and Its Canals2 (1906) and Mars as the Abode of Life3 (1908),

for seeing things continues. What makes his argument more difficult to sell is the simultaneous contention (however true or false) of the blockbuster of all conspiracy theories alleging NASA knows far more than it is willing to admit. As if these two challenges were not enough to create an atmosphere of suspicion, Hoagland determined it best also to assert *politics was in play on the Martian plain.*

In October, several weeks before the re-election of Barack Obama, Hoagland boldly predicted the "October Surprise of all time"—President Obama would disclose to the citizens of these United States that Mars in fact did hold reason for exploration... not only would life of some sort be discovered, but *evidence was now abundant that an ancient civilization once dwelt there.* About three months earlier Hoagland had announced his prediction just before *Curiosity* landed on the Martian surface (August, 2012), on George Noury's Coast-to-Coast AM. By October, 2012, Hoagland had enjoyed two months of viewing the photos sent to Earth by the Mars Science Lab. Not discouraged by what most would count as failure to see evident wreckage of an ancient city or spires from a long-gone civilization, his focus was limited to a careful study of the rocks in the foreground and the stark hills like a backdrop behind.

In a presentation featured on *YouTube*, published December 1, 2012, Hoagland showcased numerous photos from the high resolution cameras aboard *Curiosity*.[12] Slide-by-slide, Hoagland pointed out various scenes of the Martian landscape featuring Mount Sharp in the background. As always, Hoagland resorted to depicting the pyramidal shape of hills and mountains within the Gale Crater. Rock after rock held fascination for Hoagland as he called out to his audience their metallic shining surfaces as well as weird shadows cast by the remote sunlight. Select rocks seemed to "stand out like a sore thumb" mostly due to inconsistent coloration of a particular rock with its adjacent colleagues. He quickly pinpointed various items to

---

[12] "The Stealth Mission of Curiosity, Confirming Ancient Intelligence on Mars," See http://www.youtube.com/watch?v=RGucXXWm_RQ.

illustrate mangled "high tech ruins." Not that the photos were that clear-cut. There is a political agenda to keep anything clear-cut away from the public... "But the geometry is stunningly obvious."

During his presentation, Hoagland dropped hints hither, thither, and yon of why various science fiction writers (Edgar Rice Burroughs of *John Carter* fame, or more recently Ray Bradbury through his *Martian Chronicles*) had intuitively known fifty to one hundred years earlier—that there was an ancient civilization on Mars of advanced intelligence. Since they never said publicly they believed in life on Mars, how Hoagland can assert they "intuitively" knew it, amounts reading the minds of the dead. He confidently states their writings (never mind that they were intended as fiction) anticipated the discovery now made apparent by *Curiosity*. "It is obvious. You see the *sculptured geometry*—rectilinear geometry" (as if the articulate language would bestow intelligence to the rocks he described). His tone seemed to convey astonishment at anyone who would dare doubt his speculative conclusions. It was as if he were saying, "Can't you see it in these photos? You can't? What—are you blind?"

While I found myself straining for more clarity (and wishing *YouTube* provided higher resolution to enhance the pictures), I had to remind myself that what photo resolution was lacking Hoagland would overcome for me with his intricate, high-tech descriptions. After all, I'm an incurable romantic too. I want to believe, *and see.*

Hoagland cautioned that seeing things evincing intelligence would be a subtle science: "The wind excavates the mangled metal-lic ruins, like ruins of the Titanic strewn on the ocean floor. Bits and pieces of 'junk' is all we can anticipate." Somehow this caution did not seem to justify with greater weight the claims he made. The height of his argument seemed built on a few weird rocks—one that looked like a tennis shoe and another rock that looked (to him) like a pump. Were they strange looking? Yes. But were they compelling enough to rewrite history? In my humble opinion, *hardly.*

Ancient Alien Theorists must hold out hope for something more conclusive. So far, neither NASA nor Richard Hoagland has been able to deliver the goods to an audience not swayed by the lure of pure hope for an extraterrestrial explanation of humanity's genesis.

To cite Hoagland's words exactly, "I believe whoever built Puma Punku (in Peru) came from Mars." Well now, that is quite a claim. Especially since we lack unmistakable photographic evidence of artifacts Hoagland believes cinch his case. Moreover, since his claims are so monumental (no pun intended)—that whoever built ancient cities on Earth first built them on Mars—the amount of proof necessarily must be monumental too (pun definitely intended).

Somehow, to me at least, a rock shaped like a tennis shoe will not change my opinion on the origin of the human race.

Why We Want to See More than is Really There

It is true that something seems distinctly familiar about the landscape in the *Curiosity* photos. Could this be yet another trick our minds play to help us discern what we see? Some remark that

Figure 24 – Curiosity Hi-Res Photo of Mount Sharp (Mars)

looking at Mars is like looking at the Mojave Desert, which coincidentally I accomplished firsthand in January, 2013, as I drove through California on my way to my father's house in Oklahoma.[13]

Trusting our own eyes in such an out-of-this-world setting surely calls for caution. Seeing a mirage in the desert is certainly par for the course. (The reader should look at the photos adjacent to judge for themselves).

Figure 25 - Mojave Desert, Southern California (Earth)

Posted on the CBS News website, writer Benjamin Radford provided a pithy characterization of the search for life on Mars gone sideways. From his skeptical perspective, "seeing things is the essence of the problem." Radford recounts:

---

[13] As I remarked to my friend Patricia while driving through the Mojave, the biggest difference detected: "The mountains on Mars appear to have been eroded 'from side to side' by violent waters raging across the plains of Mars. The mountains of the Mojave show erosion 'from the top down' due to millions of years of rain (although it only rains there rarely now). Otherwise, they appear equally red and desolate." Neither are places I would want to run out of gas.

Photos of the surface of Mars taken by the NASA robot Spirit in 2008 were said to show a humanlike figure. Several Internet sites posted the image and suggested the figure could be alive, sparking speculation and controversy. The real explanation, according to astronomer Phil Plait of the Bad Astronomy website, is that "The rock on Mars is actually just a few inches high and a few yards from the camera. A few million years of Martian winds sculpted it into an odd shape, which happens to look like, well, a Bigfoot!"

Then in 2010 a team of psychics led by Courtney Brown, a researcher at Emory University claimed to have found evidence not only of life on Mars in NASA photos, but also a large industrial dome and a plume of waste coming from it. In a video presentation titled "Evidence of Artificiality on Mars," Brown claimed to have found "a very large dome that is highly reflective, it looks like it is made of some sort of resin material." Needless to say, no other evidence of an alien dome has ever been found.

History and human psychology tell us that sooner or later, one or more of the thousands of images beaming to us from Curiosity 352 million miles away will contain some glitch, anomaly, or trick of light that will be interpreted by someone as evidence of Martians. Of course it is possible that the rover will find real, actual evidence of life on Mars—but it probably won't be in the form of alien bases.[14]

Despite our review of historic and optimistic Martian explorers, it remains easy to forget that 60 years ago most scientists still believed in life on Mars. From *LiveScience*, 08-03-2012, Josh Bandfield a Mars expert and planetary scientist at the University of Washington made this observation: "Before the Mariner flybys in the 1960s, scientists thought Mars had water and life, even if it was just some sort of plantlike lichen. Mars' spectrum, its color in the near infrared, mimics that of vegetation. Back in the '50s and '60s, they concluded that was evidence of chlorophyll, and Mars had vegetation."[15]

---

[14] See http://www.cbsnews.com/8301-205_162-57490417/why-curiosity-rover-is-likely-to-find-martians/. Benjamin Radford is deputy editor of Skeptical Inquirer science magazine and author of *Scientific Paranormal Investigation: How to Solve Unexplained Mysteries*. His Web site is www.BenjaminRadford.com.

[15] See http://www.livescience.com/22119-mars-cultural-fascination.html.

In the article by Becky Oskin, she cites Robert Crossley, emeritus professor of English at the University of Massachusetts in Boston and author of the book *Imagining Mars: A Literary History* (Wesleyan, 2011): "The nature of people's interest in Mars has evolved in the last 50 or 60 years, but it [has] never entirely vanished." Oskin points out that the early Mariner missions to Mars dampened enthusiasm for Mars. All of a sudden, the planet looked much too much like our own moon, with craters and vast expanses of nothingness. Much to the dismay of the public, Mars appeared to be dead as a doornail.

Conclusion: The Closer We Come

To be sure, with the advent of the 1960s, the early Mariner missions prompted a radical change in our thinking *about* and our relationship *with* Mars. The images showed an apparently lifeless, highly desolate, and unmistakably cratered planet.

> "The flyby showed pictures of a very moonlike landscape, which had a staggering effect," said [Bob] Sheehan [psychologist, amateur astronomer, and author]. "It left people quite demoralized." NASA's expeditions may have killed some of the Red Planet's romanticism, Sheehan believes. "The less defined an object is like Mars, the more evocative it is. We use it as a Rorschach [the infamous ink-blot test] to project our hopes and fears on to. As Mars becomes more explored, it becomes a more quotidian setting [i.e., commonplace, unremarkable] that no longer captures the imagination," Sheehan said.[16]

In the final ironic analysis regarding whether the Red Planet harbors life of any sort, the reality of the situation now stands dismally *unromantic*. For all except the most eager to prove ET really exists, it appears more than evident that the closer we get to Mars, the worse our view becomes.

[16] Ibid.

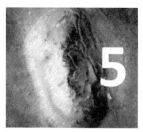

Martian "Art" and the Origin of Man

5

Just the Artifacts, Mam!

WHAT WOULD IT TAKE TO PROVE TO SCIENCE AND TO OUR CULTURE THAT INTELLIGENT LIFE EXISTS ON ANOTHER WORLD? MIND YOU: THE ISSUE IS NOT WHETHER THE WORLD IN question circles a faraway star or is a mere moon orbiting a nearby planet. The matter is whether any remote heavenly body hosts life of the intelligent kind.

Goodness knows, many readers would assert that UFOs should have done the trick. After all, the substantiation of unidentified flying objects goes well beyond hearsay. With thousands of photographs published, tens of thousands of witnessed sightings down through the ages, and too many blood-curdling stories of alien abductions in modern times to mention, a disinterested party would be led to conclude something real must be at the root of all of this commotion. Despite the fact this body of evidence is frequently compromised with hoaxes and exaggeration, to most of the population the evidence remains compelling. On the other hand, the scientific community lacks the same conviction: UFOs, Bigfoot sightings, and ghost stories are all grouped into the identical disreputable category. No matter how many photos are taken, the number of simultaneous sightings by qualified observers, or physical evidence of alien abduction (or the extensive academic research of Alien Abduction specialist, David Jacobs), when it comes to scientists and academics, UFO accounts seem to fall on deaf ears.

Indeed, despite the vast numbers of testimonies chockfull of convincing detail coming from every country on the globe, the vast majority of top scientists still refuse to believe that spacecraft from another world (manned with intelligent pilots) actually exist. The distance between star systems is just too great. There is too much space and not enough time to allow physical creatures to make the trip.

Figure 26 - David Jacobs Professor, Researcher of Alien Abduction Phenomenon

Not to be thwarted, believers in UFOs resort to another explanation for "how they get here." They postulate our visitors come from another dimension. However, this cosmic sleight of hand only complicates the debate. If anything, it solves one problem by introducing other more challenging complexities. Exactly how do you traverse dimensions? Is it not a case of prestidigitation? "Now you see them, now you don't." Doesn't this remove any possibility that UFO claims can be proven true? In philosophy when you eliminate the possibility that something can be proven false, you have made the assertion "immune to disproof." It is intellectual cheating. For in the scientific methodology, you can only prove something true, if it can be demonstrated false. Consequently, it doesn't help the argument to assert our visitors travel here from afar by moving "inter-dimensionally" (no known means exists to do that trick, hence, it is unscientific, and thus, impossible to prove). It is as believable as wizards who can dance between the raindrops.[1]

As it turns out, the opportunity to prove the theory that intelligent life exists is not really that remote. In fact, the proof we are looking for may exist in our own "backyard" (so to speak)—our own

---

[1] The notion of additional dimensions through which physical beings can travel is something that may be true and seems to be well-supported by biblical cosmology. It is just not something that science stands ready to admit.

solar system—specifically, the nearby celestial spheres we call our Moon and the planet Mars. The essential evidence convincing to most scientists is, in a word, the *artifact.*

The word artifact comes from a Latin word *artificium,* meaning either "made by craft" (e.g., a work of art) or "craftiness" which is similar to the word *artifice* (meaning "a clever deception"). Upon consideration, it is clear *artificial* and *artifact* stem from the same root word, *art.* In essence, *art* is involved in making or creating the artifact. Likewise, if something is *artificial,* it is *not* natural. It is "man made." Hence, we should rightly conclude it requires art— *creative intelligence*—to make an artifact. Another way to put it: artifacts are not random objects—they are created with a purpose in mind.

Thus, the discovery of artifacts somewhere other than earth— bits and pieces of objects made by humans (or more broadly, intelligent life of some sort)—would prove decisively we *are not* (and never were) *alone.*

Artifacts comprise the objects at the root of *archeology* (the study of ancient cultures) and *anthropology* (the study of humankind, especially its cultural development). Artifacts are the substance of both *science* (direct observation and testing) as well as *speculation,* concerning their use and place in the culture of which they were once a part. In other words, because these studies focus on empirical data (the actual objects which can be examined by various measuring tools to disclose their substance and age) *artifacts* yield "facts" *acceptable to science.* They are literally "art facts." Despite sounding like an oxymoron, *facts of art* are the proof in the pudding—like Kilroy, somebody *intelligent* has been here before.

However, the game is not as straightforward as that phrase may suggest. Any science built on artifacts is not free from conjecture. There is still detective work to do. Those who study artifacts are compelled to pass judgment on their purpose. Why such implements were created in the first place is not always that obvious.

In other words, artifacts call for speculation from the experts. In the sciences of archeology or anthropology, it takes an accomplished professional to determine what the artifacts *mean*. Questions to be asked might include: "What is the purpose the creator of the object had in mind when he or she made it? Was it a tool to simplify or mechanize a repetitive activity? For instance, was it a pot to hold water or some other important substance? Could it have been a container for food? Was it is canister used in warfare?"

Finding Artifacts Elsewhere in Our Solar System

Of course, there is a big difference evident to this author (and I assume the reader appreciates the issue as well), when *comparing artifacts on earth to artifacts on the Moon or Mars.*

On earth, ancient artifacts are studied to understand human culture in the recent or distant past. It goes without saying: we are not surprised to find them—we expect the historical residue of human activity to be everywhere. According to accepted academic science, we know humankind (*Homo sapiens sapiens*) has been here for tens of thousands of years, and the forebears of our species (*Homo sapiens*) a hundred thousand years before that.[2]

Figure 27 - The Ruins at Göbekli Tepe

---

[2] Here I am speaking as if evolutionary theory (regarding the origins of humankind) is fully true. My view is actually based upon the so-called "Gap Theory" that postulates the world is old but the Adamic race (our current human race) is relatively new (perhaps less than 8,000 years old) and is a special creation of God, directly created by Him (i.e., not evolving from lower forms of *Homo sapiens*).

Additionally, we might be surprised to learn the material composition of the artifacts we discover here on earth—how they were created, or how old they are. Such findings during the past century by archeologists at *Puma Punku* in Peru or *Göbekli Tepe* in Turkey are stunning in the complexity of the structure, their apparent "machined megalithic composition", and the fact they often testify to the ancients' sophisticated understanding of astronomy. After thorough analysis by the experts, such artifacts have stretched our understanding of "pre-history"—demonstrating advanced intelligence (presumably) of *Homo sapiens* and ancient cultures of our world.

Our history books routinely tell us civilization is barely more than 6,000 years old and that it began in "the fertile crescent"—that is, Sumer and Babylon (today's Iraq). But structures like Puma Punku may be proving our history books wrong. Experts familiar with these finds suggest they date to at least 10,000 to 12,000 years before the present (YBP). Additionally, in some cases they are at locations far distant from the "plains of Shinar" where, according to the Bible, Nimrod built the Tower of Babel commencing post-flood civilization 300 to 400 years after the flood of Noah.[3] Proof of an advanced civilization on earth 10,000 YBP would shake up both secularly-based as well as biblically-based history.

While we would be fascinated with a discovery of ancient objects on earth, merely finding any artifact *on another world* is a horse of a completely different color. Not that the idea of life elsewhere in our universe is especially new—it has been discussed for centuries. But in the age of space exploration the notion we could actually stumble across concrete evidence surely makes the heart beat faster.

---

[3] The dating of the Flood of Noah (not to mention whether or not it occurred at all) is controversial. The dating computed by Bishop James Ussher (1581-1656) dated the great deluge to roughly 2,400 BC. Some scientific geological studies suggest this flood may have occurred 600 to 1,000 years earlier than Ussher allowed. Dates derived at the city of Ur (of Chaldea) propose this population center went through several stages from 3,600 BC to 3,100 BC.

Just the presence of any object with straight lines, an explicit geometrical shape, or an extensive manufactured or polished surface would be a true game changer. If we can observe these objects "with our own eyes" (or through cameras mounted on space probes that give us a close-up look of an object with all the markings of intelligence—in effect, extending our eyes to another world), we have then demonstrated intelligent life exists beyond planet Earth and beyond a shadow of a doubt. This discovery could agitate the foundations of human culture, our self-perception, and have consequences that we can barely begin to fathom.[4]

As the fictional, lead character Dr. Heywood R. Floyd commented upon discovering the black monolith on the Moon in *2001: A Space Odyssey*, "I'm sure you're aware of the extremely grave potential for cultural shock and social disorientation contained in this present situation, if the facts were prematurely and suddenly made public without adequate preparation and conditioning."

Artifacts on another planet—even if there was no life present accompanying the "mementoes" then discovered—alters the question of origins immediately and forever.[5]

Based upon an interview published in a popular magazine, Stanley Kubrick indicated that his movie *2001: A Space Odyssey* was inspired by the Brookings Report, now over five decades old. Shared with the public on December 15, 1960, an article in the New York Times headlined the implications:

---

[4] The 1960 report by the Brookings Institute provided a strong sociological argument that may have energized a government program of hiding the truth about encounters with extraterrestrials along with a cautionary path to exploring the Moon, Mars, and other planets. The assumption the public "can't handle the truth."

[5] As I will argue, this does not mean the Bible's narrative is incorrect, just that it may have been misunderstood. Christian intellectual Michael Heiser, in an interview alongside Richard Hoagland on Art Bell's radio program in 2006, argued that Theism could adapt itself just fine with the idea of life on Mars. But Dr. Heiser tends to be contrarian when it comes to the views of this author and other close colleagues. See http://www.youtube.com/watch?v=T1ECXOGCXo0.

MANKIND IS WARNED TO PREPARE FOR DISCOVERY OF LIFE IN SPACE:

Brookings Institution Report Says Earth's Civilization Might Topple if faced by a Race of Superior Beings.

Words from the actual report itself state the following: "'Artifacts' (i.e. ancient alien ruins) are likely to be found by NASA on the Moon and/or Mars. If the artifacts point to the existence of a superior civilization, the social impact is 'unpredictable.'" The original report was astonishingly candid and confident. What changed?

Family Ties

Assume for a moment that we have established such objects exist on our moon or Mars. Then take the hypothetical discovery a bit further. What if these objects resemble artifacts on earth? What if the same shapes are common to what we see on *our* world? What does it say about life elsewhere? Would it mean that life here and there is related? Is it just *intelligence* that we have in common? Or is it more? Could certain artifacts infer that these intelligent creatures were bipedal like us, perhaps having two eyes like we do, and are chemically "carbon-based life forms" just like human beings?

Other questions might present themselves: perhaps the civilization on the Moon or Mars worshiped the stars as our ancestors did. What would that imply? Furthermore, what if these intelligent beings have a face that resembles ours? Would it mean that we have common parentage? Would we be related? Going one step further still, what if fossilized remains were located and the DNA of these other-worldly creatures was found to be similar to our own? What if it was virtually identical? To discover that we have close relatives from another planet would be astounding to say the least.

As far-fetched as this scenario seems at first blush, it comprises exactly what many outspoken authors (and a few slightly more reserved scientists) postulate. There is no telling what we will uncover when we go kicking rocks over in our own solar system.

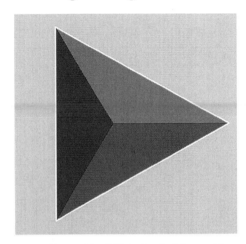

Figure 28 - A Tetrahedral Pyramid
(Comprised of Four-Equilateral Triangles)
as Viewed from Above

As we have discussed previously, Richard Hoagland is one such authority searching for these pieces of proof. He claims that his search is not just the work of an odd collection of "wanna-be" astrophysicists or sensationalist authors trying to peddle books. It is foundational to over sixty years of space exploration by the U.S. and the former Soviet Union. In fact, he speculates the search for artifacts might have been the reason NASA started up in the first place.

In *Dark Mission: The Secret History of NASA*, authors Hoagland and Bara argue that NASA has a deeper and, in not-so-subtle ways, more *mystical* mission than what the public has been led to believe. In a few words, Freemason philosophy, itself heavily influenced by the ancient religion of Egypt, compels NASA's leadership to strange, ritualistic behaviors. Even the layperson realizes the colossal monuments we call "the Pyramids" figure prominently in ancient humankind's worship of the sun and stars. Unexpectedly, the mysticism inherent in ancient mythology appears to impact mission decisions of our otherwise farsighted rocket scientists.

Ritual Alignment?

According to Hoagland and Bara, it is no accident that launches and landings of NASA spacecraft occur at key points in time. These dates and times, in which the relationship of certain stars in the sky are at particular angles as seen from our world or, in some cases, the world we are exploring. At the center of this mythology lies the belt of Orion in the constellation by the same name. In one direction it points to Sirius—the "dog star"—the brightest star in the sky; while in the other direction, a line extending from Orion's belt leads to *Aldebaran* another bright star, 65 million light years from earth. Orion is the more common name for *Osiris* while Sirius represents *Isis* in the Egyptian pantheon, the sister and wife of Osiris.[6]

In his earlier book, *The Monuments of Mars* (1987), Hoagland puts forth the hypothesis that the *Cydonia Mensa* on Mars (wherein lies the famous face with both leonine and simian characteristics), along with other oddly shaped mountains in various structures (aka "*The City*"), provide a compelling case that artificial structures exist there. As we documented earlier, because there are pyramidal shapes at Cydonia (although typically tetrahedral—

Figure 29 – The Hoagland-Carlotto Model

three-*sided* rather the four-*sided* pyramids, with four *surfaces* rather than five), and because THE FACE at Cydonia looks human,

---

[6] In ancient Egypt, when Sirius appeared first arose in the sky it marked the beginning of the new year and the flooding of the Nile, essential in the cycle of growing crops. In ancient times, Egypt was the "bread basket" of the Mediterranean world.

Hoagland has long postulated there constitutes a profound connection between civilization on Mars and on Earth. But he goes further.

The Martians were more than country bumpkins—they were highly advanced. To be specific, he argues Martians understood "hyperdimensional physics" and that *angular momentum*[7] on massively celestial objects (such as the "giant red spot on Jupiter") forms a time-space worm hole. Furthermore, Hoagland and Bara assert the structures of Mars "encode" the key to understanding this physics which transcends what Einstein taught us.

In effect, the citizens of Mars were building long lasting monuments encoding the obviously not-so-obvious truth about "the nature of nature." It is as if they had uncovered the truth and they could not stand to let the secrets die with them, lest this learning be lost to posterity (and their descendants, namely us).

This is where that intriguing number, 19.5 comes into play. It is this angle—19.5 degrees—that the tetrahedral shape exhibits extraordinary physical properties. When a the tetrahedral shape is placed within a sphere, the points "touch" the sphere at a "latitude" of 19.5 degrees above or below the "equator". Jupiter's "Giant Red Spot" lies at 19.5 degrees below its equator; Neptune's "Great Dark Spot" lies at 19.5 degrees above its equator; Earth's "hot spot" lies on the Big Island of Hawaii which also rests at about 19.5 degrees above the equator. Big objects in our solar system seem to comply with this new (but unproven) physical law (as far as we know).

Many Egyptian researchers believe the Great Pyramid at Giza also has encoded information. For instance, each side of the pyramid is precisely 365.2422 Hebrew cubits (25.20 inches), the exact length of our calendar year. The height via the slope angle of the Pyramid is 232.52 cubits. Dividing the height into two times the side length yields the irrational number "Pi" (3.14159). Many other mathematical numbers are encoded in the Pyramid making it much

---

[7] Note: angular momentum is the amount of energy created by *spin*—the more spin the more angular momentum.

more than an architectural wonder. So, does this earthly precedent suggest the "monuments of Mars" (assuming for the sake of argument they were made by intelligent beings), also encode knowledge? Hoagland and Bara attempt to prove the handicraft by working "the angle" in reverse—i.e., by demonstrating mathematical knowhow lies embedded in these structures—they are therefore proven to be artifacts, and voila, intelligence once existed there.

Hyperdimensionality implies the ability to "warp" space-time—when mass and speed are handled in just the right way. While beyond the scope of this paper, suffice it to say a civilization which understands hyperdimensionality knows the secret of "free energy" draining energy from space-itself without fission or fusion of matter) and may understand how to complete interstellar travel safely. It may also yield the ability to move backwards and forwards in time (no mean feats to be sure). [8]

The consequences are staggering because this would mean that intelligent life (if not superior intelligent life) does exist, or more likely, used to exist on Mars. Furthermore, since the shapes are "tetrahedral" (four triangularly-shaped surfaces that connect at six points or vertices), not only do these shapes prove intelligence (i.e., art) in their creation, they relate to similar shapes on earth, suggesting that life there (whether extinct or not) in some way stands connected to life on earth.

Conclusion: Picture the Possibilities

No less a figure than Sir Arthur C. Clarke commented (perhaps motivated by Hoagland's excited interpretation of numerous photographs): "I'm fairly convinced that we have discovered life on Mars. There are some incredible photographs [from the Jet Propulsion Laboratory], which to me are pretty convincing proof of the

---

[8] It is believed that Jupiter "gives off" energy from its big red spot, like a hyperdimensional power plant. The Red Spot has long been believed to be a storm, but one that exists, possibly, because of the angular momentum of the big planet.

existence of large forms of life [read: *artifacts*] on Mars! Have a look at them. I don't see any other interpretation."

Likewise, Robert A. Roe, former Chairman, Congressional House Committee on Science, Space, and Technology stated (in the accolades for Hoagland's book) asserted, "I've seen the studies and I've seen the photographs—and there do appear to be formations of a 'face' and 'pyramids' [on Mars] that do not appear to be of natural or normal existence. It looks like they had to be fashioned by some intelligent beings. For this reason, I have asked NASA to provide assurances that the *Mars Observer* mission includes this [set of targets] as one of its imaging objectives." Ironically, that spacecraft, the *Mars Observer* was lost in flight. This unfortunate incident only added to the Mars' mystery in the decade of the 1990s.[9]

Hoagland remained frustrated for years, eager to get a better glimpse of the planet's surface. He has served as cheerleader for other flights to Mars and especially to focus our reconnaissance on the specific areas he believes have the greatest promise to confirm life once existed there. The latest expedition, *Curiosity* or the *Mars Space Laboratory*, landing on the Red Planet in August, 2012, nearly made Hoagland giddy with anticipation. *Curiosity* possesses multiple high-definition cameras. It has been busy snapping photos ever since.

Curiosity touched down in the Gale Crater, near a rectangular shaped mountain, *Mount Sharp*. Because of its enormity, this prominence on the Martian surface boggles the mind. It stands 100

---

[9] "The *Mars Observer* spacecraft, also known as the *Mars Geoscience/ Climatology Orbiter*, was a 1,018-kilogram (2,244 lb.) robotic space probe launched by NASA on September 25, 1992 to study the Martian surface, atmosphere, climate and magnetic field. During the interplanetary cruise phase, communication with the spacecraft was lost on August 21, 1993, three days prior to orbital insertion. Attempts to re-establish communication with the spacecraft were unsuccessful." See http://en.wikipedia.org/wiki/Mars_Observer.

miles long and 3 miles high. Like the other structures on Mars, Hoagland speculates that this protuberance is also an artifact.

Figure 30 - Gale Crater, Landing Site for Curiosity
Mt. Sharp Stands Located at its Center.

Does *Curiosity* have the potential to find definitive artifacts and prove Hoagland's theories true? According to Hoagland's inventive review of these newest photographs (always a bit creative in his analysis and interpretation), from his perspective (and Mike Bara's), it already has. This debate, however, rages on.

In a later chapter, we will analyze the latest punches exchanged in the "photo fights"—the arguments surrounding specific photos, not surprisingly focused mostly on THE FACE. But before we feast our eyes on these most recent photos, another more provocative manner of visual exploration (to find discernible clues to whether or not life exists on Mars), demands we devote some energy (and maybe a bit of imagination) to its consideration.

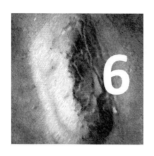

"Out of this World" Remote Viewing

More than Just another Intelligence Gathering Tool

IN THE OPENING CHAPTER, WE EXPLORED THE POSSIBILITY THAT CERTAIN SPECULATIVE *ASSERTIONS* (SOME WOULD INSIST I CALL THEM *FACTS*) ABOUT THE RED PLANET COULD BE AN IMPORTANT PART OF "THE LIE" (*"pseudos"* in the Greek—2 Thessalonians 2:13, from which our antecedent *pseudo* derives; see also, "lying wonders" or *pseudos teras*—2 Thessalonians 2:9). This cosmological falsehood will be a compelling myth that the *Man of Sin* (i.e., Antichrist) will propagate among the inhabitants of our little but cosmologically decisive planet.

The Greek words, *teras*, is used 16 times in the New Testament. Another prime example is Matthew 24:24, *"For there shall arise false Christs, and false prophets, and shall shew great signs and **wonders**; insomuch that, if it were* possible, *they shall deceive the very elect."* It stands to reason that when Paul used the word in his second letter to the Thessalonians, he was literally quoting Jesus' use from the gospel of Mark which was most likely available to him at the time of his letter writing: *"For false Christs and false prophets shall rise, and shall shew signs and **wonders**, to seduce, if it were possible, even the elect."* (Mark 13:22) The miracles of Christ attested to His being the Messiah. Peter said in his famous sermon (after receiving the gift of the Holy Spirit): *"Ye men of Israel, hear these words; Jesus of Nazareth, a man approved of God among you by miracles and **wonders** and signs, which God did by him in the midst of you, as ye yourselves also know."* (Acts 2:22). The phrase "signs and wonders" prevails through most of the 16 New Testament uses. Strong's Concordance suggests that the word is often associated with "wonders seen in the heavens." If so, wonders in the skies may be characteristic of the Antichrist himself, as he seeks, with the help of the False Prophet, to attest to his being the true Messiah of Israel and the Satanic counterfeit to save the world.

In several previous chapters, we have discussed the collection of unusual structures on Mars known as Cydonia and expressed the now commonplace notion that the odd shapes evident in multiple

Figure 31 - The Curiosity on Mars August 2012 (Artist Conception)

pictures taken by various NASA spacecraft, resemble pyramids (three-sided, four-sided, and even a five-sided one). We also referenced the outspoken and believers (like Richard Hoagland, Mike Bara, Graham Hancock, et al) who testify to ancient, albeit now extinct intelligent life once present there. The possible inclusion of mathematical "truths" built into Mars' unusual formations would reveal this to be so. No wonder then (pun not intended) that the mere possibility of this being true would motivate our government (and its power players) to search for the underlying advantages that such knowledge would afford. If such ancient wisdom provides potential military applications, the race to discover it would be a frantic one.

According to various authors who have written on the subject, our government carries out space exploration not just by expensive, robotic mechanisms launched into outer space to visit our celestial neighbors (such as NASA/JPL's *Curiosity* that landed in August, 2012), but occurs through a paranormal capability of the human mind; namely, *remote viewing*. This capability has been implemented and no doubt refined by our government (and others) for over four decades.

Remote viewing is essentially clairvoyance or *mediumship* clad in a scientific, "laboratory" guise (with a euphemistic new name) to reduce the "spookiness" of the practice.[1] This author has written extensively about the subject in two of my more recent books, *Power Quest, Books One* and *Two* (see in particular Chapters 3 and 4 of *Book Two, The Ascendancy of Antichrist in America*).

These techniques were first studied methodically at Stanford Research Institute (SRI) in 1972 by Hal Puthoff (a leading American physicist)—although in my research I trace the origins much further back in time, to 1947 and the secretive work of the infamous Andrija Puharich. It eventually led to a highly specialized (if not purely "secular" and "clinical") approach used in military intelligence.[2] It is not coincidental that SRI funded Hoagland's initial research into THE FACE on Mars.

---

[1] "Within parapsychology, *clairvoyance* is used exclusively to refer to the transfer of information that is both contemporary to, and hidden from, the clairvoyant. It is very different from telepathy in that the information is said to be gained directly from an external physical source, rather than being transferred from the mind of one individual to another... Clairvoyance is related to remote viewing, although the term "remote viewing" itself is not as widely applicable to clairvoyance because it refers to a specific controlled process (italics and bold added). From *Wikipedia*, last modified June 27, 2011, http://en.wikipedia.org/wiki /Clairvoyance. Advocates like Mr. Remote Viewing, Major Ed Dames claims that RV is scientific and technical and does not entail "paranormal" skills such as "real clairvoyants." Au contraire!

[2] Called *Coordinate Remote Viewing* (CRV), this is the dominant technique used by the team. It creates a "double-blind" method in an attempt to eliminate any interference from the impressions of the monitor or the consciousness of the remote

The gist of "remote viewing" was to serve as a weapon of war. It began with the Nazis whose clandestine channelers were part of a secret project called *Doktor Greenbaum*,[3] engaged in psychic experiments and activities during World War II.

When the Allies were splitting up the spoils at war's end, the Soviets eagerly nabbed this group while the Americans remained indifferent. However, soon afterwards, the gap in this specific area along with several other areas of strategic research (flying discs was another of particular interest) became a source of national security para-noia, compounding our worry

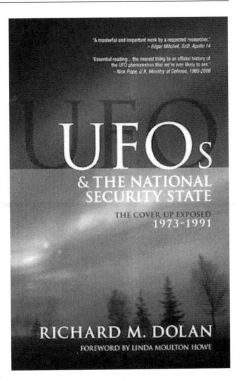

Figure 32 - Richard M. Dolan's *UFOs & the National Security State*

regarding the intentions of the Russian Marxists. Our military and intelligence communities began to fret we were falling behind in a potentially vastly superior source of strategic secrets gathering and even the ability to control of the minds of our enemies. Thus arising from this Cold War hand-wringing was born *psychic spying*.

---

viewer. The fact that latitude and longitude numbering is a human construct (and not a part of nature) makes its working all the more mysterious. Also note: The double blind methodology is not to continue to test or prove the phenomenon; it is to keep the process free of contamination by the conscious minds of the monitor or the viewer. This signifies it is intuition freed from rational faculties which is in play. Of course, Christian analysts would posit that spiritual forces may be lending a hand.

[3] **Greenbaum** being the German word for tree, the reference was most likely to the Cabala tree and the deep mysticism associated with this ancient Jewish mysticism. The fact that the Nazis tapped into a Semitic practice is a curiosity in itself.

The Testimony of the RV Community

The intriguing aspect that has been only recently unfurled, is the material related to the use of remote viewing techniques to reach out beyond our planet and seek information of other worlds. Richard M. Dolan, in his multi-volume bible on Ufology, *UFOs and the National Security State: The Cover-Up Exposed, 1973-1991 (2009)*, supplies considerable additional details on how remote viewing has been used psychically to search these worlds. To say the least, his accounts of various remote viewers, notably Ingo Swann and Pat Price, are mind-boggling.

Many regard Ingo Swann the father of the remote viewing program. In fact, one of the early experiments related to "looking" at another planet from afar. In 1973, Swann was asked to "predict" what the Pioneer 10 satellite would

Figure 33 - Ingo Swann

find when it reached Jupiter. Along with Russell Targ, Puthoff's seemingly constant colleague, Swann specified thirteen traits that the spacecraft would discover months before it arrived. Twelve of the thirteen were confirmed from Pioneers' findings, including the notable feature of a "ring around the planet."[4]

Pat Price, fresh from demonstrating the high reliability of remote viewing to a skeptic "back at the lab", also provided some surprising data which had a bearing on the issue of intelligent life be-

---

[4] Richard M. Dolan, *UFOs and the National Security State: The Cover-Up Exposed, 1973-1991* Rochester, New York: Keyhole Publishing Company, (2009), p. 67

89

yond our earth. Price indicated that, on his own, he had "psychically seen" four *alien* underground bases scattered around our world, each contained within a distinct mountain range. What nefarious plans did these earth-bound aliens have by maintaining giant subterranean encampments here? Price suspected that these bases were connected to alien "implants" and the abductions which facilitate the planting of these nano-sized devices.[5]

Fred Atwater (aka "Skip"), was the founder of the military's remote viewing team in 1977. In 1982, Atwater asked "PSI spy number one" Joe McMoneagle, to remote view "other worlds." McMoneagle confirmed Price's observations offering details about underground tubes, tunnels, and ball shaped objects. "It was a like no place I've seen before—a place I was thoroughly unfamiliar with."

Figure 34 - Joe McMoneagle

Ingo Swann had an extended experience with one Mr. Axelrod (a pseudonym), beginning in February 1975. Picked up at 3 A.M. at a location to which he was told to drive, Swann was hooded then escorted in a helicopter and flown for 30 minutes or so, then walked a considerable distance into a building. Eventually, he sensed he was descending a substantial distance underground in an elevator. Upon stepping off the elevator, he was escorted through extensive corridors only to end his journey with his hood finally removed, face-to-face with Axelrod. Swann was then informed he would receive $1,000 per day to view locations "out of this

---

[5] Ibid., p. 68. Price said, "The inhabitants of the bases looked like normal human beings, although the heart, lungs, blood and eyes were different... and used "thought transfer for motor control of us." The bases were in Spain, Rhodesia (now Zimbabwe), Alaska, and Australia.

world" on behalf of Mr. Axelrod. Apparently, Swann's new client had heard of the Saturn viewings and wanted to make use of his talents to explore specific coordinates on another world. Swann agreed.

Soon he was looking at coordinates supplied by Axelrod and viewing 100-foot towers inside large craters in which glowing green lights shone. Realizing that he was not seeing anything "of this world", Swann continuously asked Axelrod to explain what world he was observing, but with little success. Finally, caving in to Swann's persistent requests, Axelrod informed Swann he was viewing earth's moon.

At one point in the remote viewing experience, Swann became disturbed. He informed Axelrod he was saw humanoids busy at work, when *they discovered Swann observing them.* "Please quickly come away from that place," Axelrod exclaimed.[6]

Why the sudden fear? It was not so much that Swann was physically present or detectable in any natural empirical way. Nonetheless, a psychic image of his bodiless "viewpoint" would apparently be detectable to THEM.

Secretly peering over an adversary's shoulder is risky business; it is especially objectionable from the view point of the one spied upon. However in the alternative world of psychic experience and alien encounters, an intrusion like Swann's—even if such observation occurs by the distant "mind's eye" of the spy—may have consequences beyond our most apprehensive imaginings.

---

[6] Ibid., p. 70. While Swann's viewings cannot be substantiated for obvious reasons, colleagues within the RV community indicate that his observations and his integrity are not easily impugned.

What Is the Meaning of This?

So what are we to make of this curious set of events? The testimony of the Collins Elite, mentioned in our earlier chapter regarding Nick Redfern's book, *Final Events* provides a plausible answer.[7] The Collins Elite suggest that our government has played a dangerous game of deception with alien beings in something of an intentional double-cross. More plainly, this amounted to breaking a pact purportedly consummated in the 1950s between the Eisenhower administration and ET. Reminiscent of the *X-Files'* "Committee of the Elite" who made a deal with a fictional group of malfeasant aliens, our government agreed to supply access to our planet's resources (most notably, *human women for creating a race of hybrids!*) over several decades in exchange for technologies they supply along with an uneasy peace.[8] Or so the story goes.

However, in recent years fearful of the ulterior motives of this alien race, The Collins Elite stressed (according to Redfern's account) how our government literally has been "fighting back". One conscious and tactical aspect of this planetary counter-insurgency was to *use remote-viewing to spy on the aliens.*

Dolan offers this spicy bit of input:

If one assumes the reality of an ET presence, and if one further supposes that the many accounts of alien telepathic ability have some

---

[7] The reader will recall that Redfern's study focuses on this clandestine group funded by the CIA, that asserted the "aliens" are not extraterrestrial at all, but "ultra-dimensional", i.e., they are really demonic beings, not ETs, with malevolent intent.

[8] Believers in the so-called Majestic-12 documents, supposedly dating from that period, say this deal with the extraterrestrial devils is beyond dispute. One interviewee on Coast to Coast AM, from October 16, 2012, Gordon Duff, a former military "higher up" asserted that the Majestic-12 documents were intentionally leaked to X-Files creator, Chris Carter. Given the uncanny parallels between the X-Files' fictional "story arc" of alien intruders and the true testimonies of members of the UFO community supplied as true and in good faith, this would make perfect sense. This unofficial sharing of information to Carter might be pertinent whether or not the Majestic-12 documents are totally valid or partially fraudulent as opponents allege them to be.

validity, we might presume that the remote viewers were of interest to the aliens themselves. Indeed, it has been suggested to the author [Dolan] that Axelrod and his blonde, blue-eyed helpers [later we learn Swann referred to them as "the twins"—which my frequent readers might recognize the implicit suggestion of this detail] were perhaps not exactly human, either, but performing their own counter-intelligence assessment of their vulnerabilities to human remote viewers.[9]

Lest we think the most spectacular accounts only pertain to our moon, a major player who oversaw the *Stargate Program* (described in my earlier writings), Major General Albert Stubblebine relates, "I will tell you for the record that there are structures underneath the surface of Mars... I will also tell you that there are ma-

Figure 35 – Remote Viewer, Ed Dames and his Recent Book, *Killshot*

chines under the surface of Mars that you can look at."[10] We will

---

[9] Ibid., p. 70. Dolan provides another colorful and utterly provocative experience Swann had with the twins and Axelrod, when in 1979 he accompanied them to Alaska in a Leer Jet, after being plucked up from SRI where Swann was spending much of his time. After landing at an airport somewhere in the Alaskan wilderness, Swann witnessed what he depicted as a drone spacecraft, triangular in shape, arising out of a lake covered in fog. The "twins" witnessed the spacecraft through special goggles they were provided by Axelrod. Swann was told to simply observe their behavior. Soon the twins clamored that "they are enveloping the area – we will be detected!" at which point, all four split the scene. Later, Axelrod informed Swann that his group was to be disbanded and another to be formed headed up by those who would not permit "psychic'" in their presence. See Dolan, Ibid., pp. 154-155.

[10] Ibid., p. 71, quoting from Jim Schnabel's study, *Remote Viewers, The Secret History of America's Psychic Spies*, p. 213.

take up the purported existence of underground military bases on Mars in a later chapter.

Another frequently cited remote viewer, Major Ed Dames was in fact the operations officer and trainer for new recruits entering the intelligence community's psychic spy ring. Recently Dames went into considerable detail about these Martian structures on George Noory's October 16, 2012, *Coast-to-Coast AM* show (about two months before this chapter was first published as an online article).

Dames offered that vast underground structures, uninhabited, exist on Mars as a remnant of a semi-advanced civilization dating from eons ago.[11] He offered that the now extinct humanoids were composed of two peoples—both races tall and thin—as a result of Mars' physical characteristics. According to Dames, Mars was the unfortunate victim of ten consecutive years of massive planetary collisions and atmospheric storms that wiped out 85% of the population and virtually all of Mars' water and atmosphere. Given years of pre-warning, the citizens of Mars built massive underground habitations. Subsequent to this calamity they possessed limited resources to support life. Therefore, these carbon-based life forms went extinct. Only "robotic" devices remained active and presently "await the return of their creators" (obviously, Dames assumes select members of the Martian population escaped to other worlds, presumably ours as Hoagland and Bara contend). For those who study these subjects, they will likely recall the notion of a cosmic collision between Mars and a comet along with the destruction of so-called Planet K (aka Krypton which means "hidden"). This explosion

---

[11] When asked by Noury to "rate the level of sophistication" of the civilization there, Dames speculated it was equivalent to the Mayan empire; however, his remarks regarding their supposed ability to create subterranean cities, devise and develop robotic devices far more advanced than our own, and the implied escape of members of the Martian society to our world, bespeak of a civilization far more sophisticated than ours, let alone the Mayan civilization of 1,000 years ago. Like much of Dames' commentary on matters far-flung amidst the cosmos, his assessment(s) did not achieve maximum consistency.

formed the asteroid belt and may have been indirectly to blame for Mars' unfortunate fate.[12]

Related to these purported "findings," Dames claims the Russians (post-Soviet Union) contacted his remote viewing group in an attempt to determine what happened to their unmanned spacecraft, *Phobus 2*, which unexpectedly exploded when only 50 meters from landing on Mars' moon Phobus in 1989.[13] It appeared to their scientists that some sort of projectile was launched from Mars' surface destroying their spacecraft (in the manner of an anti-ballistic missile). Dames asserts a massive "sand dollar-like robotic device" was launched to intercept *Phobus 2* from the underground "command center" under the Martian surface, emphasizing that this action was taken by some type of *sentient machine* (an oxymoron?) still functioning there.

Dames also discussed ancient structures on the earth's moon. He provided an educated guess that some sort of mining activity was performed on our moon millions of years ago. As if his claims could not get any more outlandish, Dames asserted that there is an active, robotic inhabited building of massive scale on "the back side of the moon" (shades of the movie, *Transformers: The Dark of the Moon*—2011). This structure emits objects which come and go to the moon. In fact, according to Dames, crop circles on the earth's surface are the result of the activity of these robotic devices! To

---

[12] Lately there has been a spate of books discussing cosmic collisions which advance the thesis of Immanuel Velikovsky developed in his book, *Worlds in Collision* (1950). Some flesh out a different thesis, that these events were not natural catastrophes (catastrophism), but where in fact a galactic war predating human history. We will discuss in detail in a later chapter.

[13] "On March 31, 1989 headlines informed that Phobos 2, before losing contact, captured some strange photos of an unidentified object. Phobos 2 operated normally during its cruise phase, travelling the millions of miles from the Earth to Mars with no mechanical problems. It successfully gathered data about the Sun, Earth, Mars, and the interplanetary medium. On March 27, 1989, as it approached within 50 meters of the moon Phobos, it was set to drop a mobile "hopper" lander and a stationary platform. But just before doing so, contact was mysteriously lost." See http://www.youtube.com/watch?v=L_x68J3tZjY.

heighten the incredulity, Dames suggested the *Illuminati* were behind the possibility that the American election of November 6, 2012 might not come to pass. Given President Obama's second term is now ongoing, we can surmise Dames' prophecies (derived from his own remote viewing and in some cases those of "RVers" he knows), are rather "hit and miss" with more misses than hits. [14]

Nevertheless, virtually all remote viewers share Dames' notion that ancient artifacts, i.e., structures of intelligent design exist on other planets (and our moon). This surely captivates.

Ingo Swann's interest in structures on distant worlds peeked in 1976 when an anonymous party gifted him with a book by NASA photo analyst George Leonard entitled, *Somebody Else is on the Moon*. According to Dolan, the photos were very similar to Swann's drawings. In 1979, Vito Saccheri, an industrial engineer took his friend Lester Howes, another engineer, to Houston to view these NASA photos which, at that time, were available upon special request for public scrutiny. The prints were quite large and high resolution (much beyond the quality shown in Leonard's book) and provided compelling evidence of "obvious machinery" and "three surprising pyramids that prompted me later to closely study the Egyptian Giza pyramid complex."[15] Ah, there it is—pyramids once again. Proof positive we are all one big happy family. The only remaining question to be answered: whether humanity first began on Earth then migrated to Mars, or the process went the opposite way.

The revelation of remote viewing carried out by our intelligence services slowly leaked to the public within a few years of Seymour Hersch's 1974 article which broke the story of MK-ULTRA (in

---

[14] Dames' latest book, *Killshot*, predicts a rogue solar flare will devastate the earth in 2013. No "kill shot" transpired in 2013. In fact, at the beginning of 2014, the Sun has no sunspots—no solar storms. This hasn't happened in 100 years. Given two major predictions that did not happen, Dames' credibility is dwindling.

[15] Ibid., p. 118.

which paranormal abilities of certain young children were scrupu-lously and secretly studied), followed up by the 1975 Church Com-mittee of the Senate that investigated how the various intelligence organizations, especially the C.I.A. and the National Security Agency (N.S.A) had conducted illegal spying and even "drug test-ing" on unwitting American citizens in such matters as the search for "truth serums." [16] Remote viewing, which was a big part of so-called mind control experiments in the 1950s and 1960s, was seri-ous business.

The Committee that researched the malfeasance of the CIA was no small undertaking. It comprised a staff of 150 persons, conducted 800 interviews—250 executives in all, along with 21 public hearings. This investigation was ordered by President Ford and placed under the auspices of Nelson Rockefeller who, despite being a great friend of the U.S. military-industrial complex and especially its intelligence apparatus, produced a thorough and purportedly honest expose of our government's unscrupulous dealings.[17]

As this author documented in the final chapter of *Power Quest, Book Two,* although the Rockefeller Report was confirmatory in the misconduct of our government, the scope of its discussion barely began to tell the whole, sordid story. The depth of malevolent ac-tions committed by our intelligence service transcends belief. One has to review the facts personally (many included in the Congres-sional record), to believe it.

---

[16] However, it was not until the 1990s with the declassification of numerous documents that the U.S. government provided limited confirmation of the nature of paranormal "data collection."

[17] According to Dr. Stanley Montieth (a friend and frequent interviewer of this author on his nationally syndicated radio show), the restriction was that only a few copies of the report were made available and those but for a very short time. Mon-tieth has indicated to me, however, that he managed to obtain one of the copies.

Conclusion: Seeing from Afar

To recap: the door to spiritualism was opened by Nazi scientists before, during (and in some regards, after) World War II. It was clearly emphasized by the Soviets early in the game. But once the U.S. discerned how infatuated the Moscow regime was with psychic spying, our government determined it had to have its own program.

In the midst of spying on our enemies, we discovered beings exist that come from faraway places— even farther than Siberia. Indeed, sincere adherents assert and their numerous accounts confirm that our most troublesome enemies do not share our customs, our language, and especially our DNA, coming as they do from "beyond the pale."[18] Then again, as worrisome as that possibility is, beings that do share much of our DNA *but originate from somewhere other than Earth* pose even greater issues to ponder.

The CIA and the military may not have preferred to employ tax dollars to inadvertently fund a spiritualist practice in America as a means to counter the Soviets during the Cold War, but it had done so nonetheless. Indeed, it was but a singular example among many where an occult worldview (most notably prefigured in Nazi Germany), influenced U.S. behavioral science, astrophysics, and intelligence operations in the latter half of the twentieth century. As an

---

[18] An interesting phrase (*beyond the pale*), whose meaning is even more appropriate in this context. "The earliest figurative sense that's linked to the idiom was of a sphere of activity or interest, a branch of study or a body of knowledge, which comes from the same idea of an enclosed or contained area; we use *field* in much the same way. This turned up first in 1483 in one of the earliest printed books in English, *The Golden Legende*, a translation by William Caxton of a French work. This is a much later example: 'By its conversion England was first brought, not only within the pale of the Christian Church, but within the pale of the general political society of Europe' [the quotation is taken from *The History of the Norman Conquest*, by Ernest A Freeman (1867).] Our sense of it now seems to have grown beyond this, since people who exist outside such a conceptual pale are *not our kind and do not share our values, beliefs or customs.*" [Emphasis mine] From World Wide Words; see http://www.worldwidewords.org/qa/qa-pal2.htm.

unexpected dividend, our government-funded remote viewers provided cheap excursions into outer space collecting information about what may await us when we can physically inspect the most immediate neighborhood within our solar system.

This author ventures that despite the optimism of its many advocates, remote viewing remains an unlikely means to explore worlds beyond our own. It is too controversial. The military barely admits to its use even today. Plus, it lacks complete reliable—only about 80% of the time do RVers get it right. Many examples have already been adduced exhibiting its capricious findings and problematic outcomes. Might there be other ways—safer, faster, and more reliable ways—to travel between neighboring planets and beyond? Later in our study, we will discuss other possible excursion vehicles when we consider worm holes, inter-dimensional star gates, and "jump rooms."

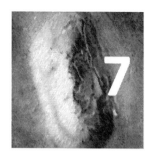

In Radio Contact with Mars

Wireless Transmissions and Martian Deception

O N HALLOWEEN EVE, OCTOBER 30, 1938, ACTOR AND WRITER, ORSON WELLES ESTABLISHED THE MOST FAMOUS CONNECTION EVER *BETWEEN MARS AND WIRELESS TECHNOLOGY*. BUT IT WAS far from the most provocative. The broadcast of H.G. Wells, *War of the Worlds* (1898), scared the pants off at least one million Americans, especially in the northeast United States. Orson Welles changed H.G. Wells' place names from England to New York and rendered the broadcast in the manner of a live eyewitness. By doing so, the program transfixed its listeners. Wireless technology in its then most ubiquitous form, the radio, proved that intelligent life ON

Figure 36 - Orson Welles on Radio, *War of the Worlds, 1938*

THIS WORLD could be duped into believing the most amazing propositions if broadcasters cleverly fashioned their production to blur fantasy and reality.

Fast forward to today: deceiving the masses with wireless technology constitutes a fully perfected science. Television, the most

101

popular wireless communication medium, seems the grand master of deception. A case in point: the line between news and entertainment has never been so thin. Research on the usage of propaganda and even the topic of mind-control has been one this author has studied and about which he has extensively written.

Welles' Mercury Theater presentation in 1938, however, was hardly the first instance where the population has been beguiled by mention of Mars amidst wireless transmission. In fact, as this chapter will demonstrate some of our smartest scientists have been guilty of letting imagination run away with *itself in the search for intelligence on other worlds.*

Figure 37 - Marconi Operating a Simple Wireless Transmitter

Not that this spectacular "astrobiological" detective work lacks enticement. The prospect of discovering life on another world, or to be more specific, to be the first scientist *to confirm intelligent life exists elsewhere,* would forever inscribe one's name in the history books.

What scientist with a larger than life ego (which seems an essential ingredient to become famous in all forms of scientific research), would not be eager to make his or her mark in this way?

To underscore the point, we will talk here about two ultra-famous scientists who invented the most important forms of both wired and wireless technology and how they romantically employed their inventions in an incredible attempt to confirm *life on Mars*.

In fact, as we recount their stories the reader should make note that these two scientists, Nikola Tesla (1856—1943) and Guglielmo Marconi (1874—1937), not unlike their predecessors, were driven over the line from *the realm of science into the murky dominion of the supernatural*. However non-intuitive this migration may appear, paranormal perspectives reign supreme with almost all exotic scientific inquiries down through the ages.

The Wireless Inventions of Marconi and Tesla

First there is Marconi. Like Bruce Wayne (aka *Batman*) and his man-servant Alfred, Marconi did science experiments in the company of his butler. When reaching only his twentieth birthday, Marconi invented the wireless telegraph. He fashioned it by connecting a battery, a spark-gap transmitter, and a bell, composing a storm alarm. When lightning would strike, the bell would ring. Eventually, Marconi made the bell chime by just pushing a button on the other side of his laboratory away from the ringer. Not long thereafter, in 1895 he took his creation outdoors. He placed transmitting and receiving antennas straight up and down (periodically increasing the distance betwixt) and soon learned that by grounding his device (making sure it touched the ground), he could extend the connection, even sending signals over a hill for a distance of up to two miles. It was such a remarkable discovery, that the head of the Italian Ministry of Post and Telegraphs took Marconi's politely letter addressed to his attention (a communiqué which explained the device) and wrote across it, *"Via della Lungara,"* a suggestion that the author should be sent straight to *Longara*—the insane asylum in Rome.

However, despite this torpid reception, eventually Marconi would acquire the respect due him. He developed the transatlantic telegraph, was credited for inventing the long distance radio, and applied this invention to notable commercial applications. For example, in 1904, ships at sea purchased subscriptions to receive news summaries. In fact, the first radio message originating in the United States was a greeting sent through Marconi's device in January, 1903 from President Theodore Roosevelt to King Edward VII. In 1909, Marconi shared the Nobel Prize in Physics with Karl Braun for his contributions to radio.

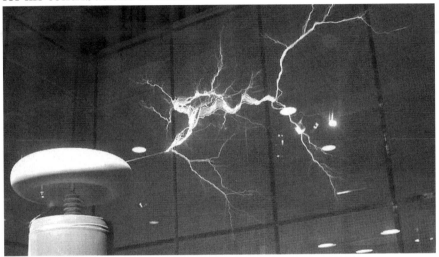

Figure 38 - The Filaments from the Discharge of a Tesla Coil

However, allow me to furnish a bit more detail about Marconi's wireless accomplishments, connecting Marconi to the other scientist of concern, Nikola Tesla. In the citation below, we pick up a few more details about Marconi and make an important connection to Nikola Tesla, allegedly a mentor to Marconi.

> Marconi studied radio transmission theory with [Nikola] Tesla and made his first radio transmission in 1895. Marconi was fascinated by the transmission of power, and in 1896 received a British patent and sent a signal nine miles across the Bristol Channel. In 1899 he successfully setup a wireless station to communicate with a French station 31 miles across the English Channel.
>
> It was thought that the curve of the earth's surface would limit radio transmission to 200 miles at the most, when, on December 11, 1901,

Marconi transmitted a signal from Poldhu, Cornwall, to St. John's Newfoundland, 2000 miles away, he created a major sensation.[1] [Emphasis in original]

In our day, Tesla's work has increasingly become subject to considerable speculation. The reader might recall that it was Tesla who played an important role in the 2006 film, *The Prestige*, as the dark, mysterious character in Colorado Springs who, circa 1901 activated lights wirelessly (which at the turn of the century Tesla actually achieved). The plot of the fascinating film hangs upon Tesla's ability to create clones of objects, even human beings, through his electrical wizardry! In many respects, compared to other astounding inventions he may have truly produced, an achievement such as the film hypothesizes may not have been entirely outside the realm of possibility. Indeed, compared to legend, seldom is the truth of one's accomplishments understated. But in Tesla's case, the folklore may pale in comparison to what he actually attained. For instance, some assert he created an anti-gravity machine that he could (and did) ride into the sky just like the Green Goblin did in Batman comic books.

Figure 39 – A 2002 Book Suggests Tesla Sojourned to Mars

---

[1] From the paper, "The Fantastic Inventions of Nikola Tesla", accessed on 3/22/2013. See http://www.biblio-tecapleyades.net/tesla/esp_tesla_35.htm.

We know for a fact that Tesla developed the so-called *Tesla Coil*.[2] Additionally, his understanding of physics, gravity, and space-time challenged the sacrosanct and celebrated teachings of Einstein. Furthermore, Tesla confronted Einstein head-on regarding the capacity of mass to *warp* space-time. Instead Tesla claimed (and may have proven) that *mass* inherits the attributes of space-time, thus reversing "cause and effect" (regarding how one effects the other) as argued by Einstein. In other words, Tesla suggested that mass acquires the *properties of space-time*. For Tesla, what we commonly describe as "mass and energy" are, in their most fundamental state (and as we might imagine, in condensed form) nothing more than *time*. Therefore, as this author has argued citing various "alternative physicists," *time* comprises the most essential building block of our universe. In essence, *the universe is time.* We can rightly understand (conceptually at least) that all substances are "knots" of time; while energy exists as "time" in an alternative form. (See my book, *Power Quest, Book One*, for an animated discussion on the alternative physics of Nikola Tesla which mirrors the work of Russian Nikolai Kozyrev, 1908—1983).

In regards to wireless technologies, Tesla discovered how energy could be transmitted through the *aether*. Indeed, it is strongly suspected that he discovered a method to leech energy from time itself, providing a means to generate free energy from the basic, fundamental substance of the creation. Many of the imaginative (but sometimes difficult) books of Joseph P. Farrell follow this line of thought.

While Tesla's benefactor, J.P. Morgan (the owner of Standard Oil and monopolist extraordinaire), must have been impressed, he

---

[2] "A *Tesla coil* is an electrical resonant transformer circuit invented by Nikola Tesla around 1891. It is used to produce high-voltage, low-current, high-frequency alternating-current electricity. Tesla coils can produce higher voltages than other artificial sources of high-voltage discharges, electrostatic machines. Tesla experimented with a number of different configurations consisting of two, or sometimes three, coupled resonant electric circuits." [Emphasis in original]
See http://en.wikipedia.org/wiki/Tesla_Coil.

was not about to let Tesla's invention crash his empire—built as it was upon the worldwide burning of fossil fuels. Furthermore, Tesla may have invented a wireless means of transmitting information that far exceeded the capability of electromagnetism (conventional radio waves). Within a mere matter of a few years from Marconi's wireless achievements, Tesla experimented with propagating *gravitic* (more properly, *electrogravitic*) energy waves.[3] This area of research opened the door to "rising above" gravity—which we know as levitation—and providing a means to propel aircraft laterally as well as vertically. In effect, gravitic energy may be *the* vehicle for powering the flying saucer and even enabling interstellar space travel.

Why the comment on interstellar travel here? Because the theory of gravitic propulsion proposes objects (and energy waves) break the barrier of the speed of light (Einstein's well-known constant). Like light, radio waves are limited to the speed of light (186,000 miles per second). But *gravitic energy* is propagated virtually instantaneously across vast distances of space. It forms the basis for the quirky connection between two particles (known as quantum entanglement), in which one particle can instantaneously alter the other although separated by near infinite distance (seemingly demonstrating a *mystical* connection).

Figure 40 - Dr. Thomas Van Flandern

According to Tesla, Einstein was simply wrong about the nature of space-time as the fourth dimension. Likewise, the late Astronomer, Thomas Van Flandern, Ph.D. (Yale), argued that gravitic energy moves through space 20 billion times faster than

---

[3] The term has been vogue since 1956. See Kerstin Klasson, *Developments in the Terminology of Physics and Technology*, page 30.

the speed of light. Later in the book we will compare the nature of gravitic waves with their mundane siblings, light and sound waves.

Tesla and Wireless Telegraphs to Mars

But for our purposes, allow me to draw attention to a self-admitted fact: Tesla believed he communicated with men on Mars after he began using his gravitic waves to send and receive "signals" to other worlds. The story goes (as related by Robert A. Nelson in his 1998 paper: "Communicating with Mars: The Experiments of Tesla & Hodowanec"), that Tesla discovered a means to detect electrical disturbances anywhere within a thousand miles of his location.

In Nelson's piece, we read about Tesla's Colorado Springs' "wireless lighting" featured in the movie, *The Prestige* (2006). Nelson notes his device was called the *Magnifying Transmitter*. When using this technology, Tesla claimed he received signals originating from Mars. Tesla speaks for himself in an article published in *Collier's Weekly* (March 1901) entitled "Talking with the Planets" in which he made this announcement:

> As I was improving my machines for the production of intense electrical actions, I was also perfecting the means for observing feeble effects. One of the most interesting results, and also one of great practical importance, was the development of certain contrivances for indicating at a distance of many hundred miles an approaching storm, its direction, speed and distance traveled.
>
> It was in carrying on this work that for the first time I discovered those mysterious effects which have elicited such unusual interest. I had perfected the apparatus referred to so far that from my laboratory in the Colorado mountains I could feel the pulse of the globe, as it were, noting every electrical discharge that occurred within a range of 1100 miles.
>
> I can never forget the first sensations I experienced when it dawned upon me that I had observed something possibly of incalculable consequences to mankind. I felt as though I were present at the birth of a new knowledge or the revelation of a great truth. My first observations positively terrified me, as there was present in them something mysterious, *not to say supernatural*, and I was alone in

my laboratory at night; but at that time the idea of these disturbances being intelligently controlled signal did not yet present itself to me.

The changes I noted were taking place periodically and with such a clear suggestion of number and order that they were not traceable to any cause known to me. I was familiar, of course, with such electrical disturbances as are produced by the sun, Aurora Borealis and earth currents, and I was as sure as I could be of any fact that these variations were due to none of these causes. The nature of my experiments precluded the possibility of the changes being produced by atmospheric disturbances, as has been rashly asserted by some.

It was sometime afterward when the thought flashed upon my mind that the disturbances I had observed might be due to an intelligent control. Although I could not decipher their meaning, it was impossible for me to think of them as having been entirely accidental. The feeling is constantly growing in me that I had been the first to hear the greeting of one planet to another. A purpose was behind these electrical signals! 4

A Wireless, World-to-World Radio

But the story goes deeper. Nelson discusses another enigmatic figure—Arthur Matthews—who claimed Tesla developed a device which Matthews labeled the *Teslascope*. Its purpose was expressly to communicate with Martians!5

However, Nelson is not the only voice claiming this to be true. In article written by Greg Brian, Brian provides this bit of corroborative analysis:

Whether Tesla really invented something called a *Teslascope*, which reportedly was an off-shoot of the Magnifying Transmitter, is still up for debate. This was basically a radio transceiver [not really—it was gravitic] that could be aimed at planets or toward direction on

---

4 From Robert A. Nelson, "Communicating with Mars: The Experiments of Tesla & Hodowanec" (1998). See http://www.rexresearch.com/hodomars/hodomars.htm. Quoting from Tesla, Nikola: *Collier's Weekly* (March 1901), p. 359-361; "Talking with the Planets."

5 But then Matthew's statements have to be taken with more than a grain of salt. He believed Tesla was from Venus (negating the more recent notion that "men are from Mars and women from Venus"). Furthermore, Mathews asserted Tesla was visited by Venetians (or is it Venusians, but certainly not the kind from Venice).

Earth similarly to a telescope. Transmitting large amounts of electric waves was the secret. Tesla though, [sic] on being able to communicate with an intelligent race if there was one. While the proof is sketchy he invented something called a Teslascope, Tesla did attempt to use his internationally famous Tesla Coil as a form of receiver to experiment with electric waves passed through the atmosphere as possible communication globally or to another planet.[6]

The colorful personage, Dr. Andrija Puharich whom I discuss at length in several of my books (an agent for military intelligence who investigated the paranormal and how it might be used in warfare), met with Matthews and did an interview concerning the interplanetary purpose of his wireless communication device (based on *gravitics*). This interview was published in the *Pyramid Guide* (not your average weekly news magazine). Puharich is quoted below:

> [Arthur Matthews] came from England. Matthews' father was a laboratory assistant to the noted physicist Lord Kelvin back in the 1890s. Tesla came over to England to meet Kelvin to convince him that alternating current was more efficient than direct current [Tesla invented the most conventional wired form of electricity, AC current which is what we use today in our homes and businesses]. Kelvin at that time opposed the AC movement. In 1902, the Matthews family left England and immigrated to Canada. When Matthews was 16, his father arranged for him to apprentice under Tesla. He eventually worked for him and continued this alliance until Tesla's death in 1943.
>
> It is not generally known, but Tesla actually had two huge magnifying transmitters built in Canada, and Matthews operated one of them. Most people know about the Colorado Springs transmitters and the unfinished one on Long Island. I saw the two Canadian transmitters. All the evidence is there.
>
> [The Teslascope is] the thing Tesla invented to communicate with beings on other planets. There's a diagram of the Teslascope in Mat-

---

[6] Greg Brian, "Did Nikola Tesla Communicate with Intelligence [sic] Beings on Mars?" See http://voices.-yahoo.com/did-nikola-tesla-communicate-intelligence-beings-1536713.html?cat=37. This is also the device that may have led to the development of the radio powerhouse we know as HAARP (High Frequency Active Auroral Research program), which some researchers believe interferes with the ionosphere to alter weather and even create earthquakes and tsunamis.

110

thew's book [*The Wall of Light*]. In principle, it takes in cosmic ray signals. Eventually the signals are stepped down to audio. Speak into one end, and the signal goes out the other end as a cosmic ray emitter. [7]

Nelson goes on to detail the work of L. G. Lawrence who described a similar phenomenon in his article, "Communication by Accident" with extraterrestrial intelligences:

> On October 29, 1971 while conducting exploratory RBS [Remote Biological Sensing] experiments in Riverside County, CA, our field instrumentation's organic transducer complex intercepted a train of apparently intelligent communication signals (tight spacing and discrete pulse intervals) while accidentally allowed to remain pointed at the constellation Ursa Major during a short rest period. The phenomenon prevailed for somewhat over 33 minutes.

> A somewhat similar phenomenon was observed on April 10, 1972. The apparent signals, aside from seemingly growing weaker, appear to be transmitted at great intervals ranging from weeks to months, possibly years. A faint, coherent, binary-type phenomenon was noted during aural monitoring. Intervals between rapid series of pulse trains ranged from 3 to 10 minutes.

> Because our equipment is impervious to electromagnetic radiation and found free of internal anomalies, the tentative conclusion of biological-type interstellar communications signals has emerged.[8]

Finally, Nelson discusses yet another electrical genius, Greg Hodowanec, who developed a theory of *Rhysmonic Cosmology,* based upon a device he designed called a *Gravity Wave Detector* (GWD). Supposedly, the device is rather simple, capable of detecting "coherent modulations" in the microwave background radiation.[9]

---

[7] *Pyramid Guide* 4(3): 1 (January-February 1976); ibid., 5(2): 5 (November-December 1976); "Letter from Tesla" (6 January 1900).

[8] Ibid. Quoting Lawrence, L.G.: *Borderlands* 52(1): 27-29 (1996); "Interstellar Communication Signals."

[9] "In cosmology, *cosmic microwave background (CMB) radiation* (also CMBR, CBR, MBR, and relic radiation) is thermal radiation filling the observable universe almost uniformly. With a traditional optical telescope, the space between stars and galaxies (the *background*) is completely dark. However, a sufficiently sensitive telescope shows a faint background glow, almost exactly the same in all directions, that is not associated with any star, galaxy, or other object. This glow is strongest in the microwave region of the radio spectrum. The CMB's serendipitous discovery

Hodowanec uses his device expressly for the search for extraterrestrial life (SETI). Nelson quotes Hodowanec from the *Journal of Radio Astronomy* (April 1986):

> The advantage of a possible gravitational technique for SETI over the radio technique is primarily one of time "propagation" for these signals. The radio waves travel at the speed of light, but the gravitational signals (per the writer's theories) are *essentially instantaneous signals* [as explained earlier]. Another advantage of the gravitational technique is the simplicity of the instrumentation required. As SARA members know, radio astronomy can be quite complicated. The gravitational wave detectors must rely largely on the Earth's mass as a "shadow" to enable the detection of gravitational radiation [the characteristics of earth gravity have to be subtracted from the signal to net out the difference]. Therefore, "objects" or signals located in the observers' zenith are best detected. Yet, the other areas are still "detectable" especially with the aid of other "shadows" such as the sun, moon, planets, etc.[10] [Comments mine]

In Nelson's opinion, the burden of proof had been met.

As far as the Martian source of his gravitic wireless correspondence, for Nelson Tesla's testimony remained vouchsafed. Nelson asserts:

> By July 1988, Hodowanec had confirmed Tesla's claims, as he announced in "Some Remarks on the Tesla Mars Signals": [Quoting Hodowanec] "Such signals are being received <u>today</u> with simple <u>modern-day</u> scalar-type signal detectors...[11] coherent modulations are being 'heard' in [the microwave] background radiation. The most prominent modulations being three pulses (code S) slightly separated in time, a la Tesla! On occasions, the code equivalents of an E, N, A, or K are also heard, but the most persistent response is SE, SE, etc."[12]

---

in 1964 by American radio astronomers Arno Penzias and Robert Wilson was the culmination of work initiated in the 1940s, and earned them the 1978 Nobel Prize." See http://en.wikipedia.org/wiki/-Cosmic_microwave_background_radiation.

[10] Ibid.

[11] *Scalar detectors* would be a sophisticated way of expressing "digital" signaling which transposes analogue or wave-like means of communications and "rounds them off" into numeric equivalents.

[12] Ibid.

The repetitive codes were only the beginning. Soon Hodowanec and his "source" began to develop a code to communicate back and forth and developed a language emulating Morse code. As if this amazing wireless exchange was beyond belief (continuing back and forth for months), Hodowanec later disclosed his personal gravitic pen pal was resident in our solar system—right next door on the Red Planet, just as Tesla asserted!

In an untitled report from 3-13-89 he wrote:

> This, in spite of NASA's denial of any life forms on Mars which situation changed in 1996. [Not really]. This possibility has been recently suspected by the writer due to the apparently very close tracking of my position on Earth by ET. ET, of course, always knew that I was on Earth (as seen by his tracking), but now he has most emphatically confirmed that he is on the 4th planet from the sun, i.e., Mars!!!

> While this release is probably a bit premature, I am so positive of these gravity signal 'exchanges' that I will stick my neck out in this instance. ET on Mars is apparently much more advanced than we are here on Earth, and he may have even previously visited here on Earth, and possibly colonized here (but who are his possible descendants?)

> It is still a mystery where ET may be living on Mars (possibly underground near the Polar Regions), and why ET doesn't use EM [traditional radio waves, i.e., *electromagnetic*] wave signaling methods? Perhaps, it is because Mars is so hostile now that ET must have developed *a very sophisticated underground civilization* which is not conducive to EM radiation systems? [Comments and emphasis mine]

To be sure, the record of the communications between Hodowanec and his Martian buddies boggles the mind. Needless to say, it also closely mirrors the typical communication between a plethora of mediums over the past 140 years and their purportedly extraterrestrial sources (a subject we take up in the next chapter).

Conclusion: Tesla, Marconi, and South America

However, given our eagerness to entertain the fantastic, legend easily overwhelms well-documented fact. When it comes to the exploits of this dynamic duo of Tesla and Marconi, whether real or imagined, hardly anything we can put forth seems too far-fetched.

113

Nevertheless, we will endeavor to conclude our story and simultaneously test the reader's credulity.

In an article entitled "Tesla and the Pyramids of Mars," extracted from "The Fantastic Inventions of Nikola Tesla," an implausible history of the collaboration of these two most famous wireless inventors takes on even greater proportion. Falling in line with the many theories of how science was exploited by fascist regimes (which this author has himself propounded), Tesla and Marconi combined efforts in an underground city in the South America resembling the scenes from the James Bond movie, *You Only Live Twice*. Material in the article originates with a French writer, Robert Charroux from his book, *The Mysteries of the Andes* (first published in 1974), who declared these two scientists worked alongside 100 others in the *Ciudad Subterranean de los Andes* (the Underground City of the Andes). Supposedly, Marconi had developed a "death ray" for Mussolini that scrambled electrical circuits and could stop automobiles dead in their tracks. It was so fearful the Pope condemned Marconi and his device. Upon papal rejection, Marconi faked his own death and fled to South America aboard his yacht *Electro* with the not-so-renown scientific 100 stashed in his cargo hold. Although no one would ever know directly about their exploits (until Charroux spilled these somewhat magical beans), the magnetic personalities of Marconi and Tesla formed a cadre destined to forever change our world.

The account chronicles the efforts of Mario Rojas Avendaro, a Mexican journalist, who investigated the city and naturally determined it was all true. In his book, Avendaro indicated he came across this unknown tale of history when contacted by an Italian, a student of Marconi, one Naciso Genovese, who also had written a most out-of-this-world volume entitled, *Yo He Estado en Marte* (*My Trip to Mars*). Unfortunately (or maybe it was fortunate), the book never made its way into English [Note: this author's research does include verifying the book exists, but does not include translation!] From Avendaro, we learn the underground city lay in an extinct volcano at an altitude of 13,000 feet (in the Andes of Bolivia, the tree line—the limit to where trees can grow—does reach 17,000 feet, well above what we see in North America). Regardless, the article ventures many flying saucers were actually the work of *Marconi, Tesla, and Associates.*

Now it is a veritable fact that South America has had more than its fair share of UFOs. Still these "facts" seem little more than speculation (being as they are based solely upon the incredible books referenced here), that the Andes-hideout-cum-science-lab was home to such amazing men and their flying machines. Nonetheless, facts should never get in the way of a good story. The article continues:

> Based upon the above scenario, it may not be totally fantastic to suggest, as some authors have, that *Tesla was picked up during the late 1930s by a flying saucer.* Yet, it would not have been a flying saucer from another planet, but one of Marconi's craft from the secret city in South America.

> In the most incredible scenario so-far, and one that may well be true, **Tesla** *was induced to fake his own death*, just as Marconi and many of the other scientists had done, and was taken, by special discoid craft, to Marconi's high-tech super-city. Away from the outside world, the military governments, the oil companies, the arms and aircraft manufacturers, Marconi and Tesla, both supposedly dead, continued their experiments, in an atmosphere [albeit a thinly oxygenated one] conducive to scientific achievement. [*Emphasis in original, comment not so much.*] [13]

Finishing with a speculative flourish, the article asks a series of hypothetical questions about the creators of these wireless wonders:

> They were ten years ahead of the Germans and twenty years ahead of the Americans in their anti-gravity technology. Could they have developed discoid spacecraft in the early 1940s, and gone on to time travel machines and hyperspace drives? Perhaps Marconi and Tesla *went into the future*, and have already returned to the past!

---

[13] From the article, "Tesla and The Pyramids of Mars", see http://www.bibliotecapleyades.net/ tesla/esp_tesla_35.htm.

Time Travel experiments, teleportation, pyramids on Mars, Armageddon and an eventual Golden Age on earth, may all have something to do with Tesla, Marconi and their suppressed inventions. While "UFO experts" and "former intelligence agents" tell us that *flying saucers are extraterrestrial* and are being currently retro-engineered by military scientists, Tesla, Marconi and their friends may be waiting for us *at their space base at the pyramids and face on Mars.*[14]

Figure 41 - Photo from the Movie, *War of the Worlds* (1953)

One can only hope that the air on Mars is at least as breathable as it was in the Andes volcano! Nevertheless, despite any exaggeration I may have allowed to infiltrate the record of verifiable history in the last portion of this chapter, we can safely and accurately attribute the miracle of wireless technology to both Tesla and Marconi. Every time we hear a radio, watch television, even use our cellular phones (another technology altogether, but erected on the telecommunications building blocks established 120 years prior), we can thank Tesla and Marconi.

At the same time, we may continue to wonder whether they actually spoke with intelligent beings on other worlds. Did Marconi

---

[14] Ibid.

and Tesla talk to the Martians-gone-underground? Or was this ultra-dynamic duo fooled by ultra-dimensional (spiritual) entities equally eager to demonstrate their own capacity *to commune wirelessly?* Was there genuine telecommunication regarding life on other worlds—even though the otherworldly responses to earthbound inquiry were generally misleading if not out-and-out poppycock?

The reader should avoid making up his or her mind at this intermediate juncture. Any verdict reached will likely be overturned when we consider even more amazing information ahead. For we have many more fantastic assertions yet to explore in this recap of Martian deception.

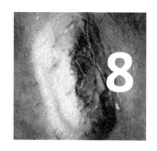

The Paranormal Martian Connection

Psychic Reality and Life on Mars

A T THE END OF THE NINETEENTH CENTURY, MANY PEOPLE—IF NOT MOST—BELIEVED INTELLIGENT LIFE EXISTED ON MARS. THE IDEA OF SMART MARTIANS WAS DEEMED INVIOLABLE AMONG THE masses, it satisfied the more discriminating tastes of the intelligentsia too. In fact, it was as fashionable to believe in human beings living on Mars as it was to believe in levitating tables and invisible spirits rapping on wood. Such "parlor tricks" were highlights among the enlightened visions as well as the esoteric entertainment sought by the rich and famous. Rest assured, mentioning these two topics in the same breath—as odd as it may first sound—foreshadows the strange subject matter of this chapter.

Figure 42 - Camille Flammarion

Given the topics of previous chapters, the reader might be surprised to learn that the personage most influencing this popular belief in life on Mars before 1901 was not the American, Percival Lowell. As noteworthy as his impact was on his culture of yesteryear and whose pursuits in Mars gazing were astronomical (if you will pardon the pun), it was a Frenchman named *Nicolas Camille Flammarion* (1842—1925), born in *Montigny-le-Roi, Haute-Marne*, France that was known far and wide, in both Europe and America, for his acumen on many matters "far out." During his amazing career, Flammarion wrote more than 50 titles probing several esoteric domains including astronomy, science fiction and psychical research. His book, *Astronomie Populaire* (1880) sold 130,000 copies; quite a best-seller in the nineteenth century. Flammarion also founded the *Société Astronomique de France* eventually boasting 600 members. Beginning in 1882, he published the magazine *L'Astronomie* and became the first citizen of France in all matters of science and in particular, the planet Mars.

Why he preoccupies us here is due to his nearly seamless interest in both the *study of Mars* and of *spiritism*, a connection author Robert Crossley in his book, *Imagining Mars*, aptly labeled a "peculiar symbiosis" which blossomed as the twentieth century began.

Crossley points out, in this extended citation from his excellent book, *the fascinating conjunction of these two realms of divergent study* whose twain one would supposed to have never met:

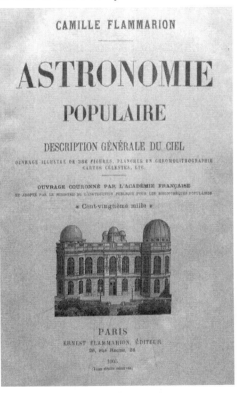

> As the fervor for Mars grew in the final two decades of the nineteenth century and into the twentieth century, there was a parallel explosion of interest in telepathy, reincarnation, and theosophy that was a cosmopolitan outgrowth of the provincial spiritualist movement that had begun in New York State in the mid-nineteenth century. In an intriguing historical conjunction, the Society for Psychical Research (SPR) was founded in London in 1882, just half a dozen years after the modern phase of Martian observation had gotten

Figure 43 – Flammarion's Nineteenth Century Bestseller

underway with the events of the 1877 opposition. Three years later, the American SPR opened in New York, under the presidency of one of the harder-nosed American astronomers, Simon Newcomb, who was determined to use his position to expose spiritualism as phony science. It was not unusual for astronomers to sign up as members of either the British or the American SPR, whose lists included both committed spiritualists and more dispassionate psychical researchers.

Percival Lowell—as his biographer, David Strauss, has explored in some detail—was intrigued by psychic research in his earlier years traveling in Japan, and consulted with members of the American SPR and with William James, who began a two-year term as president of

Figure 44 - Engraving for Flammarion's 1888
L'atmosphère: Météorologie Populaire

the British SPR in 1894. The sequence of Lowell's career as both a scientific researcher and a popular writer who was "drawn to exotic topics—trances and extraterrestrial life," as Strauss has commented, itself demonstrates the links between psychic phenomena and *Martiana*. Lowell moved from investigating Shinto mesmerism and cases of possession, recorded in his 1894 *Occult Japan*, to planetary studies begun at his observatory at Flagstaff in that same year. In fact, one hundred years ago, the two most popular scientific writers who engaged with questions about the habitability of Mars—Lowell in the

United States and Camille Flammarion in France—both combined interests in psychic research and astronomy, although their interests in the paranormal were sharply different in nature.

Lowell always remained a materialist and looked for physical explanations for psychical practices. When he was approached by spiritualists hoping to use his Mars research in their cause during the period of his fame as proponent of an inhabited Mars, Lowell made it clear that he had little patience with table-rappers and clairvoyants who sought to find in him a kindred spirit. Flammarion, on the other hand, was as devout about parapsychology as he was about Mars, and the two subjects often commingled in his books.[1]

Like two other astronomers of the nineteenth century considered previously in these articles, Giovanni Virginio Schiaparelli (1835—1910) and Pietro Angelo Secchi (1818—1878), Flammarion was trained in Jesuit schools for most of his advanced studies.[2] While attending school with the Jesuits, at the very young age, he garnered considerable attention writing a book entitled *The Cosmogony of the Universe.*[3] Like Secchi and Schiaparelli, he was an avid believer in the "plurality of worlds."

We learn from a short biographical piece published in *McClure's Magazine* (1894, written by R. H. Sherard), that his fellow Frenchmen flocked to his lectures devoted to the subject. We can safely assume that attendance at Flammarion's discourses was considerably more abundant than at church services in his home town of Paris, given the tide of public opinion in Europe had turned against Christianity as a source of answers to ultimate questions. The majority of Europeans (with America about 50 years behind) looked to science (in this case *science* so-called and even *séance*—perhaps

---

[1] Crossley, Robert, *Imagining Mars: A Literary History*, Wesleyan University Press. Kindle Edition, (2010), pp. 129-130.

[2] The connection between the Jesuits and astronomy continues to abound today. As pointed out in the article devoted to Lowell, today's Jesuits occupy the Graham Observatory outside of Tucson, and busy themselves with Project Lucifer. Cris Putnam and Tom Horn's most recent book, *Exo-Vaticana* explores this relationship and its somewhat frightening implications.

[3] Cosmogony is the study of the origin of the universe.

connected in more ways than each employing two similar sounding phonemes) to provide insights into life's genesis in the universe.

The Most Famous Frenchman since Napoleon?

On either side of the Atlantic, Flammarion's acclaim among his contemporaries was almost unparalleled. Indeed, Camille Flammarion was considered a savant, if not a genuine legend in his own time. In fact, his book by the title *The Plurality of Worlds,* made Flammarion both famous and wealthy. He told American journalist Sherard, "The book is now in its thirty-fifth edition. The subject, I may mention, had been treated about a century before by (Bernard le Bovier de) Fontenelle, but in purely imaginary style. Fontenelle's book may be described as a novel, a piece of literature, whilst mine claimed to be a scientific work."[4]

During winter days in Paris—from 1:00 PM for exactly one hour, his wife serving as his secretary—Flammarion conducted daily meetings with the Parisian populace ("he knew everyone in Paris") who wished to drop by to ask his opinion on arcane issues of mutual interest. At 2:00 PM, he would spend an hour responding to several of thousands of letters which poured in from every corner of the world. In fact, it is hard to find a singular personality in today's world that captures the imagination of the pseudo-intellectual to the extent Flammarion accomplished 120 years ago.

---

[4] R. H. Sherard, Flammarion "The Astronomer: His Home, His Manner of Life, His work," *McClure's Magazine*, 1894. Regarding Fontenelle, "Fontenelle established a genuine claim to high literary rank; and that claim was enhanced three years later by what has been summarized as the most influential work on the plurality of worlds in the period, *Entretiens sur la pluralité des mondes* (1686). He wrote extensively on the nature of the universe: *Behold a universe so immense that I am lost in it. I no longer know where I am. I am just nothing at all. Our world is terrifying in its insignificance.*" See http://en.wikipedia.org/wiki/Bernard_le_Bovier_de_Fontenelle. This perspective, an ode to awesomeness of a negative kind, anticipates the scientific materialism (and despair) implicit in the writings of American horror author, H.P. Lovecraft to which we will turn later in our study. Flammarion would publish something of a novel in *Uranie*; however, given his stated hatred for novels, he justified its writing only if he could teach science by doing so.

Flammarion was fascinated by psychic powers, even claiming he originated the use of the term applying it as he did to paranormal activities of *mediums* (whom he investigated by the dozens). Regarding spiritual realities, Flammarion found much to applaud in the work of Jean Reynaud (1806–1863) and his work, *Terre at Ciel (Earth and Sky)*. Flammarion was particularly interested in the transmigration of souls, going so far as to believe that souls on earth *progress to other planets as humans or in another life form*. Certainly Mars was more advanced than earth and it would be expected that upon death on this world, *some would wind up there* (the reader should take note that various authors published no small number of books from 1880 to 1920, employing this ancient and recurring theme of "dying and going to Mars" instead of the then already oh-so-spurned notion of heaven or hell).[5]

Moreover, Flammarion inspired the mind of Percival Lowell in the same way Edgar Rice Burroughs (through his tales of the U.S. Civil War-cum-Martian warrior—John Carter) inspired Ray Bradbury, Robert Heinlein, and Carl Sagan mid-way through the twentieth century. While Lowell was publishing his first book on the subject of the Red Planet in December 1895 (entitled simply enough *Mars)*, Lowell was simultaneously seeking out his European mentors in earnest and in person. Indeed, Lowell made his way to Europe to conspire with his aerographical superiors,[6] Camille Flammarion and Giovanni Schiaparelli, mostly to their favorable anticipation. Flammarion stated he found Lowell's theory of the canals and the life they implied with the highest interest, though certainly controversial." [7] Schiaparelli thought Lowell would make great contributions if he could "reign in his imagination." We well know Lowell's obsession with Mars built on Flammarion's conviction that life there seemed a virtual certainty. The only real question that

---

[5] The transmigration of souls finds expression early in human history, in Plato.

[6] *Aerography* is the study of the upper atmosphere. In the case of astronomy, the term was still used as scientists would be looking through and beyond the atmosphere "to other worlds."

[7] Ibid., p. 515, quoted by Sheehan and O'Meara, ibid., p 138.

remained for this triumvirate of Martian gazers: "Had that life become extinct?" Lowell's romantic poem, also simply entitled *Mars*, raised that very question while interlacing several "facts" of nineteenth century science amidst his yearning-to-know verses:

Already far on with advancing age,
Has it [Mars] passed its life-bearing stage?
And has that spirit already fled
From that planet of war, once doubtless rife
With myriad forms of happy life
Waging natural selection's strife—
But are the survivors themselves all dead?
Or is Mars yet inhabited?

When not entertaining Americans enchanted with Mars, Flammarion spent summers at his observatory located at Juvisy-sur-Orge, France, looking through his telescope well into the warm French nights whenever "good seeing" allowed him to do so.[8]   Near the village

Figure 45 - Flammarion's Observatory

of *La Cour de France*, some 30 kilometers (19 miles) by rail south of Paris, it was equipped with a 24-centimeter (9.5-inch) *Bardou* refractor. The observatory, according to authors William Sheehan and Stephen James O'Meara (whose wonderful compilation celebrates those *lured* to the study of Mars), was dedicated "like a temple to the planet Mars and to the proposition that it might be an

---

[8] *Good seeing* is a phrase used by astronomers when the atmosphere cooperates and doesn't blur their view of heavenly objects.

inhabited world."[9]   Flammarion's chateau was complete with stables, servants' quarters, and a setting reminiscent of a well-manicured park. For added color, Sheehan and O'Meara provide this bit of history of the chateau, a gift bequeathed to Flammarion by an ardent admirer!   I can only hope my books eventually lead an admirer to treat me as well as fans of Flammarion treated him.

It was a site rich in historic associations; the kings of France had rested here on their journeys between Paris and Fontainebleau, and here, too, on March 30, 1814, l'Empereur Napoleon had first learned of the capitulation of Paris, an event that marked the downfall of his empire. (Later, after his return to power for the Hundred Days and his final defeat at Waterloo, Napoleon, in bitter exile on St. Helena, would present a romanticized version of his career to an attentive British ship's surgeon, Barry Edward O'Meara" [a distant relative of the cited author O'Meara].[10]

Figure 46 - *The World before the Creation of Man*

[9] William Sheehan & Stephen James O'Meara, *Mars: The Lure of the Red Planet,* Amherst, New York: Prometheus Books, 2001, p. 122.
[10] Ibid., pp. 159-160.

Evolution—A Cosmic Imperative

Like Lowell, Flammarion was strongly influenced by *evolutionary theory*, in particular both Darwin and by the French natural scientist Lamarck. Evolution was as *second nature* to Flammarion as—well—the *supernatural*. However, the premise that captivated

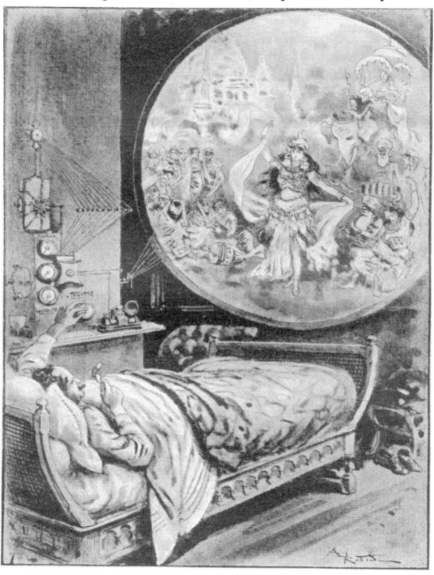

Figure 47 - "Telefonoscope" from
La Fin du Monde, 1894

127

nearly all Martian observers proceeded from an evolutionary theory whose province was the entirety of the cosmos. This is well captured in a line from Flammarion's *Uranie* where the muse of astronomy, Uranie speaks to her student non-coincidentally named Camille, whom she is taking on a tour of the universe (shades of Enoch's global tour with his angelic escorts as recounted in the *Book of Enoch*): "Life is earthly on the Earth, Martial on Mars, Saturnian on Saturn, Neptunian on Neptune,—that is to say, appropriate to each habitation; or, to express it better, more strictly speaking, produced and developed by each world according to its organic condition, and following a primordial law which all Nature obeys,—the law of progress."[11]

Apparently even in worlds beyond earth, evolutionary theory remains worthy of utmost esteem.

Because it was older than the earth (since it was farther from the sun, it is assumed Mars likely cooled earlier than earth, possibly generating life there before it did on Earth), *Mars would surely yield species more advanced than our own.* Moreover, Flammarion asserted without fear of contradiction in a Europe brimming with hope in the theories of Marx, "It would be difficult for a human species to be less intelligent than ours, because we do not know how to behave and three-quarters of our resources are employed for feeding solders."[12] Indeed, although the linkage between Mars and Marxism demands a chapter in its own right (which I did not write as it drifts too far from our interests here), we would only point out that scientific *stargazers*, whom the public fancied like it does *movie stars* today, never missed a chance to offer unsolicited comments promoting the *virtues of utopianism and socialism*. Moreover, they contended Martian society should be upheld as the epitome of civilized behavior. If only we could just find out the details of their existence, no doubt we would be challenged to advance to greater social

---

[11] Camille Flammarion. *Urania* , Kindle Locations 186-188. Originally published by Estes and Lauriat, Boston, 1890.

[12] Ibid., p. 162.

heights ourselves.[13] But alas, by commenting on political matters, I fear the pathway we follow will become infested with thorns. To get us back on track: Sheehan and O'Meara reinforce how Martian astronomers "observed" overhyped hopes beyond any manner of empirical observation:

> The idea that Mars might be a living world had been enthusiastically supported Flammarion, who had gone so far as to write: "We may hope that, because the world Mars is older than ours, humankind there will be more advanced and wiser."[14] The same idea had also been endorsed, in at least a qualified sense, by Schiaparelli, who in the 1880s had recorded changes in the dark markings on the planet leading him to exclaim: "The planet is not a desert of arid rocks. *It lives!*"[15] [Emphasis in original]

Electrifying Communiqués

In our last chapter, we delved into the fascination Mars held for Nikola Tesla and Guglielmo Marconi, two electrical geniuses to which our modern society owes debts beyond valuing. We discussed the unexpected possibility that both inventors utilized electrical (in Tesla's case, perhaps gravitic) wireless communication (otherwise known as the radio!) to dialogue with supposed intelligences on the Red Planet. It was a much more dubious supposition of writers, under the spell of Mars, to presume it possible to communicate with our counterparts on the Red Planet *telepathically*.

---

[13] Robert Crossley mentions how this was taken to an unbelievable extreme in Henry Gaston's 1880 book *Mars Revealed*:

> *Mars Revealed*, like many of its later paranormal brethren and like earlier "fantastical excursions," offers a hodge-podge of utopian vignettes of communal life, spiritualist propaganda, earnest moralizing, highly colored sentiments and descriptions, and unintended farce. Utopian hygiene and grooming tumble into this latter category when we hear that Martians "give their teeth and mouths a thorough cleansing" each morning and "comb their hair, as do all decent people on the Earth." Men and boys, we are reassured, "part theirs upon the side, like all men of sense on Earth" (200– 201).

Crossley, Robert, op. cit., pp. 133-134.

[14] Camille Flammarion, *La Planete Mars*, vol. 1, p. 591.

[15] Cited by Flammarion, p. 510, quoted by Sheehan and O'Meara, p. 131.

This would be the ultimate "wireless" medium, if we could only come to control it and put it to practical use.

Speaking of mediums, it would be this class of "good seers" who would employ a psychic, mental manner of "walk about" by which Mars would be first "explored."[16] Thanks to spirits eager to share idyllic visions of Mars (while "happy mediums" recorded such imagined explorations through channeled *automatic writing* so-called), that refracted sights of Mars gathered so feebly 100 years ago by astronomers could be supplemented through psychic "seeing"—accounts delightful in detail of the Martian expanse, sporting orange or red foliage and vast emerald colored plains. Remote viewing was hardly invented by Ingo Swann, Pat Price, and Joe McMoneagle. We learn that searching out the far corners of Mars had been a path for the mystically minded 70 years earlier than they.

One medium in particular, Sara Weiss, with her 1906 book, *Decimon Huydas: A Romance of Mars,* would combine Martian "science" and psychic expression. Crossley connects the evolutionary imperative and the sought-after wireless means to reach out and touch the Martians:

> It is a numbingly tedious recital, interrupted occasionally by a statement of spiritist doctrine about the evolution of life in the solar system. One such statement by the spirit-narrator of the romance details the expectation that at some point in the twentieth century the psychic link between the spirits on Mars and terrestrial mediums will be augmented by the invention of technology for more material telecommunication with Martians. Such a prediction rested on the two-fold faith that Mars was certainly inhabited and that wireless telegraphy would soon open up Mars to exchanges of messages with Earth.[17]

As we mentioned previously, Tesla and Marconi were up to the technological challenge and offered evidence that the utility of a wireless means for planetary communiqués with Martian society was not out of the question. Moreover, the connection proffered

---

[16] See the earlier chapter on "Out of this world Remote Viewing" which demonstrates that excursions of the psychic sort are still in vogue.

[17] Crossley, Robert, *op cit.,* Kindle Locations 3211-3223).

between mediums and Mars was not a sudden flash in the pan sponsored by an enlightened few. Believing in the superiority of Mars and in spiritualist means to apprehend it was, in fact, quite ubiquitous. Nor are we exaggerating when we underscore how this notion held sway for more than several decades.

Relying upon Crossley's superb analysis once more:

> The conjunction of Martian studies and the paranormal is most visible in a number of narratives published by mediums over the space of about fifty years from the late nineteenth century through the early decades of the twentieth. Psychologists and philosophers—at a time when psychology was still considered a branch of philosophy rather than a scientific discipline—were particularly drawn to investigation of séances and of the experiences and the claims of mediums, including those who offered accounts of their visions of Mars in the form of travelogues that were, de facto, works of science fiction.
>
> The most celebrated instance of the intersection of Mars and the paranormal appeared at the turn of the twentieth century, when Théodore Flournoy, professor of psychology at the University of Geneva and a psychical researcher, published *Des Indes à la Planète Mars* (1899), his extensive case study of a Swiss medium who called herself Hélène Smith. Smith's supposed visionary experiences, manifested in her paintings of the Martian landscape, inhabitants, and artifacts and, centrally, in the Martian language that she spoke and wrote, attracted the attention of linguists and psychopathologists, dream analysts and surrealists. Smith's visions and the fascination they generated can be more fully understood in the context of other narratives from the 1880s to the 1920s that combined the subject of Mars with psychic experience.[18]

Using Science to Vouchsafe Your Point of View

Evangelicals today (which this author calls family) are appropriately startled with so many in our world duped by the supposed surety guaranteed for their perspectives *when blending would-be science with hearty doses of the paranormal.* Science and the supernatural certainly make for strange bedfellows, but they are often found curled up together in the same bed.

---

[18] Ibid., p. 132.

Nevertheless, when we step back to take in the view we should not be all that shocked. The human race has always held a fascination for the fantastic, especially when vindicated by slipping science into the mix.

Camille Flammarion was an especially key figure in the regard— his was a venture to marry questionable psychical studies with a generally scientific search for intelligent life on neighboring worlds. However, we only have enough remaining space to present little more than his rationale and his conviction that the study of psychic phenomena constitutes pure science and builds upon an honest, i.e., *natural* reality—*not* supernatural and certainly not mere optimistic illusion.

In his book, *Mysterious Psychic Forces: An Account of the Author's Investigations in Psychical Research, Together with those of other European Savants*[19] (with all humility of course), the French savant provided a carefully worded treatise on the powers of the paranormal.

Flammarion was cautious to distinguish himself from excesses of mediums who he indicated "don't always cheat."[20] His was an apologetic effort on behalf of the preternatural. Consequently, it should be no surprise that our hero found it essential to be most circumspect in order to separate himself from the ranks of the charlatans parading around Paris at that time.

------

[19] Originally published in Boston by Small, Maynard, and Company in 1909, through the University Press of Cambridge, MA. The frontispiece includes an instructive epigraph by Victor Hugo: "A learned pedant who laughs at the possible comes very near to being an idiot. To purposely shun a fact, and turn one's back upon it with a supercilious smile, is to bankrupt Truth." Let that be a lesson to all those who scoff at psychic phenomenon!

[20] "But all mediums, men and women, have to be watched. During a period of more than forty years I believe that I have received at my home nearly all of them, men and women of divers nationalities and from every quarter of the globe. One may lay it down as a principle that all professional mediums cheat. But they do not always cheat; and they possess real, undeniable psychic powers." Camille Flammarion. *Mysterious Psychic Forces / An Account of the Author's Investigations in Psychical / Research, Together with Those of Other European Savants*, Kindle Locations 337-339.

Flammarion was proud to point out (being as it was the first statement in his book's *Introduction*) how his research into the paranormal began in earnest in 1865 when he was just a lad, authoring a 150-page book called *Unknown Natural Forces* (a title chosen to surreptitiously argue that the supernatural is not so "beyond nature" after all!) Hence, by 1909 when *Mysterious Psychic Forces* was promoted to the public in America (as I argued in *Power Quest, Book One: America's Obsession with the Paranormal*, our country always provided fertile ground for sowing psychic seeds), Flammarion was eager to share his vast wisdom—erected as it was upon half a century of experiments involving table levitation and rapping on counter-tops. In 1865, he stated the following as a premise from which he saw no need to ever depart:

> "It requires a good deal of boldness to insist on affirming, *in the name of positive science,* the POSSIBILITY of these phenomena (wrongly styled supernatural), and to constitute one's self the champion of a cause apparently ridiculous, absurd, and dangerous, knowing, at the same time, that the avowed adherents of said cause have little standing in science, and that even its eminent partisans only venture to speak of their approval of it with bated breath." [21] [Emphasis in original]

Amidst discovering several fascinating new words conveying various means of deception while accomplishing this research (examples being *prestidigitation* and *mountebanks*[22]), this author deems Flammarion was adequately acquitted of the sharp castiga-

---

[21] Camille Flammarion. *Mysterious Psychic Forces / An Account of the Author's Investigations in Psychical / Research, Together with Those of Other European Savants,* Kindle Locations 158-161. Here he is quoting from his earlier work as mentioned in my narrative.

[22] *Prestidigitation* is another way of expressing sleight of hand, specifically in the performance of magic tricks. A *mountebank* is a person who seeks to deceive others to take their money, i.e., a charlatan. Ironically, mountebank also has an historical meaning of a person who sells patented medicines to the public!

tion by a New York Journalist who referenced him as "Flimflam-marion."[23] He sought to explore the mysterious in the name of science—and not expressly to sell books nor make money at the public's expense. As additional justification, Flammarion recounted the familiar (but frustrating reality) of scientists who shun new discoveries because they don't fit "their model" of what is truth. In this matter we find the history of the steam engine put to good use.

In 1776, a young 25-year old name *Jouffroy* failed to convince scientists that his forty-foot boat was propelled by steam. Flammarion recounted: "But all ears were deaf to his words. His only reward was to be completely isolated and neglected." He continued:

> When he passed through the streets of Baume-les-Dames, his appearance was the signal for jests innumerable. He was dubbed 'Jouffroy, the Steam Man' (*'Jouffroy-la-Pompe'*). Ten years later, having built a pyroscaphe [literally, fireboat] which had ascended the Saône from Lyons to the island of Barbe, he presented a petition to Calonne, the comptroller-general of finance, and to the Academy of Sciences. They would not look at his invention! [Shades of Marconi's letter declaring his inventing the radio, addressed to the Italian Telegraph Office, and receiving the rebuke "To the asylum!"]
>
> On August 9, 1803, Fulton went up the Seine in a new steamboat at the rate of about four miles an hour. The members of the Academy of Sciences as well as government officials were present on the occasion. The next day they had forgotten all about it, and Fulton went to make the fortunes of Americans.[24]

Next, Flammarion mentioned a multi-millennium old phrase that has more truth contained within its three words than we can explore here: MENS AGITAT MOLEM (*mind acting on matter gives it life and motion*). In this specific context, Flammarion posited these words assure that our human nature seeks "to study, to

---

[23] Illustrated in a cartoon of Camille Flammarion as *Flimflammarion*, by Gordon Ross, from the illustrating of F[inlay] P[eter] Dunne, "Mr. Dooley Reviews the Year 1906," *New York Times Magazine*, 30 December 1906, 19; found by Crossley in the scrapbooks of Percival Lowell. Quoted from Crossley, Robert, op. cit., p. 133.

[24] Camille Flammarion. *Mysterious Psychic Forces*, Kindle Locations 215-221.

determine, to analyze,—elements still unexplained and which belong to the psychic realm... even if it should be proved that Spiritualism consists only of tricks of *legerdemain*,[25] the belief in the existence of souls separate from the body would not be affected in the slightest degree. Besides, the deceptions of mediums do not prove that they are always tricky. They only put us on our guard, and induce us to keep a stern watch upon them."

Despite his counsel to employ healthy skepticism, Flammarion nevertheless hoped "to convince the reader that these things really exist, and are neither illusions nor farces, nor feats of prestidigitation. My object is to prove their reality with absolute certainty, to do for them what... *I have done for telepathy, the apparitions of the dying, premonitory dreams, and clairvoyance.*" [Emphasis mine] [26] Once again, we recognize Flammarion's humility knows no bounds! Nevertheless, he goes on to provide a series of examples, some with photographs, to prove that mediums demonstrated true psychic power in his exalted presence—such purveyors of the paranormal being only too happy to do tricks in his parlor. In summary he asserted, "This phenomenon of levitation is, to me, absolutely proved, although we cannot explain it."[27]

Conclusion: The Stuff Dreams are Made of?

However, we must close now by reinforcing once more the sacrosanct link between *Martian and psychical research*—so common at the end of the nineteenth century. Robert Crossley's extended summary of Flammarion's book, *Urania* (1889) serves our purpose well:

> Of all the works of fiction that incorporate spiritualist structures or motifs, none was as influential as Flammarion's, for the obvious reason of his dual status as an astronomer and a popular writer. Be-

---

[25] Yet another word peculiar to the realm of magic and deception, meaning originally *light* of hand (as is light weight), but specifically the use of one's hands when performing conjuring tricks.

[26] Ibid., Kindle location 361.

[27] Ibid., Kindle location 381.

cause Flammarion was so attached to his theories, both on the habitability of the planets and on reincarnation, his fiction is extraordinarily didactic and autobiographical, as much personal essay as narrative. *Uranie,* published in 1889 and translated into English in the following year, is named for the muse of astronomy. A summary of the organization of this book may suggest how stubbornly the author seeks a seamlessness between astronomy and parapsychology and between romance and fact.

In part I, the first-person narrator (we eventually learn that his name is Camille) tells of his apprenticeship at the Paris Observatory at age seventeen where, Pygmalion-like, he becomes obsessed by a statuette of Urania.

In a dream, Urania comes alive to take him on a tour of the universe and to introduce him to the infinite diversity of worlds and species. The narrator's friend, twenty-five-year-old astronomer George Spero, is the protagonist of part II. After Spero and his fiancée Iclea are killed in a ballooning accident, the narrator goes to a séance and the savant has a vision of a place with cliffs and foaming seas, sandy beaches, and reddish vegetation. The landscape is Martian, and in the vision, the savant sees Spero and Iclea, who somehow have ended up on Mars after their deaths. The major portion of part III is devoted to case histories—what Flammarion italicizes as facts—that purport to validate claims of communication between the living and the dead. Some of the cases are documented in the text from publications of the Society for Psychical Research. Alternating these "authentic" stories of telepathy with passages on the telescopic observation of Mars, the narrator insists that "astronomy and psychology [read Parapsychology] are indissolubly connected."

The narrator falls asleep under a tree and awakens to the sight of two small moons in the sky. He, too, is now on Mars. He feels astonishingly light on his feet, discovers that he has acquired a sixth sense (magnetism), and observes the Earth appearing as the evening star. This last sight leads him to meditate on the failures of most terrestrials to appreciate the beauty of their planet as they indulge in soldiering and nationalist wars: "Ah! if they could behold the earth from the place where I am now, with what pleasure would they return to it, and what a transformation would be effected in their ideas."[28]

---

[28] From Flammarion's *Uranie*, p. 166, quoted by Crossley, ibid., pp. 135-136.

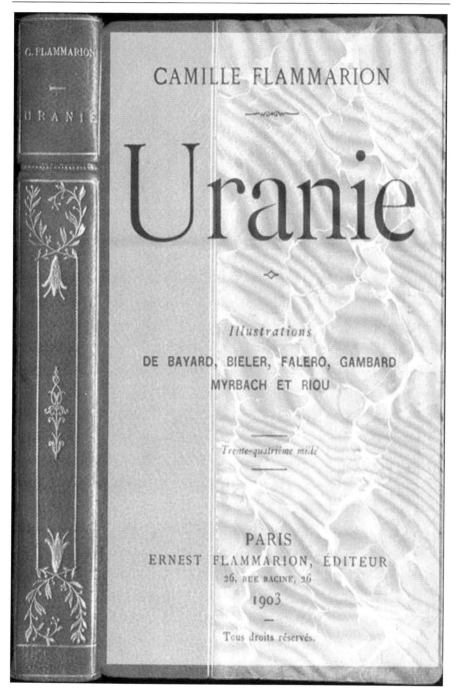

Figure 48 - Cover of Flammarion's Novel, *Uranie*

In this final evocative statement from Flammarion, one can scarcely find a more syrupy, albeit salvific passage promoting the power of science (combined with human reckoning as willing accomplice) to solve all humankind's ills. But such is the stuff that dreams are made of—especially dreams dreamt up by a savant awash in his own worldly (or should I say, other-worldly) wisdom.

Given the implications of teachings from such an esteemed and learned man as Flammarion, one is given to wonder not so much *if Mars boasts intelligent life*, but whether the best and brightest on this planet, apart from the enlightenment gained through biblical revelation, are themselves deserving of such an affirmative attribute. For in our fallen state, it most certainly seems that humankind invents all manner of misunderstanding and misconception—much to our eternal peril.

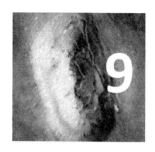

Mars and the Freemasons

The Wonderful WORLDS of Disney

I FIRST BECAME INTERESTED IN MARS AS A CHILD AFTER ENJOYING A SERIES OF WALT DISNEY FILMS MADE FOR TELEVISION. I WAS NOT QUITE OLD ENOUGH TO WATCH THEM WHEN THEY PREMIERED IN 1957 (I WAS three then). But when I was ten or eleven years old, my schoolmates and I watched these films on rainy days in elementary school. With my "inner voice", I exclaimed: "Hurray—movie time. Pass the popcorn!" I loved watching such films in school. It was ever so much better than working math problems or reciting poems.

The Disney films were especially terrific with animation surpassing anyone else's at the time. Disney based many of his early films (and television programs) on nature and science. And since science was my favorite subject, I loved watching them. Indeed, I count Walt Disney partly responsible for my continuing quest to learn.[1]

The films on outer space resulted from the collaboration between Walt Disney and the eventual Director of NASA, *Wernher von Braun*. Von Braun worked with Disney Studio as a technical director during the 1950s. Together, Disney and von Braun made three films under the collective title "Man and Space"—with the premier of the third TV film airing December 4, 1957 on *Disneyland* (which preceded for a few years the more memorable series, *Disney's Wonderful World of Color*, one of the few television shows broadcast in "living color"—and one of the first color-television shows we watched on our brand-spanking new RCA Color TV when

---

[1] There is no shortage of evangelicals who criticize Disney and his perspectives on fantasy and the mystical. This chapter will address the source of some of these criticisms. However, I remain a committed Disney fan, despite the fact I will endure some criticism for speaking a word on his behalf.

I was but knee high to a pup, all of six years old).[2] Wikipedia provides a description of the last entry in this trio, *Mars and Beyond*:

It was directed by Ward Kimball and narrated by Paul Frees. This episode discusses the possibility of life on other planets, especially Mars. It begins with an introduction of Walt Disney and his robot friend *Garco*, who provide a brief overview. It continues with an animated presentation about mankind seeking to understand the world in which he lives, first noticing patterns in the stars, and developing certain beliefs regarding the celestial bodies. Theories from scientists and philosophers are discussed, including Ptolemy's inaccurate, but formerly-accepted theories, as well as those of Copernicus. Life on other planets is considered, soon focusing on Mars. Ideas from science-fiction authors H.G. Wells and Edgar Rice Burroughs are brought to life with more colorful animation...

After this, the program adopts a serious tone as it profiles each of the planets in the solar system, from the perspective of what would happen to a man on them. The program claims that whereas most of the planets are either too cold or too hot for life as we know it, life on Mars could almost be normal, something that is of increasing importance for the future. Dr. E.C. Slipher then discusses the Red Planet and *the possibility that life is already there*. More animation speculates what the conditions on Mars might be like...

The program wraps up with what a trip to Mars would entail for a space crew and its vessels. Contributor/spacecraft designer Ernst Stuhlinger presents his design and details regarding a unique umbrella-shaped Mars Ship: "The top portion would be a revolving outer quarters ring providing artificial gravity for the crew of 20, under 'parasol' coolant tubes. At the other end would be a sodium-potassium reactor to provide power to the midsection electric/ion drive. Attached upright would be a chemically-fueled winged tail-lander. The mission shown involves six Mars Ships, ultimately reaching 100,000 mph, taking a 400 day, spiral course to Mars. There, they would spend 412 days on the surface before returning." [Emphasis added]

At the time, von Braun was the Chief of Guided Missile Development—Operation Division, at the Army Ballistic Missile Agency

---

[2] The very first "color" TV show I watched was The Perry Como Show, presented by Kraft Foods. Mr. "C" started his shows with his famous song, "Come away with me, I'm on my way to a star!" The lyrics from Como's theme song seem especially appropriate for the discussion in this chapter.

(ABMA) in Redstone Arsenal, Alabama.[3] Disney visited von Braun in 1954. The two apparently hit it off. After all, Disney's *Mickey Mouse* was already a famous American export to all nations, including Nazi Germany, where von Braun served as an officer in the Nazi SS[4] (Adolf Hitler loved Mickey Mouse). When serving the Führer, Von Braun led the German rocket program, developing the A4/V2 rockets,[5] the forerunners to the Atlas Rocket and later the Saturn V Rocket that took American astronauts to the moon.

It is no small matter Von Braun's arsenal had wreaked havoc upon London. However, we are told that von Braun's dream was space flight, first sending humankind to the moon; secondly, building a rocket ship capable of traveling all the way to Mars as well as conducting extensive Mars' exploration.[6]

Another imaginative Disney trek to outer space was "Mission to Mars," an attraction featured at *Disneyland* and *Disneyworld*, opening in 1975 and closing in 1992-3. The Disney film and theme-park attraction made liberal use of both Wernher von Braun's and another rocket scientist, Willy Ley's[7] technical planning for a Mars' voyage focused as it was on such an *out-of-this-world* trip.

---

[3] Some have pointed out that "Redstone" itself is a non-coincidence, referring to Mars and the connection between space travel and its eventual and much anticipated Martian destination.

[4] *Schutzstaffel*, abbreviated SS, translated as *Protection Squadron*. The SS wore black uniforms and a skull as the centerpiece on their caps. Most scholars believe they were "initiated" into the ranks in an ordination based upon occult rites.

[5] According to some sources, von Braun contacted Robert Goddard, the American rocket genius, and used his design for the rocket.

[6] The words below cited in Wikipedia, if true, would vindicate von Braun:

The first combat A-4, renamed the V-2 (*Vergeltungswaffe 2* "Retaliation/Vengeance Weapon 2") for propaganda purposes, was launched toward England on September 7, 1944, only 21 months after the project had been officially commissioned. Von Braun's interest in rockets was specifically for the application of space travel, which led him to say on hearing the news from London: "The rocket worked perfectly except for landing on the wrong planet." He described it as his "darkest day". However, satirist Mort Sahl is credited with mocking von Braun with the line "*I aim at the stars, but sometimes I hit London*".
See http://en.wikipedia.org/wiki/Wernher_von_Braun.

[7] An older German rocket scientist, Ley had inspired JPL's Jack Parsons.

However, the theme park "ride" was not all that exciting. Not surprisingly, it quickly became dated since the exploration of Mars via the Mariner spacecraft had begun in 1964, eleven years before

Figure 49 - *Mission to Mars*, **a Disneyland Attraction**

the attraction opened. Furthermore, in 1971 four years before its premiere, Mariner 9 photos showed Mars' rugged terrain covered with massive craters, conveying the Red Planet resembled earth's lifeless moon. The question whether life existed on Mars increasingly begged for a dubious answer.[8]

---

[8] Controversy continues whether or not life was discovered on Mars. An article appearing in *Discovery News*, April 12, 2012, presents a report summarized from scientists who believe *microbes were discovered on Mars:*

"New analysis of 36-year-old data, resuscitated from printouts, shows NASA found life on Mars, an international team of mathematicians and scientists conclude in a paper published this week. Further, NASA doesn't need a human expedition to Mars to nail down the claim, neuropharmacologist and biologist Joseph Miller, with the University of Southern California, Keck School of Medicine, told *Discovery News*. 'The ultimate proof is to take a video of a Martian bacteria. They

Nevertheless, the attraction limped along for 17 more years with few admirers, mirroring the decreased enthusiasm among the public for Mars' space flights. There were some resolute scientists like Carl Sagan, dedicated to the exploration of Mars, believing it held clues to the development of our solar system and perhaps the origin of humanity itself. This group allowed that Mars may not have life existing on its surface today—but it likely supported life in ages past. Most scientists supported the view that at one time vast amounts of water covered much of the Martian surface. This seemed apparent to scientists studying Mars from Mariner photos 50 years ago.[9] However, the verdict on the presence of water on Mars has been controversial and opinions have run "hot and cold."

This half-century-old debate actually has not been settled to the satisfaction of most experts. Furthermore, the "die-hards"—a select number of contemporary scientists—remain convinced that extant H_2O facilitates some form of life on Mars, although most admit signs of life are at best obscure. Besides the polar ice caps (now determined to be more water than CO_2, aka "dry ice"), some amount of water continues to exist below the surface in a sort of "permafrost." The supposed discovery of Methane (a byproduct of biological life) in 2003 spurred a resurgence of belief in microbial life; however, it has also given way to skepticism as recent Curiosity

---

should send a microscope — watch the bacteria move,' Miller said. 'On the basis of what we've done so far, I'd say I'm 99 percent sure there's life there,' he added. Miller's confidence stems in part from a new study that re-analyzed results from a life-detection experiment conducted by NASA's Viking Mars robots in 1976." (See http://news.discovery.com/space/ alien-life-exoplanets/mars-life-viking-landers-discovery-120412.htm.) We will discuss this topic further in a later chapter.

[9] Mariner 4 was the first U.S. craft to do a successful fly-by in 1964, five years before the moon landing. Mariner 9 was the first American craft to orbit Mars in 1971. "Mariner 9 was the first spacecraft to orbit another planet. It arrived at Mars in 1971 and changed our perceptions of the Red Planet. Mariner 9's cameras snapped close-up views of the planet's major features, including Mars' polar caps, the vast *Valles Marineris* canyon, and the Martian moons (*Phobos* and *Deimos*). It also spotted evidence of flowing water sometime in the ancient past." See http://www.space.com/18439-mariner-9.html.

tests failed to demonstrate Methane.[10] Simply put, no leading scientist actively involved in current day exploration on Mars stands firm on the conviction that life exists of Mars. Because politics and government funding are influenced, however, by this topic, it remains unlikely that a clear-cut answer with be forthcoming.

Mariner missions eventually led to the successor Viking projects of the 1970s, Viking 1 being the first spacecraft to successfully land on the planet's surface (after first taking that famous picture of the Face on Mars). Amazingly, Viking 1 continued operation for six contiguous years before succumbing to the harsh Martian atmosphere.

The Mission to Mars Project Plan

Wernher von Braun developed a proposal for a Mars mission in 1947—a propitious year for all-matters related to "outer space and space ships" with the outbreak of UFOs at "Maury Island," Kenneth Arnold's sightings over Mt. Rainer, and the most famous UFO event of all-time, "Roswell." Braun's thinking about traveling to Mars is not totally different (except in scale) from plans in the works by scientists today. To go to Mars, there are myriad logistics issues and most remain too complicated to easily resolve. At the top of the list, predictably, are provisions for food and fuel, essential for astronauts to make the trip to Mars and return to Earth with any skin left on their bones.

Von Braun's interest in Mars likely existed well before World War II, although some still question whether von Braun was being genuine when expressing that space exploration exceeded his interest in building rockets just for technology's sake (or for facilitating the victory of the Nazis over the Allies).

Details were published in his book *Das Marsprojekt* (1952); published in English as *The Mars Project* (1962) and several subse-

---

[10] See http://scitechdaily.com/curiosity-fails-detect-methane-mars/.

quent works, and featured in *Collier's* magazine in a series of articles beginning March 1952. A variant of the Von Braun mission concept was popularized in English by Willy Ley in the book *The Conquest of Space* (1949), featuring illustrations by Chesley Bonestell. Von Braun's Mars project envisioned nearly a thousand three-stage vehicles launching from Earth to ferry parts for the Mars mission to be constructed at a space station in Earth orbit. The mission itself featured a fleet of ten spacecraft with a combined crew of 70 head-

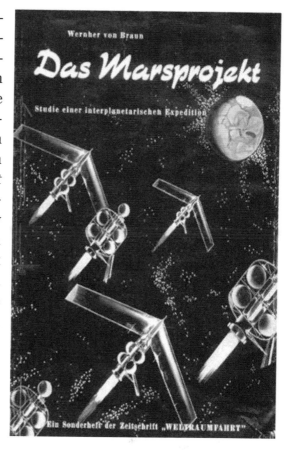

Figure 50 - Wernher von Braun's
The Mars Project

ing to Mars, bringing three winged surface excursion ships that would land horizontally on the surface of Mars. (Winged landing was considered possible because at the time of his proposal, the Martian atmosphere was believed to be much denser than was later found to be the case.) [11]

In the 1956 revised vision of the Mars Project plan, published in the book *The Exploration of Mars* by Wernher Von Braun and

---

[11] Interested readers might wish to visit the Mars-One web site. Mars-One is a not-for-profit enterprise to land humans on Mars and establish a colony there by 2023. See http://www.mars-one.com/en/. The comparisons to von Braun's plan are intriguing.

Willy Ley, the size of the mission was trimmed, requiring only 400 launches to put together two ships, still carrying a winged landing vehicle. Later versions of the mission proposal, featured in the Disney "Man in Space" film series [referenced above], showed nuclear-powered ion-propulsion vehicles for the interplanetary cruise.[12]

Was there an esoteric connection between Disney and von Braun that accounted for their eagerness to collaborate? Or were they simply "Imagineers" wanting to inspire (in Disney's case) and engineer (in von Braun's case) the exploration of outer space? Could there have been something more mystical lurking behind their effort, energizing their quest to discover humankinds' origins?

The Nazi Connection to Mars

Von Braun came to America as part of the infamous *Project Paperclip*,[13] bringing his entire rocket engineering team from Nazi

---

[12] For several years, various new propulsion mechanisms have been the subject of articles in science magazines. Here is a recap of information on one such proposed propulsion mechanism that could get humans to Mars in a mere 39 days:

"A journey from Earth to Mars could in the future take just 39 days — cutting current travel time nearly six times — according to a rocket scientist who has the ear of the U.S. space agency.

Franklin Chang-Diaz, a former astronaut and a physicist at the Massachusetts Institute of Technology (MIT), says reaching the Red Planet could be dramatically quicker using his high-tech VASIMR rocket, now on track for lift-off after decades of development.

The Variable Specific Impulse Magnetoplasma Rocket — to give its full name — is quickly becoming a centerpiece of NASA's future strategy as it looks to private firms to help meet the astronomical costs of space exploration. "

See http://news.discovery.com/space/private-spaceflight/mars-rocket-vasimr-nasa.htm.

[13] *Paperclip* was an illegal operation of America's intelligence services that I documented in my books, *Power Quest, Book One* and *Book Two*. In this activity, thousands of Nazi scientists, many who were war criminals, literally were secreted into the country by the CIA to exploit their technological know-how and help America in its cold-war fight against the Soviet Union. False dossiers were "paper-clipped" to the real ones, claiming that the person in question was not a threat and was not a significant player in German atrocities. As we later learned, many in-

146

Germany's *Peenemünde* design and manufacturing facility. The Germans had leapt ahead of American scientists during the War, developing advanced technologies in hundreds of areas, including the "wonder weapons" (*wunderwaffe*) that were Hitler's last hope to defeat the Allies. Indeed, if the war had dragged on for another six months, many scholars believe these weapons could have turned the tide and led to a Nazi victory.[14]

There has been considerable speculation regarding what enabled Nazi scientists to develop such advanced weaponry including the possible invention of "the flying disc" (which I discussed in the early chapters of *Power Quest, Book Two*). The evidence for highly advanced aerodynes built by the Nazis seems beyond doubt, although the proof that the Nazis successfully prototyped let alone manufactured flying saucers remains mostly circumstantial.

However, Joseph P. Farrell has written a number of compelling books based upon extensive research, one in particular focused on the "Nazi Bell"—a possible time machine levering a dramatically different understanding of physics.[15] Some speculate (although Farrell remains doubtful) that the Nazis learned secrets of advanced physics—including how to engineer flying saucers—*from extraterrestrials*. Others, including Farrell speculate that the Nazis possessed advanced technical know-how due to rediscovering *"prisca sapientia"* (ancient knowledge) from an antediluvian civilization, namely *Atlantis*. Like Farrell, the late author David Flynn (who we will study in the next chapter), asserts that ancient civili-

---

cluding von Braun, were very well aware of the use of slave labor, deplorable conditions, and the deaths of tens of thousands of Jews forced to assist in the building of the *"wunderwaffe"*.

[14] Joseph P. Farrell, the late Henry Stevens, and many author "alternate historians" document this in considerable details. See Farrell's *The Brotherhood of the Bell*, and Steven's *Hitler's Suppressed and Still Secret Weapons*.

[15] This physics contradicts Einstein in some respects and corresponds to the views of American Nikola Tesla, Nazi Karl Maria Wiligut, and Russian Nikolai Kozyrev. See chapter two of *Power Quest, Book One*, for a summation and explanation of the key aspects of this alternative physics.

zation employed an advanced set of technologies which have remained largely unknown to us and await our rediscovery. This knowledge far exceeds our capability today, especially in the "cosmic realm." However, whether or not this ancient knowledge was seized by the Nazis through their occult prowess, it should not be overlooked that like today, plain ol' German ingenuity (and superlative engineering) energized the many amazing Nazi advances.

It is well known and documented by many authors that Adolf Hitler was thoroughly ensconced with occult motivations, based partly upon Teutonic (German) folklore. The great mythology of the Norse (including Odin, Thor, and Valhalla), the grand tales of the *Edda*, and the myth of the Aryan Race—all were part of the legends inspiring the Third Reich. Many books have been penned on this subject by authors Farrell, Jim Marrs, Peter Levenda, Nicholas Goodrick-Clarke, and this author. Indeed, the German "volk" were steeped in such myths, with some set to music by nineteenth century German composer Richard Wagner (1813–1883). One was his opera, *Parsifal*, a Germanic version of the quest for the Holy Grail, loosely based upon the thirteenth century poem *Parzival* by Wolf-

Deutscher Orden - German Order - Teutonic Order - 1190 - 2013

**Figure 51 - The *Germanorden* or *Deutscher Orden*,
dating back to the twelfth-century Crusades**

ram von Eschenbach. The mystical mindset of the Bavarians was also influenced by the great German poet Johann Wolfgang von Goethe (1749–1832, author of *Faust*). Some were enthralled and dedicated to the *Germanorden*—the German Order of the Teutonic Knights with connections to the original Knights Templar.[16]

The Nazi hierarchy (Heinrich Himmler, Rudolf von Sebottendorf, to name but two members) was student to the arcane *Secret Doctrine* written by the mystic Madame Helena Petrovna Blavatsky. Significantly, Hitler credited another mystic, his jail mate after the failed 1923 Munich Beer Hall Putsch, Dietrich Eckart, as the father of Nazism. Eckart was the leader of the notorious Thule Society, which had earlier assimilated the Vril Society, a small coterie of mediums living in Berlin.[17]

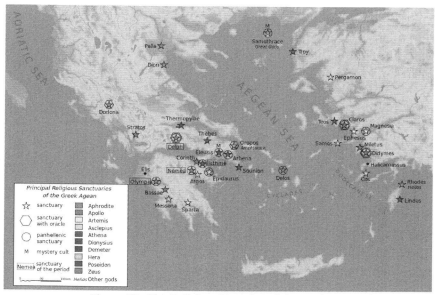

Figure 52 - The Religious Temples of the Ancient Greeks

---

[16] The Templars were founded initially by nine Frenchmen from the province of Champagne in the twelfth century. The Order was established to protect Christian sojourners and pilgrims to the Holy Land. Some, such as author Dan Brown, believe their real motive was to seize the Treasure of Solomon that they believed was hidden beneath the ancient Jewish Temple in Jerusalem.

[17] Thule was the mythical capitol of the land known as Hyperborea to the extreme north of Greece. The Vril were a fictitious race of giants living beneath the earth, entered and exited in Hyperborea, created by English Freemason (and likely Rosicrucian) Lord Edward Bulwar-Lytton during the nineteenth century.

149

In short, the supposed superiority of the Aryan race was built upon many such grandiose yet questionable myths. Trevor Ravenscroft discusses this extensively in his excellent but controversial book, *The Spear of Destiny*.[18]

Hitler railed against Freemasonry deeming it a Jewish organization built upon Jewish legends regarding Solomon's Hebrew Temple. Hitler believed that the "International Jews" were Freemasons; and Freemasonry itself consisted of an alternative belief system incompatible with National Socialism. However, reality contradicts Hitler's view. Freemasonry and Nazi mythology shared many of the same beliefs: Both believed that ancient knowledge from Atlantis passed through the Babylonians and the Egyptians to modern secret societies. This lost knowledge testified to humankind's connection to the divine. "Illumination" was the desire of a select few initiates who could be entrusted with this powerful albeit secret knowledge of the ancients. According to some, the legendary teachings of the Greek "Mystery Schools" (from Eleusis, Delphi, Samothrace, and Crete—see Map above) came to us via the Knights Templar and later their German counterparts which Hitler idolized.

The SS of Himmler was fashioned along the lines of a "Black Knights of the Round Table"—an occult society of initiates pledged to dark truths on pain of death. Von Braun, despite protests to the contrary, no doubt pledged himself to these same principles. The occult nature of Himmler, his SS, and his organization established to study Teutonic folklore, the *Ahnenerbe*, heavily influenced von Braun and many others in his organization. When von Braun was pegged to lead NASA, his Nazi occultism came right along with him.

---

[18] Many argue that the book is a fiction loosely based on certain facts about the so-called Spear of Destiny, Rudolf Steiner, Dietrich Eckhart, and Adolf Hitler. Some claim the narrative was channeled. There is no question that Ravenscroft expounded a Manichean perspective on the nature of God and reworked the theology of Christianity to include a heterodox teaching flowing from Steiner's *Anthroposophy*—an adaptation of Blavatsky's Theosophy, more honest in the sense that "humanity" (*anthro* rather than *theo*) was placed at the center. Especially noteworthy are references to the "Akashic record"—making its teaching occultic.

Nazis vs. Freemasons

Hoagland and Bara, in *Dark Mission: The Secret History of NASA*, documented the quiet conflict within NASA during the 1950s and 1960s between the Nazi "Teutonic Knights" of the SS and dozens of American-born Freemasons generously sprinkled throughout the space agency's leadership. Key Nazis included von Braun, Herman Oberth, Willy Ley, and Arthur Rudolph, leading the hundred-man plus Peenemünde rocket scientists working for the U.S. Government in Alabama and New Mexico.

Quoting from my book, *Power Quest, Book Two:*

> We learn that John F. Kennedy, at the request of Lyndon Johnson his Vice-President, appointed James E. Webb as the administrator of NASA. Webb, a 33° Freemason, appointed Kenneth S. Kleinknecht director of Project Mercury. Ken Kleinknecht was brother of C. Fred Kleinknecht, the *Sovereign Grand Commander of the Supreme Council, 33° Ancient and Accepted Scottish Rite Freemasons, Southern Jurisdiction for the United States of America*, from 1985 to 2003. Their father, C. Fred Sr., was yet another 33° Mason of the Scottish rite as well as a member of its Supreme Council. Then there are the Mercury Astronauts. Four of the original seven were Freemasons: John Glenn, Wally Schirra, Gus Grissom, and Gordon Cooper. Of the twelve who moon walked, four were Freemasons. Hoagland indicates Neil Armstrong and Alan Shepard were also likely to be members of the Scottish Rite.[19]

When von Braun took the reins at NASA, "German victory" resolved the clashing mythologies. Citing my earlier work once again:

> In this author's view, [Richard] Hoagland provides a rationale for the connection between the Nazis and the Freemasons, but fails to discern why they were in opposition from the standpoint of competitive mythologies. However, he rightly points out they share a common heritage with the Knights Templar (the German contingent of this infamous order from the twelfth century was known as the *Teutonic Knights*). Quoting Dr. Nicholas Goodrick-Clarke from his book, *The Occult Roots of Nazism* [Hoagland conveys] "Goodrick-Clarke

---

[19] Woodward, *Power Quest Book Two: The Ascendancy of Antichrist in America*, Woodinville,, Faith-Happens, 2012, p. 190, Hoagland and Bara, *Dark Mission*, p. 316.

also [along with the Freemasons] shows that Hitler and Himmler believed that these Egyptian gods themselves came from 'Atlantis'—which they believed was 'a high civilization established on Earth by extraterrestrials.'"

Hoagland surmises, "In this view, *the ancient, uninterrupted bloodline from Horus to the present* was the ultimate source of the natural supremacy of the 'Aryan race' itself. It was this 'divine right of descent' which gave the modern Nazis, in their view, their prerogative to rule all other men on planet Earth."[20] [Emphasis added]

If Hoagland is correct, and in this matter I believe he is, the mythology of Egypt as handed down through Secret Societies and their predecessor mystery schools, heavily influenced the actions and motivations of Wernher von Braun, and through him, NASA and U.S. interests. Thus, venturing into space was more of a *spiritual aspiration*, not solely a technical triumph or driven by national ambition.

Disneyland, Ley Lines, and Fairy Circles

Part of the chemistry between von Braun and Disney may have been based upon Disney's reputed Freemason membership in which he purportedly acquired its highest status: 33rd Degree Freemason.[21]

---

[20] Ibid., Woodward, p. 192, citing Hoagland/Bara, p. 318. The Norse myths were alternative and not directly derived from the Babylonian/Egyptian myths. Additional detail is provided below, citing myself from the same source:

While agreeing that the Nazis point to Atlantis as the origin of the Aryan race (one of the so-called Seven Root Races, of which ironically, the Jews also are considered a 'descendant'—but of lesser purity), there remain vivid distinctions between the two as mentioned earlier. To recall to the reader's mind, Freemasonry exalts the Egyptian origins of 'ancient wisdom'; while the Nazis combined other Nordic sources along with the fictional belief in "the Vril" (Bulwer-Lytton), and even the Manichean version of Christianity inherent in the 'German' quest for the Holy Grail (von Eschenbach's 13th century epic poem...) fundamental to German heritage. The Nazis and the Freemasons held rival mythologies. They had a common root—but the two [organisms] grew in opposing directions.

[21] However, the evidence for Disney's association with Freemasonry is sketchy; for the trail grows cold after Disney's membership in the Masonic young man's association, DeMolay; although one source indicates that even *Mickey Mouse* was made an honorary member in DeMolay! Indeed, there are many "hits" when doing a search on Disney and Freemasonry, but research proving the allegation is thin.

Walter Bosley in his book *Latitude 33: Key to the Kingdom*, provides a strong argument that Disney consulted with Stanford Research Institute (SRI), the research institute associated with "remote viewing" discussed in an earlier chapter, to locate Disneyland at the crossroads of "ley lines" in Southern California, pinpointed at King Arthur's Carousel at the heart of the theme park—a modern day vorticular "fairy circle." This location just happens to be on the 33N° latitude, where purportedly most unusual things happen. In developing his argument, Bosley references the works of Joseph P. Farrell, Sesh Heri author of *Wonder of the Worlds* (Heri is a theorist on "geomorphology"),[22] Nikola Tesla, and another German, a naturalist named Viktor Schauberger. Farrell comments on Schauberger (quoted by Bosley) that he was "deeply interested in the 'occulted physics' of arcane mathematics found in ancient doctrines and philosophies to support his research into equally ancient concepts of vorticular [spinning] motion. Schauberger's work was eventually co-opted by the Nazi SS and we are left with legendary evidence of German flying saucer technology reported since the war." Bosley speculates:

> Walt Disney once worked closely with NASA director Werner Von Braun on the popular 'Man in Space' films. Ernst Stuhlinger, NASA engineer and another war era German scientist assisted the Disney project. It is quite possible that they were familiar with the work of Schauberger, and thus may have influenced Walt Disney's interest in such ideas. More importantly, Schauberger's work would certainly

---

[22] *Geomorphology*: The study of land forms. Heri comments on Richard Hoagland's theory about hyperdimensionality and its gateway to the warping of space-time and zero-point energy:

> Anyone familiar with Richard Hoagland's work will immediately recognize here what he refers to as 'tetrahedral geometry'. I do think Hoagland is generally correct in his basic theory that the geomorphology of planets is determined by an underlying tetrahedral geometry. However, Hoagland does not explain what the lines composing his tetrahedrons represent. It is unclear whether he means to say that these are real structures in our perceived space, or are an underlying force existing in a vaguely defined 'hyper-dimension'.

See Bosley, Walter, *Latitude 33: Key to the Kingdom* (Kindle Locations 451-455). Corvos Books/LCL. Kindle Edition, 2011

have been known to an organization such as the Stanford Research Institute, and any aerospace engineers in their employ...[23]

Bosley's speculation is well-reasoned, and illustrates that Disneyland's design was crafted with great attention to detail—demonstrating an attempt to authenticity in fairy tales and legend. One can be critical of that feature. And some may find that "charming" in a literal as well as metaphorical sense. Nevertheless, Disney was an imaginative genius, well-schooled, and perhaps he was a Freemason after all.[24] Whether a Mason or not, Disney still might have shared some mystical beliefs espoused in the German SS—not necessarily the doctrine of Aryan racial superiority or the racial inferiority of the Jews—but the wistful view that *the hidden knowledge taught by the ancient Mystery Schools included an explanation for the origin of human civilization*—an origin *not of this world.*

Conclusion: Mission *from* Mars

Specifically, these Mysteries put forth evidence that civilization (and humanity) began on Mars and migrated to earth in aeons past! In other words, before there was a "Mission to Mars" there was a "Mission from Mars." Tens of thousands of years ago (potentially even a million years ago), Martians "leapt" to earth, perhaps as a result of destruction of their home planet, and built the ancient megalithic masterpieces about whose origins and originators many (including this author) conjecture today.

As we will discuss, a number of distinguished authors supply evidence they too were aware of the Mystery Schools' precept that

---

[23] Bosley, Walter, *Latitude 33: Key to the Kingdom* (Kindle Locations 954-958). Corvos Books/LCL. Kindle Edition, 2011.

[24] Bosley offers this evidence against Disney's Freemason membership: "According to the Grand Masonic Lodge of British Columbia, Walt Disney was a member of the original chapter of a Masonic-associated organization for boys known as DeMolay International. But they say Disney was not a freemason. "For reasons of their own," reports the Grand Lodge of BC, "A few anti-masons, detractors of American pop culture and conspiracy theorists have referred to Disney as a 33º freemason but this claim is unfounded." Ibid., Kindle Locations 1518-1522.

civilization began on Mars *long before it came to earth.* But exactly who were these "Martians"? Were they humanoid? Were they members of the species we know as *Homo sapiens sapiens?*

In the next chapter, we will examine the late David Flynn's intriguing research and analysis to address this incredible conjecture which finds some level of support not only in ancient mythology but surprisingly, in the Bible as well.

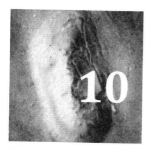

Mars and the Legend of the First Civilization

The Missing Planet Rahab

THE LATE AUTHOR DAVID FLYNN IN HIS BOOK, *CYDONIA: THE SECRET CHRONICLES OF MARS* PROVIDES A FASCINATING EXPLANATION FOR A MYTH ACTIVELY PROPAGATED TODAY BY RICHARD C. Hoagland, that civilization was first birthed on Mars and only later, out of necessity, came to earth. Exactly when this interplanetary transit took place was not precisely specified by author/researcher Flynn; but his view considers the possibility that this happened anywhere from several million years ago to as recently as 12,000 years before present (YBP). For convenience, we will refer to this voyage of intelligent "humanoid" creatures as a relocation event—a transfer *from Mars to Earth.*

Figure 53 - *Cydonia: The Secret Chronicles of Mars,* **by David Flynn**

However, referencing Mars as the source of the species which birthed civilization is not exactly what Flynn was saying. For the testimony of the Bible, as interpreted by Flynn, purports civilization developed first in our solar system on a planet named *Rahab*, subsequently destroyed by a massive cataclysm on a cosmic scale.[1] In other words, the history

---

[1] This cataclysm is discussed in detail by Joseph P. Farrell in his book, *The Cosmic War,* and his other books devoted to the meaning of the pyramids of Giza.

of how civilization developed on earth cannot be told without first understanding why civilization arose on Rahab/Mars, and why its inhabitants had to desert that planet and relocate to Planet Earth.

Where in the Bible do Flynn and others see proof supporting this unfamiliar theory? In Isaiah 51:9 we read: *"Awake, awake, put on strength, O arm of the Lord; awake, as in the ancient days, in the generations of old. Art thou not it that hath cut Rahab, and wounded the dragon?"* Likewise, in Psalm 89:10: *"Thou hast broken Rahab in pieces, as one that is slain; thou hast scattered thine enemies with thy strong arm."*

The science behind this speculation proposes Mars was in fact a *moon circling the planet Rahab*. Rahab once held the orbit now occupied by the asteroids (aka the so-called asteroid belt). Mars' two moons (*Phobos* and *Deimos*—meaning fear and terror) might only have been asteroids trapped by Mars' gravitational pull post-catastrophe. That is, their current planet-moon connection came about sometime after the destruction of Rahab.

Adding weight to this argument (pun not intended): Mars' gravity is not evenly distributed. While not exactly lop-sided, its gravitic imbalance resembles the out-of-balance density of our own moon. This suggests that Mars once faced its former "home planet" 100% of the time (i.e., it revolved around the planet once each time

---

Most recently, Farrell has expanded his views in the book, *The Grid of the Gods*. Farrell considers various scientific arguments pinpointing the cataclysm to be about 3.2 million years ago. However, like David Flynn, Farrell argues that many ancient writings, not just the Bible, testify to a vital connection between Mars and Earth, and to some manner of divine or angelic beings that have been actively engaged in influencing civilization on earth. Farrell's book, *Babylon's Banksters*, also explores this hypothesis. Farrell proposes that the infamous family Rothschild and their design on the world's monetary system is not a Jewish conspiracy, but a Babylonian one. Farrell connects the conspiracy to Nimrod and notes, "Alphonse Mayer Rothschild and Clarice Sebag-Montefiore had a son, born in 1922, to whom they gave the peculiarly Jewish-Christian-'Babylonian' (actually 'Biblical,' because there were neither 'Jews' nor 'Christians' known as such in that era) name of Albert Anselm Salomon Nimrod Rothschild (which means 'red shield')." See www.henrymakow.com/a_brief_review_of_farrells_bab.html #sthash.rkKYxqy5.dpuf

it completed an orbit; thus, like our moon its rotation was perfectly synchronized with its orbit).[2]

Flynn's supposition: *civilization began on Rahab.* Structures were built on Mars, probably observable by the postulated "Rahabians", perhaps to serve as monuments to the principals or "kings" of

Rahab. But sometime, maybe one to three million years ago (or as recently as a mere 12,000 years ago), something cataclysmic happened. A catastrophe struck Rahab, destroying the planet, and sending massive amounts of water and debris into space. Mars was

Figure 54 - Mars rover Curiosity self-portrait. A mosaic of images taken by its hand lens imager camera. (Feb.3, 2013 on Earth)

struck—inundated with debris and water—destroying many of these structures and causing massive changes to the planet's surface.[3] This "catastrophic flood" possibility may be confirmed by the most recent discoveries of the Mars Roving Laboratory, the *Curiosity*, which landed on Mars in August 2012.[4] Many scientists are now convinced that at one time Mars' surface was covered by water. However, its gravity was (and remains) so slight that most of this water

---

[2] That's why there is a "front side" and "back side" to our moon – a back-side that we never see. Sometimes the back side of the moon is referred to as "the dark side of the moon" but that is a misnomer. When we experience a 'new moon', the back side of the moon is fully illuminated – we just are not in the right position to see it.

[3] The craters and topological features of Mars suggest that only one hemisphere was devastated when struck by the cataclysm 'all at once'. This would be consistent with a unidirectional catastrophe emanating from a nearby cosmic source within our solar system. It would also explain the asteroid belt.

[4] See http://asnews.syr.edu/newsevents_2013/releases/Earth_Sciences_Mars_Lecture.html.

vaporized rather quickly, while a small portion of the water seeped into the ground and froze, creating a permafrost layer. In a manner of speaking, Mars cannot hold its water.

Therefore, it is logical to deduce that if it had water on its surface a long, long time ago, it must have come from somewhere else. This possibility also suggests the Earth could have been likewise affected by a "water-attack" from outer space—perhaps inferring that the earth was once devastated by a massive flood stemming from the same catastrophe destroying Rahab/Mars.

Figure 55 - The late author David Flynn

According to those who subscribe to this theory (that an advanced civilization once existed on Rahab/Mars), potentially artificial structures on the Martian surface are now detectable as our vision of Mars improves—thanks to the many man-made satellites which *orbit* the planet and *rove* its surface. Both kinds of robot space explorers have sent photos—hundreds of thousands of them—to give us a "bird's eye view" as well as an "up close and personal" portrait of the Red Planet.

Remember, it was from a 1976 photo sent back to earth by Viking I, that the now-famous *face* on Mars was first identified (publically). Was it merely a trick of light and shadow? Was it nothing more than an illusion caused by our "pattern finding" minds (a case of para-doelia[5], which according to Mike Bara was a term invented specifically to downplay THE FACE)? Could it have been, a cosmic *Rorschach test*—i.e., "what do you see in the inkblot?")? Or was it really an artificial structure which once existed in perfect form on Mars?

[5] See http://en.wikipedia.org/wiki/Pareidolia.

Why Was Cydonia at the Center of Things?

The face on Mars, and its surrounding area, known as *Cydonia*, particularly intrigues us because THE FACE is located at the "zero meridian" as established by Giovanni Schiaparelli, the first great map maker of Mars (Schiaparelli was a Jesuit priest publishing his work toward the end of the nineteenth century). This means that the Martian cartographer Schiaparelli coincidentally (or *not so co-incidentally!*) laid out the longitudinal lines on the Martian surface, anticipating that Cydonia (where THE FACE is located) would be the central point of interest from which everything else on the Martian surface should be reckoned. That is to say, 100 years before we could see THE FACE on Mars, something told Schiaparelli to pick

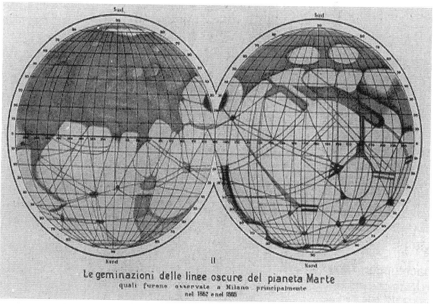

Le geminazioni delle linee oscure del pianeta Marte
quali furono osservate a Milano principalmente
nel 1882 e nel 1888

Figure 56 - The Cartography of Schiaparelli

this exact location as "zero point longitude" for future cartographical efforts. It seems hard to believe that this selection was random.

We must wonder, "What possessed Schiaparelli to be so precise, so prescient regarding his zero point meridian? For Flynn, Schiaparelli's map-making decision stands as a key impetus for his amazing theory of life on Mars. Likewise, from Flynn's perspective, the

161

fact that the face on Mars accompanies other provocative features in the Martian neighborhood comprises no chance occurrence either.

One feature that is the noteworthy is the five-pointed pyramid, the so-called D&M Pyramid, within Richard C. Hoagland's "City." A second feature is an even more suspicious structure—the *Tholus*[6] which appears to mirror a man-made hill (Silbury Hill) located near Stonehenge—a hill in England structured intentionally as massive spiral mound.[7]

Are the presence of these features proof enough that the names ascribed by Schiaparelli—based as they were on classic Greek mythology—were not randomly selected?

Figure 57 - A Stele with the Code of Hammurabi

Although not provable, to Flynn it appears that Schiaparelli had access to *very specific ancient knowledge.* In other words, *special Information from beyond this world* was at his disposal.

---

[6] A *tholus* is a dome, spiral mountain, or "rotunda." The structure on Mars and in England both appear to present a spiraling walkway up the side of the mound.

[7] The "tholus" is intriguing not just because of its apparent "man-made" shape, but because there is a 19.5 degree angle involved in both layouts on Mars and at Silbury Hill. See http://criticalbelievers.proboards.com/thread/146.

Moreover, Flynn asserts Schiaparelli understood this ancient wisdom, having an extensive classical education through the Jesuits, an education Flynn assumes included knowledge of the "ancient mysteries" managed and kept secret by the Mystery Religions of the Ancients. No doubt this speculation is circumstantial at best. Furthermore, whether Schiaparelli believed that Homo sapiens were *Martian before they were Earthling* is not spelled out either— and Flynn stops short of daring to utter what might be seen as a provocation to Jews and Christians. However, Flynn purports that Schiaparelli likely believed that *civilization with some form of intelligent life originated on Mars* BEFORE its genesis on earth.

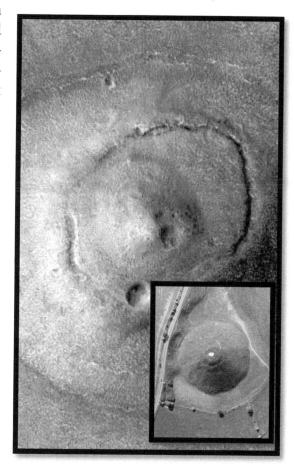

Figure 58 - The Tholus on Mars and Silbury Hill in England

Given the 150 year-old connection between the Jesuits and the Vatican Observatory (well documented in Tom Horn's and Cris Putnam's 2013 blockbuster tome, *Exo-Vaticana*), one does wonder just exactly what the Vatican knows about Mars and the secret content hidden deep within ancient Mystery Religions with which Jesuit scholars no doubt are highly familiar.

Whether in fact Schiaparelli affirmed this "ancient wisdom," Flynn certainly believes he did. However, in a somewhat predictive adaptation given his orientation to the Bible as God's revelation to humankind, Flynn did not assume that the originators of civilization in our solar system were Homo sapiens. Rather, he believed these intelligences were *angelic*. In other words, angels once existed on Rahab and built a vast civilization there. Furthermore, Flynn goes so far as to indicate that a specific type of angel—a *cherub*—was ruler of Rahab. This begs the following question: "Who was this powerful ruler?" No surprise: It was none other than the anointed cherub, *Lucifer*.

As Ezekiel stated, in the famous passage most often cited (which depicts the ancient adversary to Yahweh), it was Lucifer was "walked among the fiery stones"—the planetary "lights" which burned so bright in the night sky. *"Thou art the anointed cherub that covereth; and I have set thee so: thou wast upon the holy mountain of God;* **thou hast walked up and down in the midst of the stones of fire.***"* (Ezekiel 28:14, emphasis added)

The Real Meaning of the Mystery Religions

As mentioned in my previous article on Walt Disney and Werner von Braun, despite its frequent public denials, Freemasonry is linked to the Knights Templar and (at the very least) linked doctrinally through them to the ancient Mystery Religions. The well-known gods of the Greeks and Romans (Zeus/Jupiter, Aphrodite/Venus, and Ares/Mars) were initially based upon older, Egyptian gods (Osiris, Isis, and Horus). However, the Egyptian gods were not themselves the origin of these classic Greek and Roman mythological deities. Scholars all agree that before there were Egyptian gods, there were Mesopotamian gods existing at least from the time of Abraham—and more likely from the times before Noah—with the people known as the *Arcadians*.

By definition this would presume that the Arcadians lived *before the flood of Noah*.

Likewise, if the myths of the Arcadians influenced the development of post-flood deities in the pantheon of the Egyptians, the question is then, "How was this knowledge passed down to us?"

- Did the myths survive the flood through the stories told by Noah and his lineage (i.e., the survivors of the flood)?

- Or were there *Arcadians that survived the flood*?

- Or were there records (perhaps like the Sumerian clay tablets translated and made famous by Zecharia Sitchin, or records from ancient stele made of stone[8]) which the survivors of the flood or their descendants discovered?

Flynn describes the originators of the classic gods as the *Pelasgians*, of which there are many references in both Greek and Roman histories. Flynn depicts the origin of the Pelasgians as follows:

Figure 59 - The Nestorian Stele in China

The mystery schools were founded by the *Pelasgians*, the ancestors of the Phoenicians (Sidonians), and the original inhabitants of Arcadia. According to Aristotle, the *Pelasgians* (sea peoples in Greek) were an ancient race that occupied parts of Greece from the time before there was a moon in the sky; for this reason they were called *Proselenes* (literally "before the moon"). [Hippolytus refers to a legend that "Arcadia brought forth *Pelasgus* [progenitor of the Pelasgians], of greater antiquity than the moon." Plutarch wrote in *The Roman Questions*: "There were Arcadians of

---

[8] A *stele* is an upright stone, typically taller than it is wide, that contains an inscription to memorialize an event of historic significance. Such methods to record history exist globally, from Egyptian to the Mayan empires.

Evander's following, the so-called pre-Lunar people." Apollonius of Rhodes mentioned the time "when not all the orbs were yet in the heavens, before the *Danai* and *Deukalion* races came into existence, and only the Arcadians lived, of whom it is said that they dwelt on mountains and fed on acorns, before there was a moon." The Pelasgians existed long before the cataclysm of "Noah's Flood" (the aion alignment of 10,948 B.C.), [according to Flynn] as Apollonius suggested, before the flood of Deukalion and [his wife] *Pyrrha* [daughter of Pandora]. Remnants of the Pelasgians survived the cataclysmic shifting of the aions, preserving that knowledge of the former aions (when knowledge descended to the earth from the heavens) by establishing mystery schools, under various names, throughout the Mediterranean.[9]

According to Flynn, the notion there existed ancient knowledge that "came down from heaven" (specifically referencing the knowledge brought to humankind by the *Watchers*, i.e., fallen angels, mentioned but briefly in the Bible and extensively in the apocryphal *Book of Enoch*), was the focus of the Mediterranean Mystery Schools. Flynn summarizes the Mystery Schools' importance in regards to bequeathing the story of civilizations' origin:

Figure 60 – Honduran Stele

> The ancient mystery schools— the repositories of knowledge from the earlier aions—originated on the Mediterranean islands Samothrace, Eleusis and Crete (7 C[entury] B.C.—4 C[entury] A.D.). Though there is considerable speculation about this religion, accounts exist from ancient historians who claim to have witnessed rites, and to have petitioned to be initiated into the mysteries themselves. The mystery schools preserved the knowledge of the ancient world, as Plato described, through those ancient cycles of cataclysms by fire and water

---

[9] Ibid., (Kindle Locations 8769-8808).

that affected the advancement of civilization. Although that secret knowledge was never revealed to the common citizen, clues were left in the writings of initiates, philosophers and poets. Among those who underwent the rites of the mystery school, according to historical record, were Aristotle, Sophocles, Plato, Cicero and a number of Papyri Fragments (c. 3rd C[entury] A.D. [*Capitalization in original, bracketed comments added*]:[10]

Perhaps it goes without saying that Flynn's research and conclusions draw heavily upon detailed histories of these classic gods *as understood and explained by the civilizations which worshipped and revered them.* Of course, from this author's viewpoint, one must take these accounts with more than a measure of salt.

With that precaution acknowledged, we then proceed circumspectly: The history of the Red Planet connects to the Egyptian god *Horus*—the deity that inspired Rome's *Mars* and the Greek *Ares*. (Recall that the Eye of Horus, a familiar Freemason symbol, sits atop the Great Pyramid as pictured in America's *Great Seal*—which daily we see adorning the back of our One Dollar Bill). The now earthbound gods, Horus and his father Osiris, are linked to the (supposed)

Figure 61 - Mount Hermon in Syria / Northern Israel

distinct act of bringing civilization to humanity from heaven—obviously paralleling Flynn's contention about the angels of Rahab:

---

[10] Flynn, David, *The Cydonian Chronicles,* from *The David Flynn Collection* (Kindle Locations 8717-8752). Crane, MO., Defender Publishing. Kindle Edition. (2012)

The Martian god of Greek myth, Ares, was an ancient founder of civilization, before he became associated with warfare. Like the Romans, the Greeks considered Mars a god responsible for having introduced crop growing and domestication of animals, both necessary for community and cities. The worship of the god from the planet Mars as a builder was wide spread in the ancient world. The Egyptians referred to the planet Mars as *Har detcher*, *Horus the Red*, son and reincarnation of his father Osiris. The name 'Horus' is 'face' in Egyptian; *Har detcher* was literally 'the red face of Osiris.' *Osiris was considered the founder of Egypt's architecture and civilization*: 'Of Osiris they say that, being of a beneficent turn of mind, and eager for glory, he gathered together a great army, with the intention of visiting all the inhabited earth and teaching the race of men... after establishing Egypt, Osiris traveled abroad teaching the skills of building and society to the men scattered across the earth." [11]

Divine Wall Builders from the Land of Canaan

Most readers know that the connection between knowledge and building is at the core of Freemasonry. The *Compass and Square* are their universal symbols along with the tracing board, all tools of the Masonic craft. Another intriguing connection resides in the obvious contradiction of the "civilizing" of humanity attributed to these gods with the oft-repeated evil known as *fratricide*—a paradoxical flaw to say the least. The evidence appears that these gods were two-faced (like the god *Janus*, the god of gates, doors, and time—which reminds us of THE FACE on Cydonia!) In effect, there was a *human* (or at least *simian*) side and there was a *leonine* side (a view asserted by both Flynn and Hoagland). Flynn makes this point plain:

> [Osiris'] consort and sister Isis remained in Egypt as a resource for the skills of society. Fratricide is repeated in myths associated with the building of walls, cities, and temples. Osiris, the builder-god and founder of Egyptian civilization, was murdered by his brother Set; Romulus, the builder-god (*Mars Quirinus*) and founder of Roman civilization murdered his brother Remus; Cain, the first cultivator of crops and the first builder of a city found in the Bible, murdered his brother

---

[11] *Ibid.* The reader should make note of the curiosity that the name *Cairo* literally refers to the god and planet Mars. It is derived from the Arab, *Al-Qahir*, the Arabic name for the planet MARS. It also means "victorious."

Abel. Cain was the ancient ancestor of the Canaanites according to the Bible [although the land Canaan was named after Canaan the son of Ham]; the Canaanites were Phoenicians, that is, Sidonians.[12]

From Flynn's perspective the connection between the builder god Mars and the planet Mars stands as testimony to the descent of "gods" in ancient times from elsewhere in our solar system, possibly the Red Planet but as mentioned at the outset more likely the postulated planet Rahab. In contradistinction to the opinion of Hoagland and other ancient astronaut theorists (and admittedly repeating myself in deference to the reader's anticipated incredulity), these beings *weren't human but angelic.*

Consequently, it would not be accurate to characterize them as purely *extraterrestrial.* Their offspring however, were truly *extraordinary.* As Genesis 6:4 teaches, these were *the men of renown*—so-called gods upon which classic mythology is based. Known as the Nephilim, their story is expanded in considerable detail in the apocryphal *Book of Enoch.* While not contained within the Bible, the New Testament writers reference the Book of Enoch, and appear to accept that the original book of Enoch (which now shows obvious signs of modification) was considered scripture. References are explicitly made in Jude[13] and implicitly in II Peter 2 within the biblical canon.

However, it is the fallen angels, according to Enoch's account that were the source of knowledge of technologies that would eventually corrupt humankind. Enoch relates how the fallen angels descended upon the earth at Mount Hermon (in the area known today as the Golan Heights of Israel/Syria). From this point of origin,

---

[12] Ibid., (Kindle Locations 9597-9646).
[13] Jude 14, 15: "And Enoch also, the seventh from Adam, prophesied of these, saying, 'Behold, the Lord cometh with ten thousands of his saints, to execute judgment upon all, and to convince all that are ungodly among them of all their ungodly deeds which they have ungodly committed, and of all their hard speeches which ungodly sinners have spoken against him.'"

they began to disseminate their knowledge of civilization and to attempt to reshape humanity into their image—rather than the image of Yahweh. Flynn explains:

> Mount Hermon is on the northeastern border of Israel and Lebanon, its melting snow the source for the Jordan River—the name Jordan is derived from the root of Jared and means 'place of the descent.' The actual meaning of Hermon is from a primitive Hebrew root word *'khaw-ram'*; to destroy utterly, exterminate or consecrate, devote and dedicate for destruction. At the base of this mountain in Lebanon are the settlements of the oldest cities in the world, established it would seem immediately upon the descent of the Nephilim from Mount Hermon. This was the land that came to be called 'Sidonia.'[14] [Sidon was the first born of Canaan's *eleven* sons, a number significant to the Bible as it represents disorganization, falling one short of a number of reverence, the number *twelve*].

Figure 62 - Greek coins from Ancient Kydonia

According to Flynn, there are substantial references to these gods from mythology that constitute more than mere inference. The allusions parallel the Bible's testimony:

> The 'mighty men' described in this passage [Genesis 6:4] are called in Hebrew *Gibborim* or *geber* from *gabar* (to be strong); these Hebrew Gibborim are contemporary with the demi-gods and semi-divine heroes of Sumerian and Greek myth. This is the origin of the

---

[14] Ibid., (Kindle Locations 10074-10094).

Kibborim and *Kabiroi* known throughout the Mediterranean as *the gods of the Pelasgians*, and their descendants the Sidonians.[15]

For David Flynn, the connection with *Cydonia on Mars* and *Sidonia on Earth* constitutes much more than coincidental spelling. As stated earlier, he alleged Schiaparelli knew about the ancient legends and may have had specific insight from the legacy of the Mystery Schools that "Martians" and "Cydonians" are literally related *genetically*.[16] The notion that angels and humans mated in ancient times has, of course, gained widespread acceptance among many of today's evangelical writer/researchers (such as L.A. Marzulli, Steve Quayle, Tom Horn, Cris Putnam, Gary Stearman, Doug Hamp, Rob Skiba, and this author).

However, does this mean that the myth of civilization's having begun on Mars necessarily connects to the descent of the fallen angels on Mount Hermon? Does it prove that the Nephilim are an incarnation artifact, if you will, of the cosmic relocation effort of angels that evacuated Rahab/Mars after learning that their habitation was to be destroyed, perhaps as some form of judgment by Yahweh? Furthermore, were the giants of old, some of whose corpses are literally surfacing today (see L.A. Marzulli's new book, *On the Trail of the Nephilim* or Steve Quayle's new book, *True Legends*), related to the Sidonians of Phoenicia? Were the Canaanite giants the offspring of the Martians? If so, how much Martian genetic material actually infected the Sidonians who were associated with Tyre and Sidon (Sidonia), *Canaan* (the land named after Canaan, the cursed son of Ham and grandson of Noah), and later the land at the base of Mount Hermon, where the *Danites* settled?[17]

---

[15] Ibid., (Kindle Locations 10165-10176).

[16] Reflecting on the discussion in the earlier chaper, we could also wonder if Wernher von Braun likewise understood that *Mars held the key to humanity's past.*

[17] The Danites were known by the Greeks as the *Danians* whose thousand ships were launched in a quest to reunite Paris and Helen of Troy (the face that could launch a thousand ships!) The Danians may have given rise to *Aeneus*, the mythical father of *Romulus* and *Remus*, the purported founders of Rome. The late J.R. Church provided an outstanding study on this subject in his last book, *Daniel*

Flynn argues there exists a direct and necessary connection:

> The "Cydonians" lived on the west side of the island of Crete and even today the name of the province around Chania is *Kydonia*. Cydonia is mentioned by Homer as one of the most important Cretan cities, called, like its Canaanite counterpart, the "the mother of all Cretan cities." The port city of Cydonia according to legend was named after its founder and king Kydon, who according to the majority of mythological chroniclers, had migrated to Crete from Sidonia or from the Greek coast of Boeotia founded by Cadmus the Sidonian. Diodorus [a Greek historian writing between 60 and 30 BC] described Crete as the origin of the Mystery Schools of the Pelasgians, that is, the *ancestors* of the Sidonians of Phoenicia. [Emphasis mine][18]

To draw out the implications of Flynn's thesis: The knowledge of civilization's origin—the planet Rahab and its moon Mars where angels once dwelt, *was handed down to humanity because of the breeding between fallen angels with human women.* The offspring, the Nephilim, were proof that angels did create hybrid offspring. Perhaps these half-human, half-angel offspring propagated the stories of Martian civilization through their progeny. If so, however, this stands as no more than a logical deduction derived from Flynn's speculation. It remains fascinating conjecture, but is beyond proof.

Conclusion: How the Legend Was Handed Down

However, I would argue that both stories could be true while not necessarily connected. That is to say, the veracity of one does not prove the other. Likewise, one could be proven false while the other remains true. Each account has to be considered on its own merits.

To be more specific, surviving the flood would not be the only means for descendants of the Arcadians, Pelasgians, or *Cydonians* to transmit their stories to future generations.

Reveals the Bloodline of the Antichrist. Church believed that the Danites were in fact the descendants of the Hebrew tribe of Dan. My co-author in *The Final Babylon*, Douglas W. Krieger, has done work in this area suggesting the connection is not that clear-cut. The truth, unfortunately, may be lost in the dark mists of time.

[18] Ibid., (Kindle Locations 10433-10451).

Clearly, we really don't know whether the stories were communicated (1) directly by the hybrid offspring which may have survived the flood, (2) by the descendants of Noah who lived through the great flood and told these tales to their children and grandchildren, OR (3) because written records (cuneiform tablets, various steles, extant papyri?) were discovered after the flood by humanity—giving rise to the *legend of Mars as the genesis of civilization.* Flynn doesn't make clear his choice among these alternatives; nevertheless, it is certain that Flynn purports in some manner this information became a key tenet of Mystery Religions handed down to our day through Theosophy and Freemasonry.[19]

Whether angels begat children through human women after Noah's flood or not, Flynn's argument could still hold water (no pun intended). Certainly the possibility exists that some Cydonian giants hailing from places beyond earth, may have survived the flood to continue their hybrid breeding program.[20] On the other hand, if

---

[19] Most researcher/authors, who subscribe to the view that angels fathered hybrid children before the flood, contend fallen angels continued this practice AFTER the flood as well. Giants occupied the land of Canaan and were the primary reasons the Children of Israel refused to conquer the land (until they had experienced the punishment of wondering through the wilderness for 40 years). If all flesh was destroyed in the flood of Noah (including the Nephilim), where did these post-flood giants come from? This theory is known as the *Multiple Incursion Theory.* Angels bred with humans before and AFTER the flood of Noah. In opposition to this theory, researcher/author Rob Skiba believes the giants of Canaan may be traced to DNA associated with Ham's wife which emerged in their descendants post-flood. Skiba indicates the Scripture chronicles numerous giants through Ham's line in the land of Canaan (the land of Sidon!) Either way (one incursion before the flood, or multiple, ongoing incursions), the argument is challenging to sustain. Arguing the Nephilim are human/angelic hybrids is difficult not just because of the supernatural element (presuming angels exist), but because it assumes angels and humans can procreate hybrid offspring. But remember: all mythologies of our world assert that *gods intermarried with humans.* The term *demi-god* comes from this notion. For those who believe in the supernatural character of the Bible, the proposition that angels are made with DNA may be surprising, but not altogether beyond the pale.

[20] However take note: the Bible indicates that all "flesh was destroyed", both humanoid and animal. So if Yahweh's plans to halt the cross-breeding program were foiled this easily by angels – procreating once again hybrids after the flood – one wonders why Yahweh determined to destroy the world to "purify" the human genome in the first place. It suggests that Yahweh was easily outsmarted by the fallen

giants reappeared after the flood, whether due to Nephilim genetics being passed through one of the sons or wives of Noah or because fallen angels continued the process of procreating hybrid beings, the flood of Noah apparently *did not terminate the cross-breeding program*. Although sorely tempted, we can speculate no further in this chapter regarding the ultimate agenda of Satan and his henchmen, the fallen angels. In our concluding chapter, we will give the argument more consideration.

To summarize: it may well be that angels came to earth long before the creation of humankind—and obviously before the flood of Noah. As the *Book of Enoch* conveys, these creatures may have been the teachers of civilization to humankind (as well as metallurgy, cosmetics, and especially warfare). After the flood, all that survived were the legends of their activity. *We cannot be dogmatic about this matter: The Bible chooses not go into depth. And details are supplied by extra-biblical sources.*

On the one hand, we would be foolish to ignore the topic because it comes from many ancient sources and we hasten to point out it offers a satisfactory explanation for why a worldwide flood was deemed necessary by Yahweh to "purify" the genome of land animals and especially humankind. We would also be foolish to emphasize, however, archeology and artifacts of Nephilim at the cost of other doctrines. The topic remains most intriguing and the artifacts utterly compelling, but we best mind the guardrails and not venture too far off the main road, lest our priorities be mistaken by our peers.

Nevertheless, I will give the last word to William Shakespeare:

"There are more things in Heaven and Earth Horatio
than is dreamt of in your philosophy."
Hamlet to Horatio, *Hamlet* (1.5.167-8).

---

angels. Of course, that is only part of the story! Yahweh may have expressed his anger and his inevitable judgment. Fallen angels may have expressed their inability to contain themselves despite knowing the proven fate that would eventually befall them.

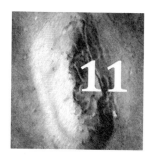

"Photo Fights:" Proof Intelligent Life Existed on Mars?

Recapping the Last Chapter

I N THE PREVIOUS CHAPTER, I SUMMARIZED THE THINKING OF THE LATE DAVID FLYNN AND HIS BOOK *CYDONIA: THE SECRET CHRONICLES OF MARS*. I DISCUSSED HOW FLYNN PROPOSED THAT

Figure 63 - The Recent Book by Mike Bara

civilization first began in our solar system on Mars (or adjacent, on its planetary partner) and later migrated to earth. This migration was forced upon the inhabitants either just preceding a cataclysmic cosmic catastrophe or shortly thereafter. David Flynn developed his thesis while maintaining a Christian—indeed, *biblical* faith.

Flynn conceived of the unexpected possibility that extinct intelligent life once thrived on Mars without compromising his view that "the cosmic chess match" (as LA Marzulli terms it, i.e., the war between Yahweh and Lucifer), continues center-stage upon our Earth. In other words, while still affirming a biblical worldview, Flynn persuasively argued that unearthly intelligence first resided elsewhere, specifically, through angelic beings that lived *not just on Mars*—but on an adjacent planet around which Mars orbited.

Therefore, to be precise, the overarching theory postulates that *Mars was a moon before it was a planet.*[1] Something happened, something catastrophic, that destroyed the now missing planet and sent Mars on its not-so-merry way alone—a diminutive heavenly body half the diameter of Earth, forever divorced of its much more massive planetary partner. Thus, Mars no longer orbited the purportedly obliterated planet (Flynn identified this planet as *Rahab*, derived from a mysterious reference in the Bible[2]). It thereafter commenced its orbit of our sun becoming the fourth planet within our solar system. In its wake, Mars left behind thousands of bits and pieces of varying shapes and sizes we know as asteroids, Ceres being the largest. Together these multitudinous space rocks formed one of the great mysteries of our solar system—the Asteroid Belt—occupying the fifth place in the sequence of planetary orbits circling our sun.

Various theories have been proposed about what happened (for instance[3], Rahab might have drifted too close to Jupiter and was pulled apart by its momentous gravitational force; or perhaps the planet was smacked by a massive comet). However, what remains

---

[1] The idea that Mars was once a moon is disputed by many scientists, one being an expert in planetary physics and interplanetary travel, as well as frequent consultant to NASA, who reviewed and supplied many helpful comments on this chapter. The outcome of the debate appears to hinge on the validity of Bode's Law. "The Titius-Bode Law is rough rule that predicts the spacing of the planets in the Solar System. The relationship was first pointed out by Johann Titius in 1766 and was formulated as a mathematical expression by J.E. Bode in 1778. It lead Bode to predict the existence of another planet between Mars and Jupiter in what we now recognize as the asteroid belt." See http://www.astro.cornell.edu/academics/courses/astro201/bodes_law.htm. Despite the much more informed opinion of my friend, I still find the data for the "moonship" of Mars compelling.

[2] "Thou hast broken Rahab in pieces, as one that is slain; thou hast scattered thine enemies with thy strong arm." (Psalm 89:10)

[3] Joseph P. Farrell proposes the timeframe was about one million years earlier, around 2.3 million years ago.

most intriguing is that, in cosmic terms, this event may have happened only very recently—(according to one expert about 3.2 million years and another, 1.35 million years ago). In a universe that appears to be at least 13.5 billion years old (or older), this means that this event happened in the last 1/10,000th of the life of the universe. Comparatively speaking, if the universe were but one-year old (a period equal to 525,600 minutes), the planet's destruction would have happened within the past 52 minutes. In the lengthy lifetime of our solar system, it is like it *just happened*. 4

As noted throughout, Flynn is not the only intellectual to conceive of this possibility. While coming from very different worldviews, authors Richard C. Hoagland and Mike Bara share Flynn's premise that humanity's past connects directly with Mars.

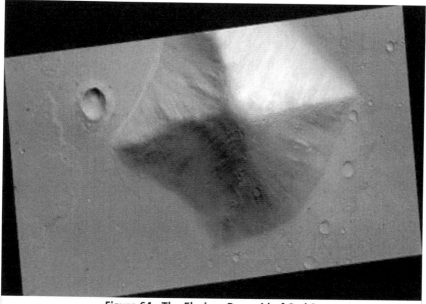

Figure 64 - The Elysium Pyramid of Carl Sagan

4 So how do we know that it was so recent, speaking in solar timeframes? The evidence amassed by Hoagland, Bara, and Farrell, emphasizes the work of the late Dr. Tom Van Flandern. Van Flandern, with a Ph.D. in Astronomy from Yale University, worked at the Naval Observatory. He developed a theory of this catastrophe based on a wide variety of arguments. I will discuss him again later in the chapter.

Advocates for Ancient Aliens

As I have unhesitatingly indicated several times before in this book, the most recognizable believer in today's newest and fasting growing undeclared cult, *ancient alien astronauts—progenitors of mankind*, is none other than Richard C. Hoagland, former consultant to Walter Cronkite and CBS Television, and for the past three decades, frequent guest on George Noory's *Coast-to-Coast AM*. Hoagland not only believes that in the distant past intelligent life once existed on Mars, he promotes the view that intelligent life on our Earth (that would be us) was first conceived and nurtured on the Red Planet.[5] Hoagland is a visible, intelligent, relentless, but perhaps unduly effusive proponent for our "genesis on Mars"—a view which continues gathering momentum among those who watch History Channels' *Ancient Aliens*.

Another top champion for the evidence of intelligent life in our solar system is his one-time co-author, Mike Bara. Together, Hoagland and Bara penned the best-selling 2007 title, Dark *Mission: The Secret History of NASA*. As noted previously, their book made a series of fantastic assertions—the most notable being the culpability of NASA in misleading the America public. According to Bara and Hoagland, NASA was initially led by a slew of Freemasons in high places. These not-so-secretive part-time mystics held sway until Wernher von Braun and his Nazi cohorts commandeered the space agency later in the 1960s. Nazi mysticism was not all that different than Masonry's; however, its mythology connected to the

---

[5] This view is decidedly different than Flynn's inasmuch as Flynn believed that humanity was a special, direct creation of Yahweh on the Earth. Flynn proposed that civilization—a society developed and overseen by Lucifer, a cherub at one time in service of Yahweh—was created and thrived first on Rehab and/or Mars, and then took up stakes and moved to Earth. Civilization was first an angelic enterprise. Hoagland, Bara, et al, suggest that humankind may have evolved first on Mars (or Rehab, aka Planet K, X, or V according to Van Flandern) and then migrated to Earth in search of a more hospitable home.

outrageous beliefs of Madame Helena Petrovna Blavatsky, believing such doctrines as (1) paranormal powers were strongest in the putative Aryan race and (2) Atlantians were the descendants of an intelligent race from another world. Based upon their respective *weltanschauungs* (worldviews), both factions equally influenced NASA decisions—and allegedly secreted away numerous discoveries regarding artifacts on our moon and the Red Planet. For all intents and purposes, from Hoagland's, Bara's, and even noted author Joseph P. Farrell's viewpoint, space exploration had become a science serving only *the interests of technocrats and plutocrats*, not the general public.

Through Adventures Unlimited Press, at the time of this writing (December, 2013) Bara has just published a new volume for which he is solely responsible: *Ancient Aliens on Mars,* [6] which serves as sequel to his other recent book *Ancient Aliens on the Moon* (2012). Both Bara books continue the story line of *Dark Mission:* (1) NASA knows intelligent life has been present in our solar system; (2) there are artifacts on the moon, Mars, and probably other planets which confirm this fact; and (3) NASA is committed to establish this truth on behalf of a select group or groups within our government, while at the same time practicing to deceive the public.

Both works aim to provide photographic evidence that aliens—and perhaps our forebears—were present on our moon and on the planet Mars. While not light on intriguing commentary, the bulk of Bara's effort displays photos, lots of them—some with bold captions and large pointers—drawing attention to what the author presumes are a series of compelling artifacts.

Bara provides the thesis of his book with these words:

> The mainstream scientists will tell you that there is not much of anything there, no buildings, no canals, not even any microbes. They will tell you that Mars has been dead for billions of years and that there is

---

[6] Mike Bara, *Ancient Aliens of Mars,* Kempton, Illinois: Adventures Unlimited Press, 2013, 218 pages.

no evidence there was ever an advanced civilization there, whether indigenous or transient. What I will tell you is that there is an unbelievable amount of Ancient Alien evidence on Mars, that it was once covered by a vast and complex civilization, one that was far more advanced than ours.[7]

Bara also chronicles and updates the three-plus-decade debate—often a vitriolic interplay as his narrative discloses—between Team Hoagland/Bara and the various front men for NASA. Sometimes the NASA parties are full-time government employees and sometimes only contractors. But all spokespersons for this supposedly civilian agency [8] are "paid shills" (according to Bara) providing disinformation and keeping the public ignorant of what has already been discovered about life in our solar system. According to Bara, the acronym, NASA, stands for "never a straight answer."

Even if true, and as we will discuss the weight of the evidence tends to suggest *it is true* (at least to a somewhat disturbing extent), the oft-deliberate obfuscation by our Government's national space agency is not the only problem complicating Bara's argument.

---

[7] Ibid., p. 78. While it doesn't necessarily concede a contradiction to his contention, it is noteworthy that the examples of habitats Bara points out reference less than advanced architectures.

[8] NASA technically reports to the White House, but its chartering document describes it as fulfilling a military purpose of developing weapons, based upon the determination of the President.: From the National Aeronautics and Space Act (December 18, 2010) Section, 20102: "Aeronautical and Space Activities for Welfare and Security of United States—Congress declares that the general welfare and security of the United States require that adequate provision be made for aeronautical and space activities. Congress further declares that such activities shall be the responsibility of, and shall be directed by, a civilian agency exercising control over aeronautical and space activities sponsored by the United States, except that activities peculiar to or primarily associated with the development of weapons systems, military operations, or the defense of the United States (including the research and development necessary to make effective provision for the defense of the United States) shall be the responsibility of, and shall be directed by, the Department of Defense; and that determination as to which agency has responsibility for and direction of any such activity shall be made by the President."

Methinks You Protest Too Much!

Like Fox Mulder, "I want to believe",[9] but this author still does not find most of the photo evidence compelling. As I have said elsewhere, to my eyes most photos continue to be murky and lacking in indisputable detail. Muddling matters further, the debate is fraught with considerable name calling, sloppy or downright intentional misstatements by NASA, and sundry sketchy suppositions from the "intelligent-life-comes-from Mars" advocates. Additionally, the lack of scientific aptitude on the part of these advocates may cast all of their thinking in a shroud of doubt.[10]

However, the biggest obstacle remains the inability to produce a photo that all can readily agree demonstrates beyond any reasonable doubt that intelligent life once resided on Mars. Instead, the debate becomes tedious with too many suppositions and convoluted explanations. Ultimately, it disappoints those who (like me) earnestly seek the photographic equivalent of "the smoking gun." When such books as Bara's are published or are subject to streamed YouTube videos, like most other curious onlookers, I inspect the photos—closely I might add—but seldom do I find those artificial structures "plain as day," i.e., structures built by intelligent beings that scream "intelligent design" and testify with certainty to its "manmade" origin. On the other hand, Bara often does.

Nevertheless, so much of the debate hangs on photographic tricks and touchups (either real, implied, or alleged) that the lay person grasps for any single object—anything at all—that amounts to an clear-cut picture of a bona fide artifact about which we can be certain. To investigate the matter, one must meander amidst the

---

[9] This was Mulder's famous UFO office poster hanging behind his desk, visible in most scenes with Mulder talking with Scully within his darkened basement location at the Washington DC offices of the FBI.

[10] A highly qualified friend says Hoagland and Bara often demonstrate a poor knowledge of physics and other scientific principles that compromise the strength of their arguments. Not being a scientist myself, I take his input seriously.

techno-jargon of "high pass filters," "elimination of digital arti-facts," or "reduction of picture noise." The reader must possess at least a modicum of expertise in Photoshop© to have any confidence that what you are being fed by the explicators of the image in question comprises the real truth and nothing but the truth. Adding to the painstaking exercise: the debate focuses on photographs (and there are many) labeled with an impersonal alphanumeric tag, yielding a narrative made even more arcane by such nondescript identification.

The photo fight has raged ever since the July 25, 1976 Viking I picture of the famous "Face on Mars" (affectionately known as 35A72). Advocates like Bara have had to wait with bated breath, usually years if not decades, between these billion-dollar episodic cosmic photo sessions. Enthusiasts predictably anticipate the next Mars mission will satisfy them—expecting the next, newer, and much higher resolution camera destined for the Red Planet—to set-tle the issue once and for all.[11] Enthusiasts, however, would have had better luck waiting for hell to freeze over.

Despite the impressive specifications for these invaluable pic-ture-takers, obfuscation has arguably never given way to clarity. Time after time, the resulting set of photos yielded snapshots *with-out* anticipated detail. No surprise then that each new photo album transmitted back to Earth, generates complaints from enthusiasts that the digital pictures were at best truncated and doctored, and at worst, purposefully corrupted by NASA (its employees or its con-tracted "imaginers"). This is not to slight the expertise of JPL/NASA's image processing experts. They are almost without

---

[11] Mariner 9 (1976) possessed resolution restricted to about one pixel per 150 to 300 meters (500 to 1,000 feet). Within the last decade or so, cameras circling Mars boasted resolutions equivalent to one pixel for each half-meter (less than 20 inches!) Ironically, when NASA presented the photos, they often looked worse than pictures released a decade earlier.

equal.[12] However, to the true believer (such as Bara and Company), the matchless skill of NASA's image experts breeds no small suspicion in its own right. They are so capable that they may discretely alter image detail effecting the veracity of any given photograph.

On the other hand, the allegations made by the life-on-Mars advocates so consistently insists that NASA misleads the public (al-

Figure 65 - A Sphinx on Mars?

ways and everywhere), that their stridency harms the advancement of their overall perspective. Does NASA mess with every photo? When you listen to Hoagland and Bara, you would think they do.

Then there is the question of whether their imagination simply gets away from them. Perhaps the most questionable claim relates to the so-called *Sphinx of Mars,* photographed by the *Mars Pathfinder,* upon its landing, July 4, 1997 (see image above). From its initial location looking toward two distant hills (nicknamed the

---

[12] Michael Malin is the contractor in question. His work received significant criticism by Bara. As I will explain later, it is possible he was asked by NASA to be slow in posting his work for public examination. Public contractors have more control over their work than government employees and agencies. His website today is most helpful and a great place to poke around. See http://www.msss.com/about-us/michael-c-malin.php.

Twin Peaks), a shapely object appeared in the mid-ground of the photograph. Bara suggests the image is a sphinx, a la the guardian of the Giza Plateau outside of Cairo. Additionally, he contends that there are pueblo-like (presumably deserted) habitations on the sides of Mar's Twin Peaks—and copious mechanical artifacts (disguised as plain old rocks) resident in the foreground.

Now, the meme of connecting Egyptian pyramids with those on Mars is familiar. As we discussed in Chapter One, this was covered by Hoagland and Graham Hancock in their respective books from two decades ago and discussed in depth by Lynn Picknett and Clive Prince via their critique of the "Pyramidiots" in their fine book, *The Stargate Conspiracy* (*Pyramidiots* is the now familiar albeit disparaging moniker applied equally to Robert Bauval as well as Hancock and several others). Nevertheless, once the jump takes place from pyramids to sphinxes (on Mars that is), this author's incredulity goes haywire. Readers should study the photograph above and decide for themselves (Note: the lack of detail in the photo here characterizes the original too). In fairness to Bara, he notes that the digital data from NASA falls short of image supplied by the European Space Agency (ESA—apparently the ESA is not so intent in keeping Europeans in the dark). Perhaps a better view exists—but we must be satisfied with a rather fuzzy image lacking in definition.

Bara comments unhappily:

> So once again we are faced with only two possibilities. Either the "sphinx" does not exist and neither do the adobe-like habitats on the Twin Peaks, or the MRO [Mars Reconnaissance Orbiter] image has simply been whitewashed. After careful consideration, I am forced to conclude the latter. Part of this "careful consideration" [his quotation marks] comes from comparing the NASA supplied super-resolution panoramas with data supplied by the European Space Agency... The ESA processing, done mostly by German scientists, showed that the adobe-like construction on the Twin Peaks was definitely valid... Other clearly mechanical objects shared the same fate. A rounded mechanism nick-named the "Turbo" took on the form of a natural rock when the NASA panoramas were scrutinized.

At this point, I am forced to go where the data pushes me and conclude that much of the imagery from the Pathfinder landing site has been tampered with to cover up the existence of both near field mechanisms and somewhat distant archologies [his term for "ecological architectures"], notably the Twin Peaks.[13]

However, while it is easy to criticize Bara's romantic (that is, enthusiast) posture on many counts, when both sides of the debate are examined objectively, the larger problem appears to rest with NASA. We will turn to their graphical prestidigitation next.

Oh, the Tangled Web We Weave

Therefore, it is not my point that Bara's complaints are unfounded. With its arrogant dismissal of the public's understandable curiosity, along with the ardent attacks on the "professional believers" whom it counts as a nuisance (that is, those like Bara and Hoagland), NASA does its best to call down ferocious fire from heaven upon itself. Sometimes the ardor comes in the form of Congressman who insist the intransigent space agency cooperate. However, most of the time NASA must field impassioned questions and generally well-reasoned technical challenges from the usual suspects; that is, incessant inquiries if not implicit reprimands emanating from the ever-vigilant Hoagland, Bara, and Associates.

Concerning the famous Cydonian "face:" well, as the saying goes—once burned, twice shy. In 1976, NASA spokespeople made the unmistaken misstatements "The face is just a trick of light and shadow." Paraphrasing what surely seemed at the time to be innocuous words: "It is no big deal. It is not a face at all. We took another photo a few hours later proving it was nothing." However, the innocent sounding phrasing turned out to be a premeditated lie. Their deception was not just dismissive but flagrantly untrue. There was no other clarifying (or disconfirming) photo. Furthermore, the "amateur investigators" proved it technically impossible

---

[13] Ibid., pp. 164-166.

for there to have been one. Why? Because the space craft did not "pass that way again" a few hours later. It did not pass that way again for several days. And despite the fact the agency continued to assert the non-existence of THE FACE and demonstrated persistent

indifference, NASA perpetuated the lie for many years afterwards. In fact, it was seventeen years later before NASA finally admitted they had intentionally lied in making this state-ment.[14] By having taken this earlier tact, even *if* there was *nothing to it*—no artificial face on Mars that is—NASA did its best to lead the public to con-clude SOMETHING REMARKABLE WAS THERE, precisely be-cause *NASA was lying.* By acting suspicious—

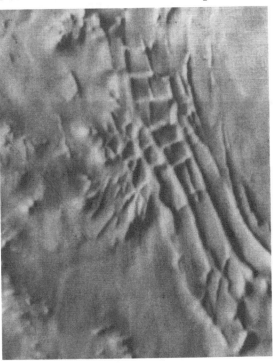

Figure 66 – The INCA City - NASA Frame 4212-15

by NASA's leadership intentionally hiding the facts—the "true be-lievers" grew irrepressible in working out the truth for themselves.

---

[14] The second photo of the face came on the 13th picture of *Viking 1*, 35 days later. Dr. Geral Soffen, a Viking project scientist addressed the press, introduced the image of the face with the dismissal statement, "Is not it peculiar what tricks of light and shadow can do...? When we took another picture a few hours later, it all went away; it was just a trick, just the way the light fell on it." Consequently, de-spite headlines around the way, no scientist took it seriously. Bara comments that even Hoagland, present at the announcement, failed to care much about it either. So "Mission accomplished!" THE FACE was a non-event—at least, initially. It was not until Senator Diane Feinstein asserted pressure on NASA that they stopped repeating the tired and untrue story. (See Bara, Ibid., p. 104).

Consequently, the falsehoods begged the follow-up questions: "What discovery about Mars is so disturbing that NASA must conceal it so nefariously? Just what is this formation on the Cydonian steppes they want to hide?"

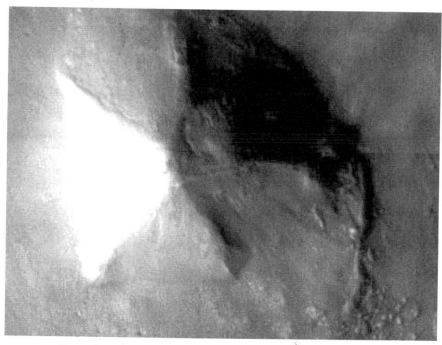

Figure 67 - The D&M Pyramid (named after DiPietro and Molenaar)

Precisely for these reasons, this author contends the strongest indication of real artifacts on our moon and on Mars may lie not the photographic evidence *per se* (although certain photographs are certainly suggestive, such as the so-called "Elysium Pyramid", the D&M pyramid—the closest element to a "smoking gun"[15], and the "Inca City" on Mars—see photos above), but *NASA's conspicuously deceptive behavior* which frustrates the sincerely curious (a group predisposed to *support* space exploration—sycophants NASA

---

[15] According to the "Ancient Alien Hunters," the D&M pyramid displays geometrical properties, including serving as the centerpiece for directing attention at the other interesting features on the Cydonian plain, such as THE FACE, The Fortress, and The Tholus, all a part of Hoagland's "City" complex.

should be doing everything they can to pacify if not recruit outright). By decades of deception, NASA has rightly earned the disgust and mistrust of the cosmically curious by frequently failing in several important regards: (1) to deliver on its promises to readily share information; (2) by supplying selected photos which have been clearly doctored; and by (3) letting contracts out to individuals or companies that hold the public hostage—that is, by releasing photos only when the contractor gets good and ready to do so.[16]

At one point, Bara cites President Reagan's science advisor, George Keyworth, who testified before Congress: "All government agencies lie part of the time, but NASA is the only one I've ever encountered that does so routinely."[17] Why lie unless there is something you don't want the public to know? In the context of Mars and the issue of whether ancient civilizations once dwelt there, *a photo withheld may tell us far more than a photo shared.*

Perhaps NASA's most obvious and blatant example of misstating the facts and misleading the public is rather stunning in its simplicity. It is the scientifically factual and proven reality: *Mars often has blue skies and not red.* Even though the Martian atmosphere is basically about 1% as dense as that of earth's, the filtering of the Sun's light works essentially the same on Mars as it does on Earth. Certain colors of the sun's rays are blocked by the molecules in the atmosphere—other rays (notably the "blue" ones) still shine through.

---

[16] This castigation is not completely fair. NASA has created a charming and detailed web site—"Be a Martian"—see http://beamartian.jpl.nasa.gov/welcome. This material provides a history of Martian exploration with a substantial photo exhibition. Granted, photos that may represent "the smoking gun" would likely NOT be showcased. But NASA is clearly seeking the public's support with this effort. Additionally, it is entirely likely that contractor Malin was used intentionally by NASA/JPL to build a wall between the Alien Astronaut theorists and a government agency obliged to make all information available to the public upon request. A private contractor has the ability to pick what it wishes to disclose and when it chooses to do so. If NASA wished to restrict access to "embarrassing photos," Malin made it acceptable and feasible to do so.

[17] Quoted by Bara, p. 93.

This produces blue skies. Bara conveys this effect is known as "Rayleigh Scattering:" In fact, every planet in the solar system with an atmosphere generally will showcase blue skies! This science has to do with the wavelength of light and how particles (be they air molecules or water droplets) interferes with light.[18] "Similar-sized molecules of all planetary atmospheres (be it the primary nitrogen of Earth, the carbon dioxide atmosphere of Mars, or even the predominantly hydrogen atmosphere of Jupiter and Saturn) all produce blue skies when sunlight passes through them."[19]

Furthermore (according to Bara), the photographic record, collected for decades by dozens of observatories around the world (inclusive of hundreds of thousands of images), proves that JPL was tampering with the truth. In other words, Bara contends that NASA was literally falsely coloring the photographs and video images.[20]

The following incident is now famous among Mars aficionados. It was documented in the book by Barry DiGregorio, *Mars: The Living Planet.*[21] We should consider the details of the story to appreciate the full impact.

---

[18] See this link for a discussions of Rayleigh Scattering principles. http://hyperphysics.phy-astr.gsu.edu/hbase/atmos/blusky.html. After reviewing the explanation, one can argue either way for the probable color of Mars' skies, although "tweaking the moniters" to make sure "they see red" colors the truth, to say the least.

[19] Ibid., p. 134.

[20] Dust storms, a frequent occurrence on Mars, will definitely tint the sky reddish brown. Consequently, blue skies and red skies are both possible for an observer situated on the Martian surface.

[21] DiGregorio's book sought to document that Viking, in 1976 carried out a series of tests invented and developed by his colleagues for Mars where it performed their function and proved (to them, not to NASA) that microbial life existed on the planet. The debate still rages today as to whether these tests did in fact prove life thrives there. NASAs reluctance to acknowledge the validity of the tests they bought and sent to Mars on Viking I and II adds additional weight to the argument that NASA *dares not admit life of any kind ever lived on Mars.* Most recently, in September, 2013, Curiosity tested for Methane in the atmosphere and officials said, "Nope, no trace" at least, not from any sort of biological source. See the link http://www.nytimes.com/2013/09/20/science/space/mars-rover-comes-up-empty-in-search-for-methane.html?pagewanted%3Dall&_r=0.

When the first Mars lander, *Viking 1*, began sending back images from the surface, the sky was perfectly blue, as the discussion above about Rayleigh Scattering suggests it would be. However, as soon as the first images were shown on the monitors at JPL in Pasadena, the project director, James S. Martin, Jr. had a technician go around to every monitor and change the colors displayed to a decided red cast. Another technician was aghast at this trickery wondering what game was afoot. He went to the monitors and changed them back to their natural color settings. The project director began yelling and screaming at a technician, Ron Levin, for doing this evil deed. Immediately, he had another engineer from TRW, Ron Gilje, return to each monitor again for tweaking so that the landscape and sky appeared red.

Apparently, Mars must NOT be allowed to look TOO hospitable. For some reason (which becomes the source of enormous speculation as the "Dark Mission" authors, Bara and Hoagland are wont to do), NASA wanted the public to hold in their minds' eye an image of Martian skies and its landscape consistent with the popular notion of Mars as "the Red Planet." Consequently, everything about it must be red—skies as well as rocks. Moreover, according to DiGregorio, since this trickery was ordered by the NASA administrator himself, Dr. James Fletcher, the case seems conclusive: *NASA has something to hide.*

DiGregorio documented this inscrutable behavior further from on a letter written to him by former JPL public affairs officer Jurrie J. Van der Woude. Van der Woude wrote that (the now late) Dr. Thomas Mutch, the Viking Imaging Team leader, had been called by the NASA administrator, Fletcher, and ordered to destroy the Mars blue sky negatives created from the original digital data. Seriously? Destroy the originals? These photographs were the very reason for sending a billion dollar space probe to Mars in the first place.

So what should we conclude? Obviously, even if "the truth is out there" it first must be filtered by the management of JPL and NASA.[22]

Kitty Litter

A more recent and especially apparent example of NASA deception toward Mars' Ancient Alien Hunters (Bara's phrase, not mine—see *Ancient Aliens on Mars*, p. 169) once again involved THE FACE on Mars. In April 1998, the Mars Global Surveyor supplied a much anticipated photo of the image from Cydonia. After considerable build-up and fanfare, the photo was released by NASA. What was finally shared with the public, to say the least, fell far below expectations. Its release seemed timed to maximize disenchantment.

Officially NASA would take no position on the merits of the photo. The picture first appeared in raw form with no tinkering—but it was also an image virtually nondescript and nearly black. It was shared by JPL scientists, more or less, on their lunch hour.

To say the least, enthusiasts were devastated by what they saw. The only picture made available of THE FACE hit the national evening newscasts with less than accompanying fanfare. Tom Brokaw said the photo "proved what we already know" while Dan Rather pronounced it "a pile of rocks." No matter that right before air time, a geologist, Timothy J. Parker, working with basic Photoshop skills, released a refined version. Nevertheless, this subsequent event was too little and too late to overcome first impressions. Furthermore, this second image made THE FACE look flat and totally unremarkable. In essence the Martian face really needed a facelift.

---

[22] Ibid., pp. 135-136. NASA's motivation could be to avoid suspicion it was willing to consider the far-fetched notions of the Alien Astronaut theorists. Funding from the Federal Government would likely dry up if NASA and JPL appeared to be "unscientific" in their efforts. From the perspective of the naturalist or the cynic, this explanation for NASA's behavior would make perfect sense.

The Ancient Alien Hunters were flabbergasted. Was this a joke? Why was the only photo NASA released far worse than what had been presented in history books for the previous two decades? Why were the image processing wizards so inept in providing a decent photograph after so much effort and expense? The later Parker photograph was certainly better than the very first photo from a few hours earlier. However, it still seemed distorted, compressed, and entirely lacking in much of any topographical quality (see photos below).

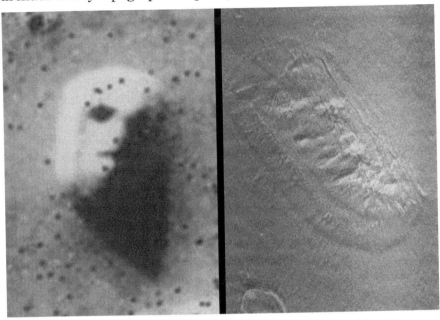

Figure 68 – The 1997 "Cat box" Image alongside the 1976 Viking I Photo

Additionally, in submitting the second photo—in contrast to the adage—"*LATE was NOT better than never.*" Timothy J. Parker, working for the MIPL (MIPL, the Mission Image Processing Laboratory, the official NASA/JPL resource) had supplied what would be the best that NASA would provide in the short-term. This version, aka the TJP version, was not an improvement—it was a corruption.

That same evening, in a conversation between Art Bell and Richard Hoagland on *Coast to Coast AM*, Bell stated matter-of-factly, "Well, looking at that (TJP) image, Richard, I'd have to conclude as well that there is no Face on Mars," and then he asked incredulously, "and my question now is, where the *hell* did it go?" Bell summarized his view of the MIPL image by remarking it looked like a pattern his kitty might scratch up in her litter box. From that moment forward, the TJP/MIPL image would be known as the "*Cat box*" version of the Face on Mars.

Something had to be done. The Ancient Alien Hunters could not sit still. Working backward, Lan Fleming of SPSR (Society for Planetary SETI Research), eventually identified the software processes through which Parker had progressed to achieve the image Art Bell's cat could scratch up.

Much to their chagrin, it was an image that would thenceforth define THE FACE on Mars for years to come. Given that Fleming successfully duplicated the look of the TJP image, the reverse engineering of the TJP image accomplished by Fleming was spectacular craftwork but a depressing outcome at the same time.

Bara listed the degradation steps that Fleming accomplished as follows:

1. (He) reduced the resolution of the original 2048 x 19200 image strip by 50% to 1024 x 9600, sometime after acqu9sition of the image;

2. Removed almost 85% of the tonal variations by using high-pass and low-pass filters on the "raw" data;

3. After initial processing, applied another high-pass filter to remove more tonal variations;

4. Applied a noise filter to induce more noise into the image than had already been created by the previous processes;

5. Used an emboss filter to delete visual elevation cues and induce false visual cues into the image. [23]

In comparing the Viking I Image (1976) to the "Cat box" version (1998, see earlier photo comparison), it does not take a Photoshop

---

[23] Ibid., pp. 178.

expert to see something was amiss—techniques were employed to intentionally make the face flatten and confuse most of its attributes. Despite the apparent dramatic software reconstructive surgery performed on THE FACE by NASA image processing, for some experts who looked at the photo, the cat still came out of the bag (or litter box to stick with the analogy). Facial features of the Cydonian formation were beyond the mundane or natural—they merited an endorsement! It was not just a pile of rocks. It was a FACE!

Dr. Tom Van Flandern, that scientist often cited by Alien Astronaut theorists, asserted the secondary facial features were demonstrable even in the ginned up Mars Global Surveyor photo. To Van Flandern, the image proved THE FACE *was artificial*. It had been constructed by intelligent inhabitants who once lived on Mars. Bara cites Dr. Van Flandern:

> The natural-origin hypothesis predicts that the 'Face' will look more fractal (e.g., more natural) at higher resolution. Any feature that resembled secondary facial features could do so only by chance, and would be expected to have poor correspondence with the expected size, shape, location and orientation of real secondary facial features. Any such chance feature might also be expected to be part of a background containing many similar chance features.
>
> In my considered opinion, there is no longer room for reasonable doubt of the artificial origin of the face mesa, and I've never concluded 'no room for reasonable doubt' about anything in my thirty-five-year scientific career.[24]

For Van Flandern, a bona fide Yale Ph.D. astronomer, *The Face was now an established fact.* Even an image kitty could scratch up in her litter box was enough proof. *Seeing was believing.* Then again, critics would claim Van Flandern lacked credibility when he beat the drum for on the "intelligent-life-once-lived-on Mars" view ever since he had previously campaigned for the "exploding planet hypothesis" which his critics judged "a now discredited theory." One does not have to look to long to discern the circular reasoning.

---

[24] Ibid., pp. 179-180.

Finally—A Face In Focus

But eventually we have to face the facts, or behold THE FACE, as the case may be. On May 24, 2001, NASA released an impressive (and clear) photo taken by the Mars Global Surveyor (MGS). Taken virtually directly overhead, THE FACE came into focus more clearly

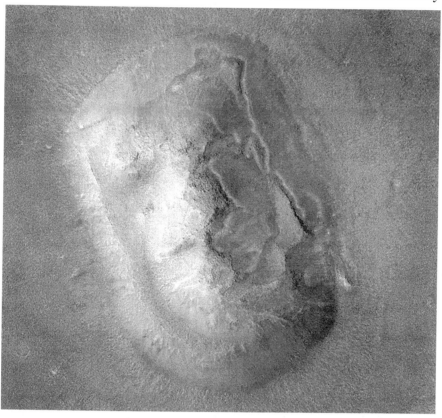

Figure 69 - The Mars Global Surveyor (MGS) Image, April, 2001

than ever before. Stunningly, to the surprise of many, it seemed that it was only a half-human face.[25] For certain observers (notably David Flynn, Mike Bara, and Richard C. Hoagland), it looked *half-*

---

[25] See http://nssdc.gsfc.nasa.gov/planetary/mgs_cydonia.html for a 5.4 million pixel image of the MGS photo.

simian (ape-like) and *half-feline.* According to Bara, however, this facial recognition development was NOT entirely unexpected:

> As far back as his U.N. speech in 1992, Richard C. Hoagland had asserted that those who expected the Face to be fully human were wrong in their assessments. Using then primitive computer technologies, he had done a series of symmetry studies of the Viking data and concluded that this human/feline hybrid appearance might have been intentional. The new image seemed to confirm this model, as updated symmetries were done and the human/lion impression persisted.

Figure 70 - Alec's Novel, *A Pale Horse*, 2012

David Flynn went to work and developed a tweaked view of this picture which drew out the human/lionesque features. For Bible believers, the image could make a lot of sense. The image might be that of a cherub. Wendy Alec, popular author who bases her plotlines on biblical themes, exploited this possibility in one of her most recent fiction novels (*A Pale Horse*—2012), stating that THE FACE was originally a monument to Lucifer. Perhaps it bears repeating for dramatic effect: this cherub may have ruled over Mars, its nearby planetary neighbor, and the entire solar system as Lucifer once *"walked amidst the stones of fire"* (Ezekiel 28:14).

Meanwhile, NASA continued to dismiss any claim that the new photographic image revealed anything but a natural formation. They actually went further in debunking the anticipated excitement about the revelations implied in the image by also publishing a paper titled, "Unmasking the Face on Mars."[26] Bara comments:

> In "Unmasking the Face on Mars," NASA used all the standard debunking and propaganda techniques they had honed over the previous 20 years of debate on the Cydonia issue. They described the Face as a "pop icon," never mentioned the existence of any of the other anomalies in the Cydonia complex like the D&M or the Tholus, pretended the geometric relationship model didn't exist and used a cartoon to ridicule the idea that the Face was anything other than a common Martian mesa.[27]

Eventually, NASA released other images of THE FACE and the D&M Pyramid that continued to increase the evidence, from the viewpoint of Ancient Alien Hunters. The single biggest "discovery" was from NASA image VO 3814003 which seemingly demonstrated a high degree of reflectivity of THE FACE when exposed to early morning light (immediately before the Martian dawn). Still, given that the reflectivity was admittedly enhanced by Hoagland's touchups, what does that mean? Is the Martian face made of metal?

Images made in August, 2005 by the Mars Reconnaissance Orbiter did not necessarily prove anything new. The far-reaching robot took pictures after a 7-month voyage with by an even more powerful camera (the HiRISE device featured a 19.5-inch-wide telescopic mirror, with a CCD camera capable of acquiring 20,000 pixels with a resolution of .3 meters per pixel (about 11 inches—compared to 48 inch-resolution by the MGS!) However, once he drills down into the close-up inspection, Bara begins to see things in the detail that suggest "right angles," "walls," and "sand-filled Middle Eastern ruins and upturned buildings seen in shattered earthquake zones on Earth."[28] To my eyes, the details look no more architected than the underside of a Nestles' Crunch Bar®. As any true lover of

---

[26] See http://science1.nasa.gov/science-news/science-at-asa/2001/ast24may 1/.

[27] Bara, op. cit., pp. 193.

[28] Ibid., pp. 209.

chocolate bars know, if you flip over the Crunch Bar and look at its underside, no longer does it remain obvious it is a candy bar made by Nestles for all the crisped rice protruding out its bumpy backside.

Nevertheless, Bara asserts correctly that if our own civilization were abandoned after several thousand years, how long would it take for the obvious signs of our intelligently designed architectures to disappear? One thinks of the fact that there remain countless Mayan (and Olmec) buildings hidden under tropical jungles in Central America as well as other ancient ruins buried under no-telling how many feet of topsoil most anywhere on our globe, representing hidden artifacts of human habitats. "What's extraordinary about the Face on Mars is that it has probably been abandoned for far longer than that, perhaps as long as 1.35 million years, and yet the signs of the majesty in which it once reveled are still visible for all to see."[29] That is, all can see it IF they examine these incredible digital images from our—at best—cautious, or—at worst—deceptive National Space Agency, AND equipped with the necessary "eyes to see."

However, this author will allow Bara the last word concerning THE FACE on Mars. Be on the alert for biting sarcasm:

> It's not a Face, in spite of the fact it rests on a bilaterally symmetrical platform, it has two aligned eye sockets, the tip of the nose is the tallest point on the structure, there are two clearly defined nostrils in the nose, the west eye socket is shaped like a human eye including a tear duct, there is a spherical pupil in the eye, there are rectangular, cell-like structures around the eye, the two halves of the Face make up two distinct visages when mirrored, one human, one feline, it is placed nearby a series of pyramidal mountains which have rectilinear cells visible in their interiors at high resolution, it is in close proximity to an isolated pentagonal "mountain" which is bilaterally symmetrical about two different axes, it has anomalous reflective properties under pre-dawn conditions, it is surrounded by a series of tetrahedral mounds which are placed according to tetrahedral geometry and in high resolution it displays features identical to ruined artificial structures here on Earth..."[30]

---

[29] Ibid., pp. 213.
[30] Ibid., pp. 213-214.

All things considered, this author admits Bara has a point.

Conclusion: Is There Reason to Believe?

Nevertheless, photo evidence—pictographic proof, if you will—fails to impress most skeptics. Even this author remains cautious in regards to the photographic evidence presented by those who argue that intelligent life once existed on Mars. There seems to be enough evidence to suspend final judgment against that assertion. But has sufficient evidence been presented to conclude sentient beings were in fact inhabitants there?

Moreover, this author remain cautious because of the nature of faith. Belief transcends empirical examination—even when the inspection confirms the facts. Arguing in favor of religious relics as well as artifacts on distant planets constitutes the reliance on tangible "proofs" evincing "ultimate matters." For the most part, belief doesn't rely upon tangible objects, much less controversial photographs. That is why authentic faith requires more photographic proof than any picture can muster. Despite the claim to holding a purely scientific mindset, Ancient Alien hunters draw conclusions that life once existed on Mars based upon *inconclusive data.* Their favorable determination includes some definite measure of *faith.*

Additionally, as the oft-quoted principle conveys, "Extraordinary claims require extraordinary evidence." Even if we receive the most vivid and detailed photo of ancient artifacts on Mars, the committed skeptic will find a reason NOT to believe. That is the nature of *skepticism and unbelief.* If someone is unwilling to believe in something, there is no proving to that someone anything to the contrary.

Philosopher and Christian, Søren Kierkegaard—aka SK—preached that (paraphrasing), "the moment we base our faith on *approximation knowledge* we cease to believe." Approximation knowledge was SK's way of depicting evidence collected to "prove a case". "SK may have been overstating his position (in my humble opinion he was). For Christian faith doesn't deny *a posteriori* knowledge, but authentic "saving faith" extends well beyond it.[31]

Perhaps there will always be a subjective element when attributing authenticity to any fantastic assertion, even if a good picture pops up and lends support. Faith in the *incredible* ("that which is too implausible to be credible") stands as a certainty only for those *with eyes to see*. Faith, like beauty, exists "in the eye of the beholder."

That is why the verdict on whether artificial structures exist on Mars may never be proven solely by photographs taken by robots on that distant world. Try as we might, we can never eradicate the human element in the photo taking, photo transmitting, photo editing, and especially photo viewing.

Verifying life on Mars ultimately comes down to trusting those in whom we assign the task to do such far-fetched reconnaissance, evaluate the results, and report back to the rest of us. If, in their opinion there is no reasonable justification to conclude life once existed there, we should question anyone who tells us otherwise. Now, should our ambassadors who quest for knowledge of faraway places chose to disseminate corrupted information or misguide us with the data they collect, we can still choose to believe in spite of the data presented or without sufficient reasons given. That is our choice. But we must not be bothered if others disagree. That is their choice.

In regards to NASA and its leadership, for all intents and purposes, the public remains practically incapable of squeezing out the truth. That doesn't mean we should stop looking for signs of life (extant or extinct), or considering whatever digital data they do make available for our review. But we must approach the issue with caution. Unlike many Ancient Alien Hunters, jumping to conclusions

---

[31] The late Christian intellectual, Francis Schaeffer, doubted the authenticity of SK's faith, inasmuch as SK emphasized the "leap of faith"—i.e., believing not because of evidence, but in spite of the evidence. SK's comment is derived (if memory serves) from *Concluding Unscientific Postscript*, a second book written in the nineteenth century to append his famous *Philosophical Fragments*.

and seeing things that others cannot see will not make the case for life on Mars more solid.

In conclusion, each of us must make up our own mind—we must choose between these three options:

1. Can we trust NASA, an agency that seems committed to hiding data (whose gathering was paid for by hopeful taxpayers); and which just might answer the all-important universal question in the heart of humanity, whether we are alone in the universe?

2. Or should we believe the Ancient Alien Hunters who seem incurably romantic in "wanting to believe" even while habitually ignoring most disconfirming science (such as the completely inhospitable environment of Mars or the questioned outcome of scientific tests to prove life exists there today)?

3. Or must we remain in the camp of the undecided, being unwilling to place our trust in either point of view despite the graphic evidence one side or the other has claimed proves their position to be true?

One thing seems certain: the issue of whether life exists on Mars stands as a far-reaching matter in which everyone has a stake. For our final destiny may depend upon what Mars tells us about life on Earth. That is, whether we believe in Ancient Aliens as the progenitors of humankind or alternatively profess faith in the God of the Bible and reject the implications of Ancient Alien Theory—the choice we make regarding these contrasting worldviews constitutes THE ultimate cosmological but highly personal issue that, figuratively speaking—extends well beyond the aphelion of Mars itself. [32]

---

[32] Aphelion is the point in a planet's elliptical orbit where it is *farthest* from the Sun. In Mars' case, that is approximately 250 million miles.

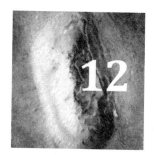

Jump Rooms, Time Travel, and Military Bases on Mars

The Real Fake Film behind *Argo*

A
RGO WAS A HIGHLY ACCLAIMED FILM, NOMINATED FOR EIGHT OS-
CARS AND WINNING THREE INCLUDING *BEST PICTURE*.
CO-PRODUCED BY GEORGE CLOONEY AND DIRECTED BY BEN
Affleck, the story recounts the
smuggling of six Americans
out of Iran with the help of the
Canadian embassy in Tehran,
during the 1979 Iranian Hostage Crisis. The terrific screenplay was adapted from two fine
sources: Anthony Mendez's
book, *The Master of Disguise*
and Joshua Bearman's 2007
article in *Wired Magazine*,
entitled "The Great Escape."

Mendez, the protagonist of
the actual historical incident in
1979, was a CIA agent secretly
awarded the Intelligence Star
by President Jimmy Carter,
but unable to keep the medal
until the details of the case

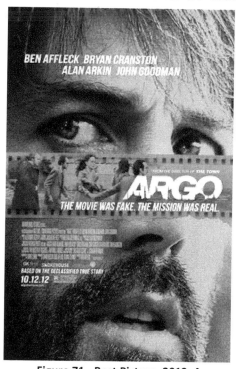

Figure 71 - Best Picture, 2012, Argo

were released to the public in 1997, 18 years later.

If Mendez did half of what is represented in the fictionalized version of the story, he stands out as a genuine American hero. But
what interests us here is not Mendez, nor the film *Argo*, nor its primary sources that eventually led to the 2012 Oscar for Best Picture.

We care about the "film within the film" that wasn't named *Argo* and wasn't ever intended to be made at all. We care about the historical fact that the original story was part of an intelligence ruse.

The would-be film was based upon the actual book *Lord of Light*, a 1967 novel reminiscent of the film *Star Wars*. Like Lucas' famous film set "a long, long time ago, in a galaxy far, far away..." *Lord of Light* was a fantasy/science fiction novel, authored by one Roger Zelazny. It was chosen by the CIA not only because was it a science fiction book (a timely subject matter helping the "believability" of the scenario in the CIA "op"), but because it had a "Middle-Eastern" religious tone—although it employed notions from Buddhism, not Islam. Nevertheless, *Lord of Light* was the 1967 novel turned into a 1979 screenplay, comprising the real fake movie portrayed "in pre-production" within the real 2012 film *Argo*. Hopefully, my efforts to explain has clarified rather than confused.

Comic Books and the CIA

However, as if that was not already opaque enough, our deepest interest lies not with the book or fake film *Lord of Light* per se. It is with the real-life artist that was tasked by the CIA to create bogus artwork promoting the fake film—a creative type named Jack Kirby. Importantly, before he was an artist creating artwork for a fake movie in a clandestine CIA operation, Jack Kirby created comic books with a no less noteworthy comic book artist than Stan Lee. In particular, one 1958 comic book was called, interestingly enough, *The Face on Mars*. Now with that sensational disclosure, the reader begins to sees the connection to our study.

Nick Redfern provides the "story behind the story" of the comic *The Face on Mars*, the comic book artist Jack Kirby, and the common connection of the CIA to both. In his book, *The Pyramids and the Pentagon: The Government's Top Secret Pursuit of Mystical Relics, Ancient Astronauts, and Lost Civilizations* (2012), Redfern supplies this outstanding "find" and this pertinent recap:

In Kirby's story, an American astronaut named Ben Fisher leads a team to Mars, where, dominating the Martian landscape, they are astounded to find a gigantic human face carved out of rock. The adventurous Fisher elects to climb the huge face, and in doing so finds to his surprise that the eyes of the immense creation are actually cave-like entrance points to a vast kingdom hidden deep inside the face itself.

While investigating the old, long-abandoned structure, Fisher has a vision in which he sees ancient Martians doing battle with hostile aliens whose home world, interestingly, was a planet whose ultimate destruction by the Martians led to the creation of the Asteroid Belt. And here's the kicker: Jack Kirby had secret associations with officialdom—in fact, with none other than the CIA.[1]

The plot thickens.

However, could this connection be coincidence? Or did the CIA know something about Mars in the 1950s that they wanted to leak to the public as part of conditioning our response to the possibility that life had been discovered, as least to the satisfaction of some, on the planet Mars? Remember this was two years before the 1960 *Brookings Report* had called for special handling of any extant extraterrestrials artifacts on nearby planets (or our moon). Their instructions were simple: keep it all secret.

Granted, comic books wouldn't be the first place we go looking for trustworthy information about our solar system. But if the Government's goal was to prepare the public for an eventual disclosure that intelligent life once existed on Mars, telling the story to kids might not be a bad idea. Children would grow up seeing the possibility of extraterrestrials being not necessarily such a fearful thing. Given their parents reacted in terror to the 1938 radio broadcast, *War of the Worlds*, dropping hints about aliens to the *next* generation might be an effective antidote.

---

[1] Redfern, Nick, *The Pyramids and the Pentagon: The Government's Top Secret Pursuit of Mystical Relics, Ancient Astronauts, and Lost Civilizations* (2012). Career Press. Kindle Edition, pp. 159-160.

Figure 72 - Jack Kirby's Comic book story, *The Face on Mars* (1958)

After the panic which ensued from Orson Welles' famous broadcast, it would be obvious to most any government on the face of the globe that such unexpected, worldview altering information could lead to some dire consequences for the State.

We can safely surmise that no government wants to deal with terror on a massive scale. Should the existence of extraterrestrials prove true, planning by our leaders for how to tell the public would be prudent. Certainly the only thing worse than an 800 pound gorilla in your living room is a twenty-ton flying saucer from Zeta Reticuli levitating above your front lawn—especially if government leaders have been working with ET behind the backs of the citizenry. If discovered to be true, a good old fashioned lynching might not be out of the question.

Furthermore, as to what the CIA knew and when it knew it, is it not *a little too coincidental* for an artist with CIA connections to tell a tale where astronauts stumble across a giant face on Mars? Does it stretch coincidence further that this face was the entrance to a colossal underground base? And that these explorers from Earth discovered massive remnants of their sophisticated technologies? And that these beings were humanoids? Moreover, that these humanoids had once fought a cosmic war with hostile aliens from a much more distant world—humanoids that had to escape to Mars because their planet was destroyed by those aliens? This sounds a bit familiar. Where did we heard these things before? But then, maybe these ideas are all obvious and without connection to "the real world." Maybe, just maybe *you can make all this stuff up*.

As they say, "truth is stranger than fiction", especially when that nonfiction tells the most amazing tale—placed within a comic book for kids—so that "the older and wiser ones" can prepare the children for the future while they don't scare their parents to death today. It makes sense. Just because we assess an account strange does not make it untrue. Just because we find something unbelievable, does not mean it has not happened. We are, after all, creatures that filter information. We certainly pay little mind to the implausible—nor do we have the inclination to be bothered with the remote possibility that disaster from beyond the stars could actually strike us dead. Likewise, stumbling across giant faces as monuments on distant planets is not an everyday, run-of-the-mill occurrence.

Nor is discovering there might be *underground U.S. military bases on Mars.*

Deep Underground Military Bases

For years, conspiracy theories have been rife with accounts of "deep underground military bases"—DUMBs—which has to be one of the most apt acronyms ever. Or so we thought. Nowadays these formerly fantastical accounts have considerable credibility. Given the photographs of the enormous rock-eating machines that create massive tunnels underground, the idea of developing military outposts deep below the Earth's surface proves to be logical and should come as no surprise.[2]

An underground, enclosed, mile-deep base provides shielding from the enormous power of "bunker buster" bombs, even nuclear versions, and would provide a means to preserve life and continuity of government should the worst of worse case scenarios comes to pass—such as an asteroid or comet striking the earth. The 1998 movies, *Deep Impact* and *Armageddon* painted this picture in graphic detail comprising some of the latest and greatest entries into the "disaster movie" genre. This idea has led to practical action. We now monitor asteroids and comets closely. We have taken steps to protect ourselves. Should they come calling, there are now means to face down these doomsday rocks falling from the sky. Undoubtedly, by now we have surely established many underground bases for self-defense. So DUMBs are not so dumb anymore.

What seems much less believable, however, is that such outposts exist on Mars. And yet, we have already come across this testimony before. Remember the remote viewers and their accounts of doing mental walkabouts on the Moon and Mars? In earlier chapters, we shared Ingo Swanns' experiences and cited Major General Albert Stubblebine who stated, "I will tell you for the record that there are

---

[2] See photos of such tunnels and tunnel making at http://gizmodo.com/8-massive-tunnels-being-built-right-now-under-a-city-ne-1493440920.

structures underneath the surface of Mars... I will also tell you that there are machines under the surface of Mars that you can look at."[3] Recall that before Viking I's 1976 photo, mystic James Hurtak had gone on record saying he "saw" THE FACE.

Did the U.S. Military Build Mars Bases after WWII?

A search of videos on YouTube provides dozens of lectures on the subject, with self-described experts supplying colorful and detailed accounts claiming we have been encamped above and below ground on Mars since the 1960s.[4] One such account in particular stands out. This is the testimony of William Cooper who publicly declared this tale to be true in 1989, or so says one reporter of the truly strange, Alfred Lebremont Webre, in his lengthy article about Mars bases, time travel, and jump rooms:

> In Mr. Cooper's 1989 lecture and affidavit, the full texts of which are made available at the end of this article, Mr. Cooper states that the U.S had first landed on Mars on May 22, 1962 and that, by the time the U.S./NASA public space program landed on the moon in 1969, the U.S. already had a moon base there, since the mid-1950s. In his lecture, Mr. Cooper states,
>
> TRANSCRIBER: "Regrettably, the next question was totally unintelligible, but thankfully Mr. Cooper had a good public address system to amplify his reply."
>
> COOPER: "The first moon landing was May 22, 1962 ... or excuse me, that was the first landing on Mars. I'm sorry, May 22, 1962, was the winged probe that used a hydrozine [sic] propeller, flew around approximately three orbits and landed on May 22, 1962, was a joint United States/Russian endeavor. The first time that we landed on the moon was sometime during the... probably middle 50s, because at the time when President Kennedy stated that he

---

[3] Quotation from Jim Schnabel's study, *Remote Viewers, The Secret History of America's Psychic Spies*, New York: Bantam Doubleday Dell, 1997, p. 213.

[4] In fact, some accounts assert that the Nazis were trekking to Mars using anti-gravity flying saucers before the end of World War II. Even the most open-minded person, a person like this author who believes the Nazis were testing jet-powered flying saucers at War's end, finds this speculation a bit too over the top.

wanted a man to set foot on the moon by the end of the decade we already had a base there."

"What about Mars?" came another quick question.

"We have a base on Mars also," Cooper calmly replied.

"When did that happen?"

"I don't know the exact date but I know the project's name, it was 'Adam and Eve.'"

"How long have you known about this?"

"Well, I revealed it publicly for the first time on July 2, 1989, and within three weeks of the time I revealed it publicly, the government, to get the American people not to listen to me, came out and said that they planned to build a base on the moon and a colony on Mars. Now, three days previous to my speech, representatives from NASA said, 'We can never have a colony on Mars, it's impossible that there's a colony on Mars because Mars is a dead planet.' And it's not a dead planet, they've lied to you about Mars." [5]

Given the late William Cooper was one of the nation's most outspoken conspiracy theorists, his testimony may *not* be *totally* inadmissible, but he would hardly be the sole witness the defense would call to the stand in an attempt to prove bases exist on Mars.

Other Witnesses Testify to Having Been There

No matter how remarkable, given the far reaching consequences if proven true (regarding Mars' underground cities and military bases), we might want to listen with an open mind before we dismiss so many accounts scattered about the Internet.

In one of the more detailed tales, Michael Relfe claims to be a member of US armed forces that served at the Mars base for twenty

---

[5] Accessed 12-14-2013: http://ufodigest.com/article/naval-intelligence-officer-corroborates-us-mars-bases-and-time-travel. Cooper was suggesting, of course, that the "they" is someone or some group within the U.S. government

years, from 1976 to 1996.[6] He discusses his experience in two lengthy books available for download at http://themarsrecords.com/download.html. Relfe went from the Earth to Mars via teleportation. Yes, Scotty beamed him up. As with another even more controversial figure we will discuss later in this chapter, Relfe stepped into an elevator on Sepulveda Boulevard a stone's throw from LAX (the Los Angeles International Airport), and in a matter of minutes with the help of an engineering feat developed in the 1950s by U.S. Military (based on Nikola Tesla's research of course), Relfe was walking on Mars. Although he spent 20 years there, in the final analysis and happily for him, he really didn't give up that much of his life to aid the Mars mission—since he was teleported back to Earth from 1996 to 1976! It seems worm holes allow quick travel—from place-to-place—and from *this timeframe to another.*

After coming home, Relfe still spent six more years in military service finally culminating with an honorable discharge in 1982.[7] His time of service was, however, erased from his memory until recalled through a manner of deprogramming (or memory recall—reminiscent of the movie, *Total Recall*, a movie no doubt the reader will totally recall, as it was coincidentally set on Mars). This technique is known as "clearing" and was accomplished with the help of his wife Stephanie (B.Sc.).

In their book, Michael Relfe explains:

> To clarify: there are two kinds of people that I remember.
>
> 1. People visiting Mars temporarily (politicians, etc.) – They travel to and from Mars by jump gate. They visit for a few weeks and return. They are not time traveled back. They are VIP's. They are OFF LIMITS!!
>
> 2. Permanent staff – They spend 20 years' duty cycle. At the end of their duty cycle, they are age reversed and time shot back to their space-

---

[6] Another public witness was Command Sgt. Major Robert Dean, now a professional UFOlogist, who described sophisticated structures at a U.S. military base on Mars. See http://en.wikipedia.org/wiki/Robert_Dean_%28ufologist%29.

[7] This seems like a lot of trouble to go through just to cheat someone in the military out of 20 years' worth of pension—since his Mars service was not counted.

time origin point. They are sent back with memories blocked. They are sent back to complete their destiny on Earth." (Vol. 2, p. 204)

The technique used by Stephanie included a biofeedback meter to help detect buried memories and to free the subject from the mind-control mechanism blocking their recall. For those familiar with the secret mind-control programs of U.S. intelligence (a subject I have written about in *Power Quest, Book Two: The Ascendancy of Antichrist in America*), what the Relfe's disclose about "clearing" is not that off the hook. However, if the reader is unfamiliar with the evidence for Monarch programing, the Relfe's story will probably be too much to take in.[8] Even if their account is completely accurate, it is correct only to the extent that the "facts" are what have been surfaced in the memories of a mind-control victim. Other factors which surround the memories in question must be taken into account to determine whether the information has any correlation to the truth. As one practitioner informed me, a friend of this author, his first job is not to pass final judgment on the validity of the memory recollected, but to help the survivor of the mind control freely remember what has been stored in his or her mind.

What makes Michael's account most difficult to swallow in one big gulp regards his testimony to various types of aliens who occupy the Mars base along with their human partners. Nonetheless, the "typical" observations concerning Reptilians and Greys, to say the least, make for lively conversation. Below is an extract from their book, an interview taken from *Examiner.com*:

EL: What about the Reptilians?

Michael Relfe: Yes. They are racially related (Draconians, Reptilians, Grays.)[9]

---

[8] The Relfe's give witness to their belief in Jesus Christ, give thanks to evangelical author Terry Cook for his help in deliverance from demonic influence, and seem as genuine as can be verified without first-hand knowledge of the couple.

[9] The notion that 39" tall Greys are racially related to giant Reptilians would seem a strong disconfirming factoid! The *lack* of resemblance is most striking!

EL: Do any Grays and Reptilians live on the Mars Base?

Michael Relfe: Yes, some are stationed there. I remember the Grays as doctors or technicians. I believe the Reptilians stay camouflaged (cloaked) most of the time. They prefer to appear human because they are naturally fierce-looking." (Vol. 2, page 205) [10]

What should be kept in mind is that the stories told by the Relfes are consistent with alien abductees—and again, what is recalled by the victim of mind-control may not be the truth, it may only be the "level" of recall that the programmer allowed the victim to access—and therefore, their practitioner who seeks to "deprogram" (or in this methodology, "clear" them). As the work published by Dr. Corydon Hammond (and others) has well documented, Monarch programming comprises multiple levels and even specially constructed "trap doors." Breaking through all the levels to encounter the whole truth comprises a multi-year process and takes a herculean effort on the part of the victim and their practitioner.

Therefore, building a cosmology based upon the testimony of abductees or military personnel claiming to be former Mars-based service personnel is not only problematic, it is most unwise. Even if Relfe served on Mars and encountered THEM there, that does not mean these entities were who they said they were or even who they appeared to be. The Relfes' account is most sincere. Based upon my review, however, it does not consider "Total Deceptive" a possibility. These subjects are difficult to accept but they are well studied and discussed by dozens of authors (such as Dr. David Jacobs).

Industrial Sites on the Surface of Mars?

However, the incredible present-day first-hand experience on Mars are not limited to witnessing the Martian underground. We also must factor in the testimony of the remote viewing community.

---

[10] See http://www.examiner.com/article/basiago-and-eisenhower-reveal-marsgate-and-make-case-for-alternative-4. Published March 28, 2010.

A genuine expert and frequent speaker regarding remote view-ing is one Courtney Brown, professor from no less a school than Emory University in Atlanta.[11]

Now there was a time when admitting to practicing a medium-like technique would not only get you fired from a professorship in a respective university (with or without tenure)—it would gain admit-tance to an asylum. But times have changed. Remote viewing com-prises an accepted spying method by our military, practiced for over 40 years in the U.S.[12] And as stated earlier (tongue-in-cheek), it sup-plies a very low cost method to gather data from distant worlds.

In another *Examiner.com* article published by the Internet re-porter mentioned earlier (no stranger to the highly strange), Alfred Lebremont Webre, on July 28, 2010,[13] we read his account of Court-ney Brown's lecture in which Brown discussed a remote viewing session involving multiple RVers who supplied these most contro-versial discoveries from their remote "seeing" the surface of Mars:

> An apparent active industrial site on the surface of Mars with a "large nozzle shooting a liquid spray" onto an apparent industrial waste area has been successfully located and explored in a remote viewing study conducted by the Farsight Institute in March 2010 us-ing nine highly trained remote viewers and methodologies developed by the U.S. military.
>
> According to the Farsight Institute, the original discovery of the active industrial site and giant nozzle spray "was made by [Mars

---

[11] From his personal website, Brown offers an extensive biography. Here is the opening paragraph: "Courtney Brown is a mathematician and social scientist who teaches in the Department of Political Science at Emory University in Atlanta, Georgia. Independent of his work at the university, he is also the leading scholar on the subject of "remote viewing" as it is done using procedures that were developed by the United States military and used for espionage purposes, or procedures that are derivative of those methodologies."

[12] I wrote about it extensively in his previous books, *Power Quest Book One and Two*, and discussed its use with one person in the military who informed me they sought out this group of specialized spies and relied upon the information acquired from the RV unit. The information was termed "most useful."

[13] See http://farsight.org/demo/Mysteries/Mysteries_1/Mysteries_Pro-ject_1.html.

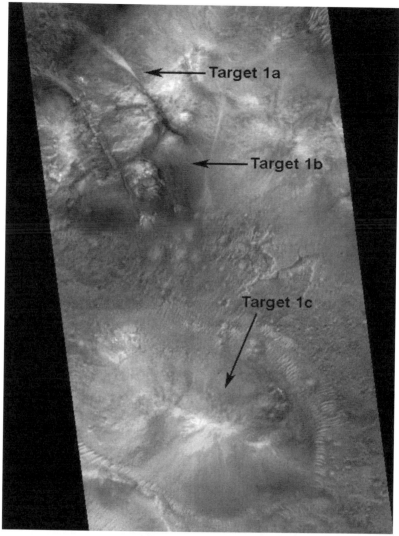

Figure 73 - An Industrial Site on the Surface of Mars?

anomaly researcher] Patrick Skipper" from photographs of the site taken by Jet Propulsion Laboratories (JPL). The JPL photos were taken 16 October 2000 at Mars Longitude of image center: 19.73°W, Mars Latitude of image center: 3.08°

During the presentation, Dr. Brown indicated that tentative results of the study, based on high clarity scores of the remote viewing sessions, included the following:

- A large dome at the site is an artificial structure;
- Tunnels connect various chambers at the site
- The original builders of the site were ancient;
- The level of the original technology is high;
- There is a shortage of spare parts at the site;
- The site may be used for power or energy generation;
- There are intense flashing lights at the site;
- There is a sense of despondency among the occupants of the site;
- There is a laboratory setting at the site, occupants wear uniforms, and there are more men than women;
- The site occupants view this as a hardship post;
- The site occupants cannot return home and knew that when they accepted;
- There is No ET (extraterrestrial) content detected at the site;
- The occupants at the site could be human;
- The occupants of the site are of unknown origin;
- The site may be a black budget operation.
- The remote viewing interpretations of the site may be a decoding error.

Is the data regarding spewing hoses on the surface of Mars factual? The validity of remote viewing as a means of exploring space can only be proven out when objective parties "with their own eyes" verify the perceptions of the viewers. There is no way to satisfy skeptics although the photograph provided seems more difficult to explain away than many other claims about experiences on Mars. However, we know how Photoshop creates its own graphic reality.

Nevertheless, we cannot rule out the findings of remote viewing altogether unless, *a priori*, we:

- Assume this form of "knowing" lies beyond the ability of humans,
- Impugn the reliability of those whose remote viewing indicated it was "for real," or

- Prove the technique wholly unreliable. For if the photographs prove genuine, skeptics should at least acknowledge the possibility.[14]

On the other hand, a simple answer to the question "Is there or isn't there life on Mars?" eludes those who seek it. Far-fetched notions abound from many quarters supporting the idea of underground bases on Mars, so many in fact it might overwhelm most anyone's incredulity.

Spiritualist Viewing of the Martian Underground

One of the more extravagant claims this author has discovered proposes Mars will be the internment camp for a hundred thousand who will be kidnapped and flown to Mars via flying saucer in days not too distant. This crime of astronomical proportions comprises one aspect of a fake-rapture event heralding the coming of Antichrist and the establishment of the New World Order, known as *Project Blue Beam!* This allegation comes from one Sherry Shriner (without bothering to supply much to document her claims). Never mind that PBB has failed to materialize more often than Santa Claus coming down the chimney.[15] We had better make sure we update our Last Will and Testament to account for the possibility we could be "Shanghaied" to Cydonia at any moment.

> Mars contains military bases, captives, abductees, aliens, humans being held there against their will and more people will be joining them as those caught off guard and kidnapped via the False Rapture of the Blue Beam Project when the Antichrist, posing as the messiah, descends to earth. "UFO's" will be snatching over 100,000 people off the earth to mimmick [sic] the rapture that the modern church has been conditioned to believe will happen.

---

[14] Trusting in any sort of channeled information remains questionable for those who base their worldview on biblical cosmology, inasmuch as we are on the lookout for our adversary who continually attempts to fool us. His customary practice to deceive remains intact, especially when it amounts to serving up information about the cosmos and our place within it.

[15] For those inclined to read the details of this most over-the-top conspiracy, see http://rationalwiki.org/wiki/Project_Blue_Beam.

> And who said government and religion are separate. It makes you think that they've been working together all along to perpetrate the biggest hoax of all time. In fact, they have. The pre-tribulation teaching and the Blue Beam Project go hand in hand in working together to make thousands of people disappear, and then the world will witness the arrival of a "Messiah."[16]

And yet not every offbeat claim lacks the sophisticated touch of an accomplished writer. There exists no shortage of purveyors of vastly oversized remarks. A most intriguing account of Martian underground cities (coming from a spiritualist point of view) resides in the *Fire Docs Collection* of Palyne 'PJ' Gaenir.[17] For those wishing to study the phenomenon more deeply, you will find scores of documents detailing remote viewing at his website (see footnote).

My search for RV material on Mars was especially satisfied by discovering an account from Ernest L. Norman (published and copyrighted in 1956) regarding his astral travel to Mars in the 1950s. Below I include a small portion of his personal recollection near the outset of this novella confidently entitled, "The Truth about Mars." I provide it to the reader to convey a sense of the calm and clear writing of author Norman—despite his other-worldly, out-of-body excursion—and keeping company with an odd tour guide, *Nur El*. Nur El was Norman's "favorite Martian"[18] who was impeccably dressed in vivid red lengthy coat from his head to his feet (but wasn't covered in soot nor did he have a belly that shook when he laughed like a bowl full of jelly). This visitation and tour would have grounded most astral travelers due to speechlessness and loss of capacity to detail the trip. However, Norman retained his lucidity:

---

[16] Accessed 12-14-2013: http://www.thewatcherfiles.com/sherry/planet-mars.htm. Ms. Shriner likely would accuse me of challenging her views since I happen to believe in the traditional Pre-Tribulation rapture. So be it. Sticks and stones.

[17] See http://www.firedocs.com/remoteviewing/pjarchives/.

[18] A nod to the popular 1960s television show, My Favorite Martin, starring Bill Bixby and Ray Walston as Uncle Martin (the Martian). When I was 17, I flew to Hawaii in 1972 with my parents and Ray Walston, who I recognized when he stepped on the airplane at LAX. It is a small world—and a small solar system too.

During the last twenty-five years of so, there has been a tremendous impetus given to astronomical interests [that would be from about 1930 to 1955 according to Norman—as discussed earlier the timeframe more inaccurately began about 1900]; perhaps this is partly due to the approach of the conclusion of a great cycle and the actual beginning of the Aquarian age. There are numerous monthly publications which deal in a fictional way with interplanetary travel and life on other planets [the pulps of course]. There likewise are other articles and stories which have appeared from time to time dealing with flying saucers and space ships, etc., which claim to be true, and as a small lad I shared this common interest in the heavens. Often I would peer through my father's telescope (which was of very modest power) at the moon or other bright points of interest; winter nights would often be devoted to pouring over any book or article containing anything of astronomical nature.

It was not, however, until the close of World War II and the sudden influx of flying saucer stories, that time and circumstances permitted resuming this fascinating subject. Along with metaphysical work which I did both in churches and independently, the planets, space travel, etc., all became an integrated part of this work [as this author asserted, Mars and the paranormal were typical bedfellows].

It was inevitable that sooner or later I should actually take a "flight" to some planet, not that this would be done in a rocket or some such machine; man has not progressed to such an advanced state of engineering as yet [apparently Norman was not aware of the saucers then known to William Cooper]. So any such trips would be in a clairvoyant state. I am not the only one by far, who has had such experiences; the persons both known and unknown who have made such flights and contacts are too numerous to mention at this time. I might add that much of what is written in the following pages has since been corroborated by some of these persons, without my previously having read any articles so written by them.

It has been my consistent habit to spend an hour or so of the late evening time in meditation. During these hours I have made innumerable contacts with those who have passed from this plane of existence. However no serious attempt at interplanetary contact was tried until the second month of the year of 1955. At that time I began to be increasingly aware that something like this was being attempted by the peoples of other planets. One evening, about the first part of May, of this year, while in a deep meditative state, I suddenly perceived a rather strange looking man standing before me. At first I thought him to

be Chinese, as his dress and general appearance was somewhat similar to that of a man of ancient China. After introducing himself as Nur
El, however, he quickly explained that he was from the planet Mars,
and that if I so desired, I could go there with him, to his city (in astral
flight) and that he would be my personal guide. He explained that his
people were very desirous in view of all the controversy going on, to
clear up some of the so-called mysteries of Mars. He further assured
me that it was quite obvious that a complete understanding was not
possible in one visitation; therefore as the first contact was made, it
would be comparatively easy to establish other contacts, as was con-
venient and necessary. Since this first contact and trip was made, I
have returned on several occasions; in fact, Nur El often stood beside
me as I wrote, to further clear up, or refresh my memory regarding
any details which were not entirely clear.[19]

"The Truth about Mars" then provides elaborate descriptions of
the Martians, their cities, animals that inhabit the surface, the
means of transportation between the cities, and all manner of facts
that testify to how evolved the Martians were in the 1950s. Norman
never misses the chance to embellish his tale with admiration for
the accomplishments of our not-so-nearby neighbors. Of course, it
is best if we ignore a number of scientific details that are far off the
mark (a good example would be the assertion that the axis of Mars
stands at 6 degrees inclination instead of 22.8, supposedly produc-
ing little in the way of seasonal distinctions, also inaccurate[20]).

Not to despair: we should recall that channeled material seems
impervious to the facts of most any matter (with a particular preference to miss by a long shot the timing of oft-predicted events).
And like most mediumistic authors who travel about in astral manner, humility remains in short supply. From his partner Ruth E.
Norman (this author supposes her to be Mrs. Norman), we learn
that his twentieth-century incarnation not only suffered a distract-

---

[19] Ernest L. Norman, *The Truth about Mars*, Glendale, California: UNARIUS—
Science of Life, 1956.
[20] Since Nur El provided this information I question the rest of his counsel.

ing circular mark on its forehead, but his misfortune included a major drop in status. In this manifestation, we learn Norman stooped rather steeply from his once lofty identity two thousand years prior:

> On the forehead of the author is a large welt, in a perfect raised circle. This becomes activated at time when he is inspired or attuned, as though it is a necessary factor in making contact, mentally, with the intelligences of other dimensions or on other planets. Another strange phenomenon is the nail holes in the palms of his hands, which appeared physically during a psychic working out with his previous life in Jerusalem and the crucifixion and are most surely points of great interest in showing that he is indeed a most unusual soul, mentally and spiritually and has reached a very rare, if ever duplicated, state of consciousness through his countless thousands of lifetimes of endeavor in these fields.

For those attuned to channeled material, it is no surprise that Norman's claims (or his wife's) know no bounds. He maintains more composure than most. But his story smells of the very same smoke.

Wormholes, Teleportation, and Time Travel

But the rabbit hole goes even deeper. In the spirit of saving the best for last, it has come time to share the details of Project Pegasus.

Project Pegasus was, purportedly, a 1950s project of the U.S. Government to develop the ability for humans to travel to specific points in time in order to collect vital information useful for national planning. Armed with this data about past or future events (supplied by fresh first-hand witnesses charged with making extensive mental notes), our leadership could better predict mega disasters, take steps if possible to avoid them, and prepare the public when not.

The principal player in this unfolding drama is Washington State attorney Andrew Basiago. On his behalf, let me first praise Basiago's courage to face ridicule by going public. Whistleblowing, if you will, rightly deserves special recognition. It is not easy to tell the world you were selected to be one of a few less-than-cherished children who would be put at risk when teleported back and forward in time, and later when a teenager, be placed in a "jump room" in El Segundo from whence, in the words of an old *Chicago* tune, you would be transported in a high speed "motorboat to Mars." That defines true gumption.

Providing a few of the more interesting details:

- Basiago was a child participating in the DARPA21 program in 1968-1972). He teleported to Mars in 1981.

- Basiago states he teleported from a CIA facility in El Segundo (Los Angeles) California. He was recruited by a CIA operative, Courtney M. Hunt due to his childhood experience in Project Pegasus.

- The Mars colony was funded by black budget military dollars to provide a survival mechanism for the human race in the apparently likely event our Earth would be hit by solar flares, a planet-killing comet, or a life-ending nuclear war.

- Individuals were trained by Major Ed Dames, the master of remote viewing on behalf of military intelligence. Despite the risks associated with the excursion, the lads were dropped off at the U.S. underground base on Mars. What were the risks? The hard-shelled, reptilian-like creatures (the Plesiosaur) that inhabit the surface make mince-meat of any humanoid they can catch.

- The teenagers were destined for great things. According to Basiago, two of them would one day become President. The first was one Barry Saetoro (aka Barack Obama) who already has become President (in case you had not noticed); while the second, Andrew Basiago himself, indicates he will run for President in 2016.

- The two were trained at the same time with their parents in attendance at *The College of the Siskiyous*, a small school near Mt. Shasta (perhaps no coincidence that it remains to this day a known haven for "new-agers"). The class also included Regina Dugan who would in 2009 become the nineteenth (and first woman) director of DARPA, appointed by President Obama.

- Basiago's father, Raymond F. Basiago supervised his son as did the mother of Barry Saetoro, Stanley Ann Dunham, who coinci-

---

21 DARPA is the Defense Advanced Research Projects Agency created by President Dwight D. Eisenhower in 1958.

dentally "carried out assignments for the CIA in Kenya and Indonesia." Also attending the school was Thomas Stillings, who had worked for the Lockheed Corporation and the Office of Naval Intelligence. Stillings has also gone public with the story.

- Jumping to Mars from the CIA facility near LAX (999 El Segundo Blvd, so we are told), the *chrononauts* (as Basiago depicts himself) soon made contact on the Martian surface when Saetoro meandered across the Martian terrain, walking up to Basiago saying, "Now we're here!"

Basiago provided a detailed statement confirming the above:

In a statement made Sept 20, 2011, Mr. Basiago confirmed Mr. Obama's co-participation in the 1980 Mars training class, stating: "Barry Soetoro [sic], a student at Occidental College, was in my Mars training class under Major Ed Dames at The College of the Siskiyous in Weed, California in 1980. That fact has been corroborated by one of my other classmates, Brett Stillings. Two years later, when he was taller, thinner, more mature, a better listener, using the name 'Barack Obama,' and attending a different college, Columbia University, we crossed paths again in Los Angeles and I didn't recognize him as the person that I had been trained with in the Mars program and encountered on the surface of Mars. In fact, doing so would have been virtually impossible... because measures had been taken to block our later memories of Mars shortly after we completed our training in 1980."[22]

Like Mike Relfe, Andy Basiago indicates his memories of Mars had been cloaked with some method used in mind control.[23] And like Relfe, Basiago gives detail accounts of intelligent life on Mars.

However, he asserts there are *humanoids native to Mars*—real, live Martians. In fact, he had been unexpectedly introduced to these Martians when he was yet a child by his father.[24]

"Mr. Basiago has publicly confirmed that in 1970, in the company of his late father, Raymond F. Basiago, an engineer for The Ralph M.

---

[22] See the article, http://exopolitics.blogs.com/exopolitics/2011/11/mars-visitors-basiago-and-stillings-confirm-barack-obama-traveled-to-mars-1.html.
[23] The principal means to program children is trauma-based mind control to create "alters" that are then programmed to accomplish very specific things.
[24] And I kick myself for taking my kids to scary movies when they were too little.

Parsons Company who worked on classified aerospace projects, he met three Martian astronauts at the Curtiss-Wright Aeronautical Company facility in Wood Ridge, New Jersey while the Martians were there on a liaison mission to Earth and meeting with U.S. defense-technical personnel."[25]

During interviews reviewed by this author, Basiago's evaluates his Martian acquaintances as constituting attributes very similar to our own. He suggests Mars and Earth humans must have common ancestry—the races were likely separated millennia ago.

Basiago is not the most noteworthy of individuals who publicly discuss their experiences, although arguably he remains the most articulate and earnestly continues the public campaign to force the federal government to tell the truth about Mars. Laura Magdalene Eisenhower, great-granddaughter of President Dwight D. Eisenhower, contends she refused to become a member of the Mars colony, resisting the advances of intelligence personnel in 2007. This experience led Eisenhower to be outspoken on the subject of efforts to secure the preservation of our human genome (the so-called Alternative 3 and later Alternative 4).[26]

In a wordy, mystical statement on her web site (emphasizing her "chosen" character), Eisenhower explains herself interweaving the account of her life with her esoteric new-age philosophy. Her biographical account includes what she labels "soul-alchemy", encounters with aliens, past lives, 2012 optimism (revelation now classified as not-so-relevant), and a husband who "had issues."

> My ex-husband, I came to discover, was giving his sperm to an alien race and had been abducted numerous times. He was very out of control with their frequencies and it was beyond a challenge for me to handle. At night sometimes he would say that he could see them and

---

[25] See http://ufodigest.com/article/naval-intelligence-officer-corroborates-us-mars-bases-and-time-travel.

[26] *Alternative 3* was a plan to protect the human genome "off-world" on Mars while *Alternative 4* has been promoted by Eisenhower to find a safe and foolproof way on planet Earth to secure the future of humanity.

that they were around us and some nights he refused to even sleep. He had extreme paranoia and shifts in behavior that just happened out of the blue and the erratic nature of his character was very unsafe and at times life-threatening to me. It was sort of by accident that we came together and seemed too random to have been destined, but nevertheless it showed me that something of alien nature was affecting his body, heart, and mind deeply.[27]

Eisenhower indicates that despite her own challenges, "someone who has psychically read the Dalai Lama confirmed me as the Magdalene-Sophia just a year or so ago and told me I was the only one who could open the gateway for our liberation." She is special. [28]

Her nemesis was a character she calls Agent X, her "handler" seeking to enlist her celebrity in the Mars' colony project:

"He knew a lot about me from numerous sources that overlapped with one another – from Freemasons, Knights Templar, to this hidden branch of the government that was behind creating this Mars mission. They understood me based on remote viewing and time travel devices and they also seemed to recruit people from the Freemasons and Knights Templar who were well aware of the Magdalene path."

There it is—all wrapped up in one nicely paranormal package. "All I ask is that the secret Mars colony and related issues be further investigated." I am doing my best to comply.

Eisenhower avoided Mars, choosing residence on Earth. Now she continues her campaign for truth, armed with her "Sophia" persona which energizes her philanthropic efforts.

What is most remarkable of all disclosures, however, is the provocative pronouncement of several researchers, most notably author David Wilcock (whom this author has generously cited in his other books on the paranormal), who stated the U.S. colony of Mars may be as high as 500,000 persons! Given five people have a hard

---

[27] See https://sites.google.com/site/lauramagdalene/home/2012-and-the-ancient-game, accessed December 18, 2013.

[28] Or adapting what Bill Murray's character mumbled in the movie *Caddy Shack*, "The Dalai Lama thing. She got that goin' for her."

time keeping a secret, 500,000 persons effectively sworn to secrecy stretches my credulity to a breaking point.

Unfortunately the future might not be so bright for those off-planet colonists. According to Basiago, their life expectancy has been dramatically reduced.[29] You would think with their life expectancy greatly shorted by doing "government work" the colonists would have unionized by now and made their story known to Oprah or Anderson Cooper. Granted, the reader should find all of this bizarre. Yet take note: the story found its way to the White House and has been officially denied by the President.

According to Amir Khan in his article posted on January 4, 2012, "The United States government, obviously, denies this allegation, saying Obama [has] never been to Mars. "Only if you count watching Marvin the Martian" [so said] Tommy Vietor, the spokesman for the National Security Council told *Wired* [Magazine]. [Khan continues] But that's exactly what they'd say if they were trying to cover something up." Amped up with a double dose of sarcasm, Khan goes on:

> Obama didn't use his real name of course. Traversing the universe as Barry Soetero [sic], Obama was one of 10 people who was teleported to Mars via a jump room. And though Basiago or Stillings didn't say what exactly Obama did on Mars, Retired Army Maj. Ed Dames allegedly told Obama, "Simply put, your task is to be seen and not eaten." Basiago and Stillings said the CIA's goal was to establish a defense regime protecting the Earth from threats from space, and also lay claim to territorial sovereignty. They also said that Obama acted almost as an ambassador, and had to secure a U.S.-Martian alliance. [30]

---

[29] Basiago suggests there are few that have lived more than five years. As the reader likely recalls, Michael Relfe was a notable exception, since he says he served on Mars for 20 years. Maybe there weren't on the same planet? Also note that Basiago has been public about his Martian visits for more than five years, although he would no doubt point out that he did not stay long enough to be effected.

[30] Cited from http://www.ibtimes.com/government-denies-teleporting-obama-mars-390782, accessed December 18, 2013. Basiago also offered an explanation the need to acclimate the Martians underground and the creatures above to our presence on the planet. As Bradbury predicted in his Martian Chronicles, two

226

That seems an amazing request to ask of a 19-year old, even if he was supposed to become President of the United States one day.

Conclusion: What Do We Make of These Accounts?

The controversy regarding the claims of Andrew Basiago and the broader subjects of jump rooms, time travel, and underground bases on Mars no doubt will continue for an indefinite period. Given all that we have covered in this study of Mars' influence on our culture, what best explains what is happening here? There remains only one reasonable explanation—*deception*. Figuratively speaking, when it comes to asking and answering ultimate questions, *Mars has always meant deception.*

From yet another article by Webre which recorded a panel discussion of the three fellow whistleblowers on the topic of *where in the universe the chrononauts had actually traveled*, we learn that supposedly a government investigator (obviously not associated with the officials behind the Mars jump room program), concluded all three had been *taken to somewhere other than Mars.*

> Mr. Basiago states, "A third plausible explanation [for where they were teleported] is that the CIA jump rooms, given to the United States by the Grey extraterrestrials, were devices that were sometimes being diverted by the Greys. Sometimes we were visiting Mars, and other times the jump rooms were teleporting us to the kinds of micro-Universes that CIA whistleblower Bernard Mendez is describing..." [Mendez was one of the three panelists]

> He [Basiago] also cites the fact that power losses were being recorded during times when the jump rooms were ostensibly functioning normally. This could be evidence that during operation, the Greys were diverting the jump rooms from Mars to elsewhere.

world were coming to collide, in a manner of speaking, and the Martians would be the worse for the encounter.

Mr. Basiago states that since NASA has been lying about natural conditions on Mars, determining whether Mendez' "elsewhere" interpretation of the CIA jump room program or Stillings' "Mars" interpretation is the correct one will hinge on official declassification.

Mr. Basiago observes, "What we have now is three fellow jump room participants sharing their experiences... We were trained for Mars in summer 1980 and the domain that we were visiting from 1981 to 1983 was certainly understood to be Mars. What we are grappling with now is Bernard's claim that as the U.S. government investigator tasked to study the project he discovered that we were not visiting Mars but a... simulation of Mars architected by the Greys in a bubble Universe... [A place outside of space-time?] That's a highly provocative claim, but since Bernard Mendez and Brett Stillings and I were project participants together, in the interests of truth, I have facilitated all three of us coming forward publicly and sharing our understanding of what we were part of... Even if it was not Mars that we were visiting, all three of us agree that it was an off-planet location in time-space."[31]

Readers should be struck by the alleged deception (alleged by Basiago in this example) perpetrated by the "Greys"—their typical modus operandi. Those familiar with alien abduction studies recognize the unswervingly bad behavior of these beings, based on hundreds of abduction accounts, that has led authors like Jacques Vallée, L.A. Marzulli, Thomas Horn, and this author, to judge the "Greys" to be (forgive the expression) *demons in drag*. Perhaps the three amigos of time travel were hoodwinked.

As we noted at the outset, the deception inherent in the cosmology of Ancient Alien Theory comprises the final one-world religion. We should expect that the prestidigitation would be like nothing the world has ever seen before. The sophistication of the trickery should not be all that surprising, for we were warned by the Lord

---

[31] Cited from http://ufodigest.com/article/naval-intelligence-officer-corroborates-us-mars-bases-and-time-travel. The "bubble universe" comment would appear to this author to conflict with a "place in time-space." The first describes a location existing inter-dimensionally, perhaps where "angels fear to tread" but where they are left to hang out until they can find a body to possess.

Jesus himself that, *"... if it were possible, they should deceive the very elect."* (Matthew 24:24, Mark 13:22)

It should also be underscored that Michael Relfe, Andrew Basiago, and many others who are caught up in this Lovecraft-life drama, profess faith in Jesus Christ. The details of their belief systems, however, cannot help but be dramatically affected by the incredible complexity of what they may have been "led to believe." Indeed, they may have arrived at conclusions from actual experience—be they psychic experiences or having taken place in spacetime. Either way, those events were likely engineered by demonic powers. Alternatively, they may believe based upon mind-control

Figure 74 - Valles Marinaris: As Big as America

techniques utilized by bad actors within the clandestine services (false memory implants). These individuals appear to be sincere and trustworthy—but that does not mean what they believe to be true about their experience actually is. "Testing the spirits" demands we examine these testimony in the light of what the Bible teaches about our adversary and his stratagem for the last days. Discernment remains mandatory—now more than ever.

Is it possible that bases, colonies, or Martian underground cities exist on Mars? As they say, anything is possible, however, sometimes are much more plausible than others. We can assume that it has only been within the past two to three decades that we have had the ability to create deep underground bases on Earth—and that is under the best of "planetary conditions." The logistics of transporting the means to construct sophisticated structures on another world surely defy imagination (they could not fit on the elevator!) Then you must factor in all the particulars about the environment on Mars: there is next to no atmosphere, no proven source of accessible water, and lastly the surface of the planet is constantly bombarded by ultraviolet radiation (since Mars has no magnetosphere to protect carbon-based life forms).

And then there is the constant threat of being hit by meteors. Mars has about 99% less shielding than Earth (having little atmosphere to burn up meteors before they hit the ground), and is far more proximate to the source of such hard rocks from outer space—namely, the asteroid belt. Mars hardly supplies the best of circumstances! Rationally, we must ask why our leadership (or the "shadow government" of the elite), would seek to protect life on Earth from a cosmic catastrophe by seeking shelter on Mars, when Mars has been shown to be subject to cataclysms far more destructive and frequent than Earth. It has the scars to prove it (namely, thousands of visible craters as well as *Valles Marineris*, a mysterious trench whose origin begs for a catastrophic cause—a canyon four times as deep as the Grand Canyon, and as long as the U.S.A. is wide).

Next, we must consider whether it reasonable to suppose we have mastered time travel through the use of "worm holes." Once again, experts who understand the physics involved in "devices", could offer up dozens of reasons why it could not have happened up to now. It transcends any reasoned pace of human technological advancement. If we possess the capacity for time travel, it must have resulted from some sort of Faustian bargain with players

230

whose technical capabilities far surpass our own. Of course, the most popular theory of those who believe we can travel in time.

From what we know about the bad behavior of ET, the question that remains unanswered is, "Why would any advanced civilization travel many dozens (or hundreds) of light years to play tricks on us?" No advanced civilization would go to that trouble. Pranksters are unlikely astronauts. If deception is the goal, entities of another kind come to mind who would instigate a paranormal practice to deceive.

As the Apostle Paul argued almost 2,000 years ago, humankind is not warring against flesh and blood, humanoids from Mars, or extraterrestrials from Zeta Reticuli. We are dealing with devils in disguise. *"For we wrestle not against flesh and blood, but against principalities, against powers, against the rulers of the darkness of this world, against spiritual wickedness in high places."* (Ephesians 6:12) They may choose to look like ET today, but that doesn't mean they have always looked that way. Isn't it interesting that leprechauns, fairies, and other unusual mystical creatures from hundreds of years ago, also had a proclivity to tell lies?

Not that doing a deal with the Devil is out of the question. After all, humanity has been negotiating with that crafty serpent for our entire history—however long that has been—attempting to find an alternative means to achieve godhood. The serpent may have beguiled Eve with the knowledge supplied by a magical apple. But the Devil in our day tempts us with scientific marvels promising military advantage (on a national level) and personal immortality by supplying medical miracles. Still, the possibilities regarding the truth about ET are legion. In the next chapter we will examine one of the most sophisticated myths concocted over the past few decades. Like most myths, truth rests right alongside fabrication. The trick lies in picking out what you should believe and what you should reject. For a Christian, our guide is the Bible. As we will see, the light that scripture shines on Mars—what is true and what is not—is surprisingly bright despite its considerable distance from our home.

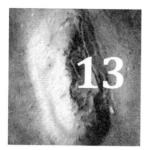

Mars, Advanced Civilizations, and the Real Star Wars

When Scientists Could Believe

ONCE UPON A TIME, EVEN CARL SAGAN COULD OPENLY CONJEC-
TURE ABOUT INTELLIGENT LIFE WITHOUT WORRY IT COULD GET
HIM FIRED. THIS WAS 1966, WHEN HE WAS A PROFESSOR OF
astronomy at Cornell. At that
point, he wrote a book with a
provocative title, *Intelligent Life
in the Universe* with a Soviet astronomer, I.S. Shklovskii, a
member of the Soviet Academy
of Science. It was a challenging
time to team with anyone from
behind the Iron Curtain since it
was at the height of the Cold
War. The fact they jointly speculated Mars' two moons—*Phobos* and *Deimos* were *not* naturally formed moons—no doubt
also raised a few eyebrows.

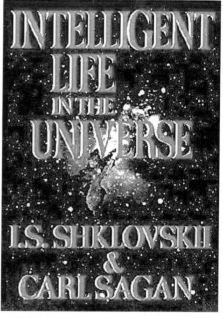

Figure 75 - Sagan and Shklovskii, 1966

Shklovskii and Sagan asked,
"Could Phobos be indeed rigid,
on the outside—but hollow on the inside? A natural satellite cannot
be a hollow object. Therefore, we are led to the possibility that Phobos—and possibly Deimos as well—may be artificial satellites of
Mars."[1]

---

[1] Carl Sagan and I.S. Shklovskii, *Intelligent Life in the Universe*, Holden-Day,
1966, p. 373.

Manufacturing moons is no easy business, even for superpowers. To contemplate such things had some scary implications. Whoever made those moons must have vastly superior capabilities and thus, there could be a frightening threat facing Planet Earth. The fact that a U.S. and Soviet scientist came together to write such a book when it was politically incorrect even to be seen in the same venue, much less share a geopolitical opinion, raises intriguing questions: "What could cause the U.S. and Soviets to find it imperative to race to the moon when they were about to blow each other up? It had to be something big. Were they worried that ET was a threat to the human race? Shouldn't the Soviets and US ally to protect our planet?"[2]

By 1980 when Carl Sagan wrote *Cosmos*, he had toned down the rhetoric about life existing elsewhere. Despite writing the fictional book (later made into a 1997 movie, *Contact*), he was much more publicly skeptical, not just about life on Mars, but life most any-where else.[3] It seemed scientists had forever learned their lesson. The example of Percival Lowell was not to be forgotten: *never talk about life on other planets—people develop unreasonable expecta-tions.* Likewise, through the example of Camille Flammarion they learned it quite unwise to mix planetary science with the paranormal. Speaking about ANY life beyond our globe was, well, crazy. Just look

---

[2] One of the reasons that Kennedy was assassinated, according to some Ken-nedy conspiracy aficionados, is that Khrushchev and Kennedy had agreed they would work together to reach the moon. Khrushchev's son, as I documented in *Power Quest, Book Two*, confirmed they reached this agreement. This alliance rep-resented a threat to American contractors in the Military-Industrial Complex.

[3] As authors William Sheehan and Stephen James O'Meara said regarding the "tests for life" executed by Viking I, "For Sagan, the results were depressing. A few scoops of Martian soil, and *poof!* Mars was once the advent of the Space Age (in fact, just up until the Viking Mission), the universe had been a playground for all manner of imagined life. Lowell had his intelligent race of civilized Martians, while Flammar-ion believed that even Venus and the other planets had inhabitants. In the 1700s William Herschel believed that extraterrestrials might live inside the cool core of the Sun, looking out at the universe through sunspots... Ironically as technology brought us ever closer to achieving the summit of our "mountain Mars," our visions of life on the planet diminished proportionally. It was as if we were looking for life through the wrong end of the telescope." (Sheehan and O'Meara, op. cit., p. 287).

what happened when average folk listened to Orson Welles' 1938 fictional radio show broadcasting that the Martians had landed. The fuse of panic was easily lit.

All things considered, scientists should keep their mouths *shut* about what REALLY might be out there. There is no upside.

Subsequently, the experts grew so cautious when talking about the possibility of life on other worlds that the experiments to test for life on Mars, although first thought a success, were later rejected as inconclusive. In a book published in 2003, *The Microbes of Mars*, Authors, Barry E. DiGregorio, Dr. Patricia Ann Straat, and Dr. Gilbert V. Levin discuss the scientific tests for life aboard the Viking I spacecraft, our first soft lander on the Martian surface (1976). Levin was the principal designer of several tests. Despite showing positive results for the existence of life, due to a growing consensus (later reversed) that Mars had no water, test results performed on the Martian surface were dismissed. Not to be forever thwarted, Gil Levin released a study in 1986 and then another statement in 1997 to reopen the issue. He asserted, despite arguments to the contrary, that to his satisfaction the tests carried out by Viking 1 *proved* living microorganisms existed on the surface of Mars. DiGregorio quotes Levin as follows:

> The failure to pursue NASA's highest priority (the search for life in the solar system), and the goal NASA once described as "probably the greatest experiment in the history of science," cannot be logically explained. It results from NASA's fear of finding out that its original conclusion about Viking was wrong, supplemented by philosophical and religious elements who insist, for non-scientific reasons, there can be no life elsewhere but Earth.[4]

And I would add, the politically incorrect pressure to avoid making the same mistakes that Lowell and Flammarion made. Conjecturing about life on Mars at NASA could be a career limiting move.

---

[4] Barry E. DiGregorio, *The Microbes of Mars: A 2011 Addendum to Mars: The Living Planet,* Middleport, New York, Barry E. DiGregorio, Kindle Version, Location 217.

But the point here is not to join the debate—rather, it is assert that even if life was discovered on Mars, we would likely not be allowed to know that fact. Scientists believe for a variety of reasons there is no advantage in getting the populace stirred up about life elsewhere. Likewise, public officials regard the public to be so panicky that the cat better NOT come out of the bag. It is best kept secret.

Dr. John Brandenburg in his book, *Life and Death on Mars,* offered the same assessment—that NASA is prejudiced against ever finding evidence of life on Mars. "This reflex rejection of 'life-as-never-the-simplest-hypothesis' became ingrained in Mars science. Just about any hypothesis, no matter how arcane, will be entertained at a Mars conference, as long as it does not involve biology or the conditions conducive to it. This mindset has continued since the Viking Life experiments in 1976 and led to a crisis in science."[5] The ghost of Vatican verdict against Galileo still haunts science.

The biggest and best kept secrets, however, involve much more than mere microbes on Mars. Scientists won't talk much about them. Yet, writer/researchers (whose career is not directly tied to funding from grants and professorial peer pressure) are willing to investigate these best kept secrets. This group (which includes yours truly) are generally denigrated as "alternate historians" and "conspiracy theorists." Despite developing a persecution complex, this group labors on. This irrepressible contingent finds bushels of facts—and even an occasional scientific paper—to back up the story. These alternative theories are not always right, but they still deserve serious consideration instead of being dismissed out of hand.

The Secret Space Program

One of the more intriguing topics that these alternative historians and conspiracy theorists address, concerns whether the race to the moon between the Soviets and the Americans was "for real."

---

[5] John Brandenburg, Ph.D., *Life and Death on Mars: The New Mars Synthesis*, Kempton: Adventures Unlimited (2011)

Debates have raged for years (and still do in some quarters) that we didn't really put men on the moon. For one thing, the dubious assert we lacked the technology to do it. Then there is another factor: these same "doubters" assert that human beings could not pass through the Van Allen Belts (now known to be three radiation blankets—shields really—that help protect Earth from cosmic radiation). Be that as it may, the matter goes far beyond the moon landing.[6] The mystery is how we acquired so many advanced technologies in the 1950s and whether we were in fact *threatened by aliens from another realm.* Several best-selling authors take up this conjecture under the collective moniker, *The Secret Space Program.*

One of these authors and researchers, Joseph P. Farrell (whom this author has cited on many occasions), discusses this so-called "Secret Space Program" and its implications across several of his

tomes. In particular, Farrell's 2013 book, *Covert Wars and the Clash of Civilizations,* has to do with global "oligarchs" and how they financed advanced technology development "off the books." Untold fortunes would be essential to pull this off. Perhaps secret assets in the Far East were leveraged (caves full of gold may be hidden in the mountains of the Philippines— a grand story in its own right). The effort demanded creating technologies sufficiently advanced to neutralize the threat of ET. In other words, enormous effort

Figure 76 -Joseph P. Farrell

has been expended for over five decades to demonstrate to ET that if they dared attack Earth, they would pay a heavy price.

On the surface—that is, the overt "space race"—constituted a high stakes competition between the U.S.A. and the U.S.S.R. The

---

[6] Please note: this author remains fully satisfied that Neil Armstrong and Buzz Aldrin did walk on the moon in July, 1969.

covert race, however, required "Earth" (the combined forces of humanity) build up enough real technical capability (or apparent capability for bluffing the enemy) that we could persuade would-be alien adversaries to judge us *invulnerable* to attack. Thus, if the overt space race was for high stakes, the covert space race was for even higher stakes—our leaders determined it was a matter of life and death for the entire human race.

With the following analysis, Farrell recaps the storyline:

> Examining the UFO phenomenon and the USA's space program, many researchers, including this one, have advanced the hypothesis that there must be a secret space program, with hidden and very advanced technologies and agendas. It is one thing, however to maintain this hypothesis, but it is quite another thing to maintain that the needs and requirements of such a secret space program led to the development of an entire "state within the state," as it did in Nazi Germany's case with the SS, or subsequently (and on an even larger scale) in the United States of America, with the creation of vast intelligence, covert operations, and military black projects bureaucracies to deal with the twin threats of Soviet Communism and the more long-term threat of the UFO. As I argued in the previous book of this small series, *Covert Wars and Breakaway Civilizations*, all this in turn required the creation of enormous and completely hidden and secret systems of finance.[7]

Secret finance and the creation of a hidden branch of government, analogous to Himmler's SS—all to fight a war that the public did not know was taking place. Conspiracies get no better than this!

The Triggering Event

Although Farrell is not unaware that most experts doubt the testimony of Lt. Col. Philip Corso (and the claims from his controversial book, *The Day after Roswell*, 1997—a book this author feverishly read when first published), Farrell nevertheless sees more than a kernel of truth in the colonel's story (pun reluctantly admitted).

---

[7] Joseph P. Farrell *Covert War and the Clash of Civilizations, UFOs, Oligarchs and Space Secrecy*, Kempton, Adventures Unlimited, Kindle Version, 2013, Location 108.

Corso explains why he tells his tale with these stimulating words:

> The full story behind the SDI [Strategic Defense Initiative, aka "Star Wars" program of Ronald Reagan] and the way it changed the Cold War and forced the extraterrestrials to change their strategies for this planet is a story that's never been told. But as spectacular and fantastic as it may sound, the story behind the limited development of the SDI is the story of how humanity won its first victory against a more powerful and technologically superior enemy who discovered, to whatever version of shock it experiences, that there was real trouble down on its farm.[8]

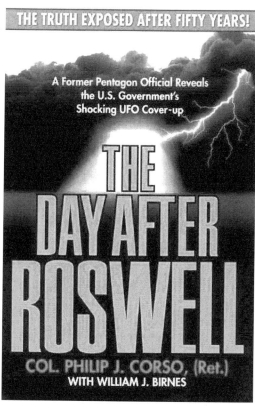

Figure 77 - The Day after Roswell

What Corso said was spectacular enough—a covert war is being fought between Earth and the "aliens"—a war supposedly managed by the U.S. military. Yet, what he said in passing was also stunning in betraying the cosmology behind the war. The "earthlings" were now fighting back against the threats posed by aliens. In Orwellian motif, the farm animals were rebelling against the "owner" of the animal farm.

So were key members of the U.S. government operating from the perspective that humankind was birthed or at least nurtured by aliens? Were the slaves revolting against their masters?

---

[8] Col. Philip J. Corso, *The Day After Roswell*, New York: Simon & Schuster, 1997, pp. 249-250.

For the sake of argument, we assume Corso supplied an accurate account of how the U.S. government captured "foreign-made" technology when the world's most famous flying saucer stopped flying and crashed in 1947 outside of Roswell, New Mexico.[9] Corso was named the primary military officer-in-charge of taking this "Roswell" technology and exploiting it for the benefit of the United States. That is, Corso became responsible for privatizing these advanced technologies captured from the Roswell crash site—wherever they originated—and putting them into play for practical purposes. His job was to place them in useful applications, whether for military designs or private use.

It wasn't until years later, however, that we might have discovered what was going on, when President Reagan opaquely spilled the beans about the U.S. and the Soviets working together—sharing the technologies created by SDI—one day in 1987 when speaking at the U.N. In his now famous speech for UFOlogists, Reagan hypothetically conjectured the Cold War would end the instant we discovered we shared a mutual enemy from outer space! Should we figure out that ET was eyeing our world (in the manner told us 90 years earlier when H.G. Wells wrote his novel, *War of the Worlds)*, there would be little doubt it would put into perspective how much we held in common with our mortal enemies—the Soviets.[10] Of course, Reagan might have only been talking *hypothetically.*

Recall SDI's ostensible purpose was anti-missile defense. But the ultimate reason, if we caught the implications of Reagan's chat, went far beyond creating a missile defense shield to nullify the use

---

[9] In using these words, I'm accounting for the fact, as Farrell himself argues, that the technology in the 1947 Roswell crash may have been manufactured by Nazis (rather than aliens as Corso asserts), who escaped Europe after World War II and set up shop somewhere in the Americas.

[10] General Douglass MacArthur was much more emphatic, as he was prone to be, at a WestPoint speech in 1955: *"The next war will be an interplanetary war. The nations of the earth must someday make a common front against attack by people from other planets."* In 1955, the U.S. Military was already thinking alien attack!

of "strategic" nuclear weapons (i.e., inter-continental ballistic missiles). With SDI deployed, not only would a surprise attack be rendered effectively impossible, it would eventually spell the death of such weapons altogether. Moreover, since the "accelerated particle beam weapon" of SDI could shoot down approaching enemy missiles, it could also (more importantly) shoot down flying saucers! Finally, according to Corso, by the time he wrote his book in 1997 SDI had already done just that. A UFO or two had been shot down.

Perhaps it was no surprise that only a few years after Reagan's speech (with SDI now proven against the *real* enemy), the Cold War ended. Was it coincidental that at the same moment we effectively neutralized ET's threat (to the satisfaction of certain key government officials within the two "superpowers"), the Cold War thawed out?

For decades before Corso wrote his book, according to Farrell and others who subscribe to the notion of a Secret Space Program, there were myriad clandestine duties carried out by, note carefully, *non*-U.S. military personnel. Efforts involved far more than the singular Roswell-connected actions managed by Corso. In fact, the lion's share of projects dealing with ET's threat were black-ops programs run by scientists and militarists *outside the control of our government* (or *any* official governing body foreign or domestic).

In his books, Farrell goes into considerable detail explaining that the strategy involved *hiding an anti-alien defense initiative within the conduct of the Cold War.* He borrows a seminal phrase coined by author and UFO researcher, Richard M. Dolan from his multi-volume work, *UFOs and the National Security State (Volume 1 published in 1973)* who argued that a "breakaway civilization" had taken charge of the overall program. This civilization was "breakaway" because it was not controlled by any known public governance. It may have begun under the auspices of major governments. But once it overcame bureaucratic inertia, it became impossible to "reign in." The breakaway civilization began with many of the best and brightest working together across national boundaries, perhaps for the protection of "Planet Earth." But it is now, according to these researchers, fully untethered and primarily protecting the interests of globalists and "international elites."

According to Dolan, Farrell, and others who contend this civilization exists, there are identifiable persons who "interface" with this covert set of out-of-control institutions. While Farrell suggests who might be involved—that is of no particular concern to us here. The issue that is pertinent: a covert war exists, it involves advanced technologies, it is being fought against extraterrestrials, and we are "learning a lot more as we go forward." Not only are we *fighting the future* (the final outcome of the administered plan by the power players—as the first "X-Files" movie was sub-titled), as we progress along the way, we marvel at the additional insights uncovered concerning the history of ancient civilization on our planet, our solar system, and even the galaxy we call home.

Perhaps we should pause here to catch our breath for a moment and to recap what we have covered. We have seen several examples of key persons who stated aliens were at the door, the evidence indicates they are powerful enough to build moons, and then, the alarmists went silent. The most vital effort in the history of mankind went off the radar and a "Secret Space Program" was unofficially (but factually) put into action.

We have outlined so far, however, only the first portion of the colossal "mythos" of Joseph P. Farrell. It now seems justified to consider Farrell's take on Ancient Alien Theory because, simply put, his views go in a very different direction from "standard theory" and in many ways ring far truer. His perspective also comprises a more frightening narrative. Moreover, it entails a much more complex tale than the standard theory. And as we are about to see, it comprises a vast, multi-layered saga. We should also note: some aspects of Farrell's take on Ancient Alien Theory reflects the Bible's account—at least as explored by the late David Flynn—regarding cosmic powers and their ulterior motives.

242

Therefore, we turn next to what Joseph P. Farrell believes comprises our most essential history with ET.

The Cosmic War—A Real Star War?

As reprise, *traditional* Ancient Alien Theory (admittedly, a strange word to use in this context) holds that ETs are our space brothers. They have come to Earth to keep us from blowing each other up given our misappropriation of nuclear energy. It seems WE are a race that declares war at the drop of a hat; THEY are far more civilized. THEY settle their disputes, so we are told, without warfare. The story of Mars follows the same plotline. From the writings of the nineteenth century to the "Marxist" utopian theories of the early twentieth century, the intelligentsia argued that Martians were older and wiser than we, their younger and less so-

Figure 78 - The Cosmic War

cially advanced humanoid siblings. We could learn from THEM. We must learn from THEM.

In current Ancient Alien Theory, humankind's religions are regarded as early attempts by simple-minded people of ancient times to come to grips with alien visitors. Our connection to ET is, however, most intimate. Aliens supposedly tampered with our genetics, improving our genome. According to many Ancient Alien theorists,

243

especially Zecharia Sitchin and his followers, we are today already *chimeric*; that is, we are hybrids of alien and Homo sapiens ancestry *now*. We are way past mere mentorship—*we are into motherhood*.

In our day, however, ET still continues to be maintain his technological advantages—he remains much more advanced than we. Those that believe in the Gospel of ET maintain that in every sense, aliens are grander, more peaceful, and have mature values. Now ET stands ready to return, to facilitate our transition to the next phase of evolution. Advocates ignore any evidence to the contrary—and *there is considerable contradictory evidence*. Proponents overlook alien abduction victims who testify of brutal experiments, harvesting human eggs and semen, gestating hybrids, kidnappings, and unwelcomed nighttime visits. All of these behaviors are dismissed or downplayed by advocates for the "Space Brother" point of view.

With Joseph P. Farrell's perspective, however, the benign alien postulate gets tossed out the window. The answer to the challenge of "from whence intelligent life hails," appears derived as much from beings who have been resident on earth for millennia (perhaps ten to twenty) as it does from locations beyond our earthly realm. The point is not so much that ET is not coming someday soon—he is here and influencing our civilization for millennia—if not millions of years.

For Farrell, the elite on this planet may be descendants of intelligent beings originally spawned (I use that word intentionally) on a "planet far, far away," but more likely came from a planet within our solar system—namely, the missing planet postulated by Dr. Tom Van Flandern (as touched on two previous chapters). This elite has been operating for aeons, from a point in the past Farrell depicts as "high antiquity"—a time long, long ago for which he also coins the term "paleoancient." Like classic Ancient Alien Theory, Farrell's proposal combines a lost advanced civilization with activities occurring in outer space—but on a scale that far exceeds the traditional theory. From this author's perspective, that does not necessarily mean that Farrell's mythos is more likely to be true than the traditional theory—

but it stands as a far more interesting alternative, accounts for anomalies left out of the standard theory, and may be reconciled (not perfectly but substantially) to the biblical record. But what is the evidence for this connection?

First, Farrell argues that various physical realities of our solar system are better explained, not by natural processes, not just by cosmic catastrophes, *but by a cosmic war*—a true "star war" that encompasses the entire galaxy,[11] enlists the use of galactic energy, and places the Earth at the center of the conflict. As just mentioned, we encounter the exploding hypothesis of Van Flandern once again, but in this scenario the annihilation does not result from a random collision with another world—as the reader may recall in the theory of Immanuel Velikovsky (18995-1979, made famous through his 1950s' book, *Worlds in Collision*). Instead, the explosion results from a powerful planet busting beam—think the "Death Star" in *Star Wars*. Here, as per usual in his books, Farrell explains the science behind his theories—which I won't delve into here with much detail. However, at the risk of losing some readers, we must digest a few technical elements not only to satisfy the curiosity of those readers up to the task, but to appreciate the broad strokes of Farrell's theory.

Farrell begins by ruling out various explanations that do not have the inherent energy to bust a planet. He explains no known example exists of natural processes exploding a planet. An asteroid impact would not generate enough kinetic energy to do the trick. Nor would it be possible for any mere incident involving the (natural but rare) occurrence of nuclear fission be sufficient to blow up a planet. To destroy a planet, we need a powerful explosive, one that stretches the limits of our know-how. So get ready to have your mind blown.

---

[11] I will not discuss an element theorized by Farrell and a few others, that the "pulsars" (those supremely fast rotating stars detected by radio telescopes) are non-randomly placed in the galaxy. They could serve as a network of beacons for interstellar travel. In effect, beings who do interstellar travel, assuming for a moment that such beings exist, would navigate by referencing this set of pulsars.

It is most significant, however, that high levels of Xenon 129 exist on the Martian surface—three times the levels known to be present on any other planetary body. So while Farrell makes the point conditions could randomly coalesce to allow for spontaneous nuclear combustion, such conditions would not produce the levels of Xenon 129 we detect on Mars. Consequently, according to Farrell, we know of no model which allows for a massive nuclear reaction capable of exploding a planet. And yet, Mars appears to have been affected by some form of nuclear blast. How could this be so?

Farrell postulates that proximity to an exploding planet, done in by an engineered explosion (making use of a form of nuclear fusion we will discuss next) could very well explain the presence of this isotope. On this point Farrell cites Van Flandern once again, as the late scientist proposed that active *intervention* by an "intelligent" agent should not be ruled out as explanation for an explosion big enough to destroy a whole planet. Therefore, Farrell concludes that *only a weapon* can blow up a sizeable heavenly body. Once destroyed with the weapon he describes (employing this most sophisticated nuclear technology), radiation residue would linger in the vicinity for quite some time. In fact, on Mars we may just have a case of interplanetary nuclear fallout.

Ion Canons in the Cosmic War

So what weapon could accomplish this mother of all cosmic cataclysms? In a phrase: *a plasma pinch*. What pray tell, is a plasma pinch?

To begin with, we must acquaint ourselves with a scientific fact not taught to my generation in elementary school: there are four, not three, states of matter: solid, liquid, gas, and *plasma*. Plasma is a state of matter that only exists inside nuclear reactions. The dictionary in Microsoft Word 2013 defines a plasma as "a fourth state of matter distinct from solid or liquid or gas and present in stars and fusion reactors; a gas becomes a plasma when it is heated until the atoms lose all their electrons, leaving a highly electrified collection of nuclei and free electrons." Forget for now that you might want to buy a plasma television.[12] We are focused here on much bigger (and hotter) plasmas.

The plasma "pinch" more or less conveys the notion of compressing a nuclear reaction into an elaborately structured nuclear containment unit of sorts, squeezing the nuclear activity in such a way that a "longitudinal pulse wave" is created. A longitudinal pulse wave is different from a run-of-the-mill-latitudinal sound (or light) wave. As Farrell explains, a sound wave may be compared to throwing a jump rope up and down. On the other hand, a pulse wave likens to a pushing a yard stick. Working in tandem with your hypothetical jump rope partner, you expend energy lifting the jump rope up and pulling it back down. Generating a wave in that manner wastes most of the energy just by creating the wave—the wave itself is not that stout. In contrast, a *pulse wave* would be like pushing the yard stick directly at the person on the other end of the stick. All of your energy, the force you create, is felt directly by your partner. Because you and your partner are connected (in our analogy, you have "addressed" your partner by the connection between you— each holding one end of the stick), therefore, your energy (all your effort) is put to work. If you are not careful, you might just knock your friend off his or her feet.[13]

In our elegant hypothetical particle beam accelerator (in Farrell-speak, also known as a *scalar weapon*), the device allows particular particles to escape at either end. Electrons go out at one end and fused nuclei, aka *ions*, go out the other (in this discussion, *ions* are fused protons and neutrons; therefore ions are separated from their typical electron partners). Importantly, ions contain the *mass* of

---

[12] This type of flat panel TV is called a "plasma" display since the technology utilizes small chambers containing electrically charged ionized gases.

[13] Recall we discussed Tulsa purportedly created a *pulse wave radio* to talk to the Martians!

any atomic particle—as electrons have no mass. Therefore, being hit by ions (the so-called *ion canon* we hear tossed about in science fiction television shows and films) packs quite a punch. Targets hit by a sufficiently robust ion beam would be obliterated.

Imagine for a moment harnessing the nuclear reaction of a star and squeezing that energy through our ion canon. Farrell explains how that can be accomplished theoretically (which I won't explain here—I've risked losing enough readers already). Suffice it to say, a star turned into an ion canon would be the *ultimate death star*.

So how does one aim this radiation beam? By knowing the atomic "address" where your target resides. Aiming the beam requires "connecting" your canon with your target. Remember the yardstick analogy. Once you connect, the force or energy expended on your end can be applied directly to the target on the other.

Addressing particles or collections of them (even a massive collection as in a *planet*) can be accomplished by detecting its *resonant* signature. To explain: understand that each atom in the universe has its own unique atomic signature—which amounts to its very own *resonance*. To impact it, to target the beam at it, one needs to know its signature. I would use the phrase "being on the same wave length" as your target, but that might actually be confusing latitudinal waves with longitudinal waves. It would be more accurate to say being "connected" with your target—your weapon holds one end of the yard stick and your target holds the other. To repeat, despite being infinitely larger than a single atom, planets and stars each have their own signatures (aka resonances). Dial in their exact resonance, release the massive particles through your beam weapon, and *wham*: you have destroyed a planet (or a sun if you are really *shooting for the stars*—which brings a whole new meaning to that phrase too).

Of course, it is not that simple. I have skipped quite a few steps here, which reading Farrell for yourself can remedy. However, for our purposes in this chapter, my explanation should suffice. But be warned: according to another expert Farrell cites, Lt. Col. Tom

Bearden, if you aren't careful, your particle beam weapon can back-fire. This could result in the greatest case of shooting yourself in the foot ever seen in the history of the universe. Bearden cautions:

> If the discharge happens to tickle the Sun and Moon's feedback loops the wrong way, you'll get convulsions of the earth, mighty burps of the sun raining fire and brimstone on the earth, and a violent increase in the interior heat of the earth's molten core, with a concomitant eruption of that core right up through the mantle... (Whenever) one activates a large scalar (electromagnetic) weapon, one immediately places the entire earth in deadly peril. The slightest misstep, and it's curtains for everyone. And it's curtains for the earth as well.[14]

When Did this Cosmic War Happen?

If you were stationed on Earth when a cosmic war transpires, and one of the planets orbiting our sun is taken out by an ion canon, you would see enormous aurora displays in the heavens. Plus, these

Figure 79 -Examples of Rongorongo Petroglyphs

---

[14] Farrell, Ibid., p. 47. Citing Tom Bearden, *Fer De Lance*, p. 408.

displays would hang around for quite some time. Eventually, everyone around the globe would see the aurora as it produces a persistent magnetically induced image—with one particular shape resembling a humanoid. Consequently, hiding the fact you annihilated a nearby planet would be most difficult—using this scalar weapon would create witnesses everywhere. And if the warfare happened within, say, the last 12,000 years as Farrell speculates it may have, our forebears on every continent[15] would have taken note of the event and recorded it in the artistic medium most readily available to them: image painting on the walls of their cave dwellings. Based on the work of a plasma physicist Anthony Peratt, Farrell conjectures this is exactly what happened.

These underground notations were the focus a scientific paper developed by Anthony Peratt while working for the government at Los Alamos Labs.[16] The fact we had a plasma physicist working for the government and doing papers on plasma events dating back to pre-history, raises interesting questions in its own right. We will not have the time to investigate that matter. Suffice it to say that our government might know about "paleoancient weapons" that an advanced ancient civilization used—and may be seeking to discover the technology behind such planet busting potential—before someone else does. Farrell pays particular attention to ancient texts and the so-called Tablet of Destinies. This record (a tablet made of some type of resilient substance) supposedly contains the secrets of this "scalar" technology.[17] Farrell suggests it may still be buried in the

---

[15] Were cavemen Homo Sapiens? Were they annihilated in this Cosmic War? Were Adam and Eve successor Homo sapiens sapiens modeled after their predecessors but given a genetic upgrade by Yahweh which advanced intelligence and the capacity to commune with Yahweh? All good questions. No firm answers.

[16] Anthony Peratt's paper proposes a connection between plasma displays in the atmosphere with ancient petroglyphs. His paper may be found at the following link: http://www.scribd.com/doc/14145750/Anthony-Peratt-Characteristics-for-the-Occurrence-of-a-HighCurrent-ZPinch-Aurora-as-Recorded-in-Antiquity.

[17] Farrell guides the reader for a lengthy analysis (too long for my taste) of the Edfu texts, Egyptian *Book of the Dead*, and the Sumerian *Enumu Elish*,

sands of the Middle East and might have been the true "weapon of mass destruction" that America sought when it invaded Iraq. If not in the ancient land of Sumer/Babylon, Farrell suggests this ultimate recipe book for destruction could be buried on the moon or Mars!

To flesh out the speculation a bit more: Human beings saw this stunning display in the skies—an aurora borealis surpassing any semblance of what they had seen before. Additionally, they may have been physically impacted by this plasma event (by feeling great heat or experiencing resultant earthquakes). Regardless of the physical threat (which ultimately may have destroyed ancient civilization on earth), the troubled population recorded these awesome sights worldwide in petroglyphs where they dwelled. To be clear, caves might not have been their normal abode. They may have taken to the caves for protection (shades of Revelation 6 and the opening of the sixth seal!)

Figure 80 - Easter Islands Moai

Another scientist, Robert M. Schoch, corroborates the world-wide witness of this major plasma phenomenon. The reader may recall it was Schoch who famously dated the Egyptian Sphinx to a much earlier date in antiquity than conventional history allowed (dating this signature icon of Egypt all the way back to 7000 BC). Schoch's archeological investigation demonstrated the Sphinx showed signs of rain erosion—which could only have occurred during a much wetter time—9000 years ago when it could rain torrents in North Africa. Besides his studies at the Giza plateau, Schoch has researched ancient civilizations in various corners of the world, including the indigenous people of Easter Island in the South Pacific. Schoch studied the famous Moai and images of the Rongorongo petroglyphs. According to Schoch, images exist in that pictorial language which match those cited by Anthony Peratt. Schoch discusses this connection and the great plasma event of 9700 BC on his website:

> Oddly, the indigenous Easter Island rongorongo script may hold the answer. But first we have to consider the concept of the fourth state of matter—plasma. Plasma consists of electrically charged particles. Familiar plasma phenomena on Earth today include lightning and auroras, the northern and southern lights, and upper atmospheric phenomena known as sprites. In the past, much more powerful plasma events sometimes took place, due to solar outbursts and coronal mass ejections (CMEs) from the Sun, or possibly emissions from other celestial objects. Powerful plasma phenomena could cause strong electrical discharges to hit Earth, burning and incinerating materials on our planet's surface. Los Alamos plasma physicist Dr. Anthony L. Peratt and his associates have established that petroglyphs found worldwide record an intense plasma event (or events) in prehistory.
>
> Dr. Peratt determined that powerful plasma phenomena observed in the skies would take on characteristic shapes resembling humanoid figures, humans with bird heads, sets of rings or donut shapes, and writhing snakes or serpents—shapes reflected in countless ancient petroglyphs. The Easter Island rongorongo script, recorded on antique wooden tablets, is composed of similar shapes as the petroglyphs. Studying them in detail... I concluded that the Easter Island rongorongo tablets (the surviving tablets are copies of copies of copies...) record a major plasma event in the skies thousands of years ago. This, I believe, was the event that brought a final close to the last ice age. [18]

Schoch does not connect the great plasma event with Farrell's Cosmic War. But his research at Easter Island at least confirms a cataclysmic event took place and was registered by an intelligent race of beings who liked to paint on the walls of their homes (caves) all around our globe in a timeframe that might correspond to a destruction of all earths' life forms explicated by the so-called Gap

---

[18] Citation from Robert M. Schoch's website: http://www.robertschoch.com/plasma.html.

Theory.[19] Could this same event have been the obliteration of Mars' planetary partner? Could this have led to the destruction of a possibly-not-so-mythical Atlantis as many speculate? For Farrell, the timing of his Cosmic War ranges from millions of years ago to a time much more recent—such as an event from 9700 BC. In his book, *The Cosmic War*, he considers the timing:

> Once this highly speculative concept is entertained [of a Cosmic War], it opens the door to a resolution of other chronological issues, for it allows the war to have occurred at any stage that such a society [here on Earth] might have emerged. In short, and barring the consideration of other types of evidence for the moment, the door is open for the cosmic cataclysm to occur anywhere from millions, *to mere thousands*, of years ago [emphasis mine]. And as has already been seen from the evidence presented in this chapter, there are two loci around which a chronological resolution must be orbited: on the one hand, it must account for the existing planetary data of such a catastrophe, from the asteroid belt as remnants of a missing exploded planet in our solar system, to the electrical discharge scarring on the various moons and planets—most notably Mars—in our solar system. The evidence necessitates a much later dating [closer to today], for once one adds intelligent observers into the mix to observe and record these events, one perforce cannot be dealing with the primordial conditions of the solar system... the petroglyphic evidence compiled by [Anthony] Peratt, and the textual evidence of the myths themselves, fix another terminus a few thousand or tens of thousands of years ago. [20]

Despite the argument he advances for a planetary explosion represented in humanity's "cave paintings" referenced as the "problem of Peratt," (which means the evidence demands there were sentient, intelligent beings who could observe the event). As an academic hedge of sorts, Farrell does not consistently argue that this event was this proximate to our day. In fact, he may be slavishly reliant

---

[19] Referenced earlier, The Gap Theory conjectures that between Genesis 1:1 and 1:2, there was a gap of thousands, millions, or billions of years. The current earth was not an event of creation, but re-creation, reclaiming an earth that had been turned into a chaotic wasteland, perhaps as a result of Lucifer's rebellion.

[20] Joseph P. Farrell, *The Cosmic War: Interplanetary Warfare*, Modern Physics, and Ancient Texts, Kempton: Adventures Unlimited, 2007, pp. 78-79.

upon Van Flandern's proposed timeline for a cosmic event involving Mars, and not just one but two exploding planets. The problem with Van Flandern's timeframe: it does not allow for humans to be advanced to the point where they could witness and record the event. Unless intelligent humans existed on Earth over 3 million YBP.

Assuming a traditional evolutionary scenario for the sake of Farrell's argument, humanity did not awaken to abstract thinking until the last 100,000 years or so. Van Flandern had suggested the timing of a second exploded planet was 3.2 million years ago (he proposed a first planet may have blown up 65 million years ago related to the now-accepted catastrophe on earth that ended the dinosaurs' reign). Farrell defaults to the 3.2 million year timeframe through of the rest of his book.[21] This includes a positive review of Michael Cremo's "hidden history of the human race"—an unusual "alternative" point of view contending a sophisticated humanity, capable of abstract thinking, has been resident on earth for millions of years. Now that perspective comprises a true minority report. Still, it constitutes one way to reconcile cosmic events with human artifacts.[22]

Conclusion: The Cosmic War and Its Implications

Summarizing the points Farrell makes regarding the Cosmic War, including a couple we haven't mentioned yet (in a feeble attempt to streamline my compilation of this rather difficult subject).

---

[21] Farrell comments that if Van Flandern's "original Planet V supported intelligent life, then Mars may have been inundated with debris of a very different, artificial, nature." Ibid., p. 22. As to Van Flandern's thoughts on whether there was intelligent life on Mars itself, he "believes that these structures, if artificial, were built by some civilization prior to the event at 3.2 million years ago." Farrell here quotes Tom Van Flandern's book, *Dark Matter, Missing Planets, and New Comets,* p. 435.

[22] A quick note in passing: no one can say that Ancient Alien Theorists are obliged to defend evolutionary theory—they are as prone to call out Darwin as Theists are. As with Theists, for Ancient Alien theorists, Earth is not a "closed system." Consequently, most prefer to keep their feet in both circles depending upon what best suits their purpose.

First, geological support exists for a "cosmic catastrophe" on Mars; specifically, scars on Mars suggest a planet exploded nearby:

> Mars along of all the planets in the solar system has the best geological evidence for the type of Flood described in the Old Testament and in other ancient legends and traditions. Indeed, the severe hemispherical disparity one encounters on Mars [the southern hemisphere has few craters, the northern hemisphere is covered with them] is exactly explained by the hypothesis, for "one hemisphere would have been heavily bombarded, and the other barely touched by the explosion."[23]

Second, there is the exploded planet itself: Farrell conveys that (1) it was large with the same mass as Saturn; (2) it was solid, for the debris consists of carbonaceous asteroids, and (3) it "was very likely a water-bearing planet, since Mars exhibits definite and distinct evidence of sudden, massive flooding across its entire southern hemisphere."[24] Mars was permanently scarred by the Cosmic War, but its neighbor was destroyed in a plasma discharge that could be "seen" and felt on Earth.

Only briefly mentioned before, we must make a few more points about the mechanism for accomplishing this "Death Star" function. It was, Farrell asserts, recorded on a *Tablet of Destinies,* and discussed in the ancient texts of Sumer and Egypt that Farrell reviews in *The Cosmic War.* The ultimate trophy in the space race today (joined by India and China) may be finding that "tablet" and its planet-destroying technologies expounded thereon. In regard to this tablet, Farrell compares what happened in ancient times with the masters who held the tablet, with the Allies at the end of World War II. He summarizes this analogy as follows: "The Tablets were inventoried, and some carted off and used elsewhere by the victors in a kind of "paleoancient Operation Paperclip," some were deliberately hidden because of their potential destructive power, and be-

---

[23] Ibid., p. 21. Farrell here cites Tom Van Flandern's book, op. cit.,, p. 427.
[24] Ibid., p. 14. I believe Farrell has the Martian hemispheres reversed.

cause of the impossibility of destroying them, and some components were permanently destroyed."[25] There is, of course, no compelling evidence offered by Farrell that proves the Tablets ever existed, other than considering the testimony of the ancient texts themselves. Of course, if a crime was committed, there has to be a motive. And without the hunt for the Tablets and the information they supposedly contained, his theory of the crime lacks a motive—this crucial element goes missing.

Fourth, we must touch on another element not mentioned up to this point in the context of Farrell's mythos. This issue connects the players of the Cosmic War to the issue of the Nephilim—those giant beings that resulted when the *Bene Elohim* came into the "daughters of men" and begat children through them (Genesis 6:4). Farrell supposes that if intelligent beings escaped from the exploded planet to our own, those beings would have been a much larger size, possessing a robust skeletal structure with "muscles to match", in order to deal with the much higher level of gravity they would have experienced there. "In short, such creatures would be, by modern human standards, giants." No surprise then that Farrell cites the research of noted evangelical author Steven Quayle; specifically, his extensive studies on giants[26] referencing many classic (Greek and Roman) sources. Quayle's work is called upon in his study of *The Cosmic War* to help substantiate Farrell's adjunct theory that these giants arrived on earth sometime in pre-history (the reader will recall we discussed this in detail in regards to David Flynn). According to Farrell's hypothesis, the Nephilim were instrumental in building a "high civilization" incorporating advanced technology and enormous monuments, including such structures of the Pyramids.[27] They were not big, ugly, and dumb. They were quite smart.

---

[25] Ibid., p 382.

[26] Quayle's latest research is now presented on his nicely updated website: http://www.genesis6giants.com/.

[27] When I met Steve Quayle in Oklahoma City back in the fall of 2013, he was unaware of Dr. Farrell's research and reference to his material.

His theory does not entirely correspond to the views of Quayle, L.A. Marzulli, and this author, as Farrell interprets the concept of the *Bene Elohim* ("Sons of God") figuratively while we interpret the phrase literally. That is, we believe the Sons of God were fallen angels—perhaps occupying another planet but more likely, originating and residing in a different realm altogether. Farrell suggests instead that these beings were very large humanoids, racially like us (inasmuch that we could beget children together), but who came to Earth as a result of the Cosmic War. Farrell supposes the beginnings of our race may have dated from millions of years ago. Additionally, he even theorizes that our species may have originated somewhere else in the Cosmos. Nonetheless, while rejecting most of these suppositions, I remain fascinated that Farrell comes as close as he does to the perspective of this author (which I, of course, contend conveys the orthodox meaning of the Bible regarding the Nephilim).

Farrell connects another set of dots that, to say the least, adds yet another level of intrigue. Farrell notes the fact Egyptologist and mystic James Hurtak had published his remote viewing experience, "seeing" the Cydonian "face" before the 1976 Viking 1 photo of THE FACE generated so much popular interest. Farrell worries that remote viewers may have been contracted by national governments (or the "breakaway civilization" itself) to search for the secret (perhaps only hypothetical) Tablet of Destinies. He comments:

> Hurtak's viewing of the Mars' Face thus raises another disturbing possibility, one known to be in use presently by the various countries' militaries and also by large corporations researching exotic technologies, and that is that such technologies might be located via such processes. And it raises the possibility that such processes were being used to guide technological exploration of Mars long before probes were actually sent [recall the 1958 comic book, *The Face on Mars*, and the possible connection of mediumistic spying with the CIA]. If so, it casts another shadow on the Two Space Programs Hypothesis. It will only be a matter of time before someone, somewhere, attempts to use the same process to view and generally locate the missing components of the cause of that Cosmic War, the Tablets of Destinies.

Should that search be underway and exist as a motive for what continues to transpire in the strange and bizarre world of UFOs and ET, we can only hope that the Tablet remains lost and not found.

Finally, Farrell considers the possibility that a super-intelligent evil personage has been involved throughout the history of the Cosmic War and whose threatening presence may lurk still.

> If there was such a war, it implies a celestial extent to humanity, or "whomever," and a sophistication of technology and a potential for destruction that we can scarcely imagine. If one adds into that volatile mix the clear indications of our most ancient myths, that there was also an ancient and preternaturally malign intelligence behind the most primordial revolt; that it is a frightening scenario indeed.[28]

This author does believe that such a malevolent intelligence continues to carry out his plan for the deception of humanity, and ultimately, to transform humanity into a form resembling his nature and not that of our species' actual creator. This story may link to our ancient past, but it surely portends profound connections to our future.

According to Ancient Alien Theory, humankind has been altered genetically in ages past by beings other than the God of the Bible. Is that likely? Is it possible that there lies hidden in us the evidence of past tampering? Could it be that this program to alter our genome has commenced yet again? Could aliens have actually been present with us all along and we didn't recognize them for who they were?

As we move toward the end our study, we will take up these questions and bring our chronicles of the lying wonders of the Red Planet to their disquieting conclusion.

---

[28] Ibid., pp. 413-414.

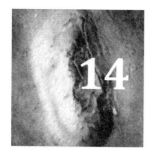

Mars, The Dark Lord, and the Aeon of Horus

Crowley, Lovecraft, Grant—ET and the Great Old Ones

IN HIS LATEST BOOK, OCCULT RESEARCHER PETER LEVENDA TAKES HIS READERS INTO THE DARK MIND OF THE PAST CENTURIES' MOST NOTE-WORTHY OCCULTIST: THE BEAST, ALEISTER CROWLEY. LEVENDA'S book, *The Dark Lord*, explains the esoteric connection between Crowley (1875-1947), his follower Kenneth Grant (1924-2011), and the horror/science fiction writer H.P. Lovecraft (1890-1937).

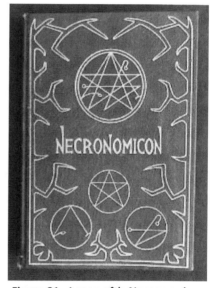

Figure 81 - Lovecraft's Necronomicon

Levenda's book is not for the faint of heart. He intends to teach the dark truth about Crowley's and Grant's religion, the real god they worship, and the relevance of the *Necronomicon*, a fictional Bible of a sort, but more accurately a *grimoire* (guide book to magic),[1] written by H.P. Lovecraft and whose English version was dedicated to Aleister Crowley. Their linkage, although strange and diabolical, reveals the meaning of Ancient Alien "theology", and its transcendent origin.

---

[1] The dictionary from Microsoft Word 2013 provides this summary: "A grimoire is a textbook of magic. Such books typically include instructions on how to create magical objects like talismans and amulets, how to perform magical spells, charms and divination and also how to summon or invoke supernatural entities such as angels, spirits, and demons." Not exactly recommended bedtime reading.

Thelema—A Legacy of the Plymouth Brethren?

The infamous Englishman Crowley grew up in the home of devout Christian parents, followers of the Plymouth Brethren founded by the great dispensational teacher, John N. Darby. Crowley's father was a minister for the Brethren. Crowley came to call himself

Figure 82 - Aleister Crowley and H.P. Lovecraft

"The Beast" and saw his life's purpose to incarnate the dark being who opposed the God of Christianity. Using his own elaborate Gematria (a Kabbalistic method for discerning the numerical value of Hebrew words and their mystical meaning), he tied himself to the number of Antichrist, 666. Likely due to her frustration over the difficulties of rearing him, Crowley's mother called him *the Beast*. We can safely say that Crowley did not follow in his father's footsteps. For members of altruistic religions, but especially those who consider themselves evangelical in orientation, Crowley stands as a stark reminder that how we exemplify our beliefs—what we teach our children by example (especially and the self-image we instill), can help, hinder, or even haunt generations that follow.

Crowley believed that his writing, *The Book of the Law*—from which Crowley's religion *Thelema*[2] derives—was channeled through him in 1904 while he and his wife, Rose Edith, were tourists in Cairo.[3] Simply stated, the law of Thelema asserts (paraphrasing) "What one wills is the only law that matters." In other words, true religion should be freed from dictates of what another wills (your parents, an institution like the church, or even God Himself). We should heed *only our will*. But Crowley did not restrict his religion to a mere state of mind. What he revealed through his channeled writings was a "metaphysic"—something ultimately true for all humankind. That is, Crowley believed that through his experience and writings a new aeon of humanity was revealed to the world—the Aeon of *Horus*. Supposedly, this new aeon Crowley announced superseded the former age of Osiris. Although Horus is the Egyptian god equivalent to Mars, and Cairo means "the city of Mars"—those "Martian" connections are only tangentially associated with our study. For Crowley, the meaning of Horus was "the child" (as the Son of Osiris and Isis), symbolizing the break with *patristic religions*—Judaism, Islam, and Christianity—doctrines in which neither the *child* nor the *feminine* is emphasized.

---

[2] Thelema comes from the writings of François Rabelaisa, a French Franciscan of the sixteenth century, who created a satirical fiction set in the Abbey of Thélème, a place where men of virtue, placed under the burden of the law, lose their virtue. Crowley stated Rebelaisa was the first Thelemite. Today's Master of the Lodge of *Ordo Templi Orientis* denies the importance of that connection, indicating Crowley's writings only are considered guides to creating a Thelemite-oriented society. See http://en.wikipedia.org/wiki/Thelema#Historical_Precedents. An interesting synchronicity: Rabelaisa's story centers on a *giant* and his son. The giants' name is *Gargantua*, from which our word Gargantuan derives.

[3] From the dictionary in Microsoft Word 2013, we read regarding Thelema, "By his [Crowley's] account, a possibly non-corporeal or "praeterhuman" being that called itself Aiwass contacted him and dictated a text known as *The Book of the Law* or *Liber AL vel Legis*, which outlined the principles of Thelema."

On the other hand, for author H.P. Lovecraft, an aeon had no lasting significance other than its contemplation might drive one mad. Lovecraft used the notion of aeon as an element to add drama to his horror stories. His evil anti-hero, Cthulhu, lay asleep, lurking in the deep of the ocean, having been there for aeons, waiting for the "stars to be right," to be awakened from his near eternal slumber. But for Crowley an aeon involved much more than endless time. It connected to the meaning of *aeon* as taught by the Gnostics in the days of Jesus and especially, His apostles.

As the reader likely knows, the Gnostic gospel (unhappily celebrated by modern popular theologians like Bart D. Erman and Elaine Pagels) became the primary enemy of orthodox Christianity.[4] In Gnosticism, God was revealed through these aeons—emanations of the divine that came forth from the *pleroma*, the totality of God's being, the effulgence or radiation of all that conveys what God is. [5] Each successive aeon was less pure than the aeon "higher up" or closest to the pleroma. Recall that Gnosticism asserted evil existed in the world because matter itself was tainted with evil.[6] By separating the goodness of God from the evilness of matter, aeons enabled God to keep His distance from the creation. Important in

---

[4] The earliest known Christian Gnostic was Valentinus (c. 100-153 AD). The Gospel of John and John's letters anticipate Valentinus and for a period, John and Valentinus may have been contemporaries. Valentinus denied that Jesus had come in the flesh. This says John is *the spirit of Antichrist.* 1 John 4:3: *"And every spirit that confesseth not that Jesus Christ is come in the flesh is not of God: and this is that spirit of antichrist, whereof ye have heard that it should come; and even now already is it in the world."*

[5] Paul uses the word *pleroma* in Colossians 2:9. *"For in Him dwells all the fullness of the Godhead bodily."* Christ is the pleroma, the totality of all that God is— and in Christ the Godhead [the pleroma] dwells bodily." Elaine Pagels falsely assumes that by using this word Paul was a gnostic. Exactly the opposite is true. Paul was employing the word as a means to interpret what the actual meaning should be, not how it was being used by Gnostics. That God could dwell in the flesh, the *entire pleroma in one human body*, would be impossible for the Gnostic.

[6] In a deep sense, the religion of the Antichrist is a religion that declares the creation is NOT good. Lucifer attacks Jehovah "in the beginning." It is significant that the Bible begins by reinforcing that all that God creates IS GOOD.

this depiction of the Cosmos: this "line" was not t
mained a line distinguishing God from creation.
derstood a border or a *limit*. And this line was
known as the *horizon*.

The reader should recall from Egyptian mythology Horus was the avenging son of Osiris who sought after Set, the evil brother of Osiris and Isis, who murdered Osiris and sliced him into 13 pieces. Isis re-assembled the body parts of Osiris, and supposedly Horus resur-rected him. Thus, for Thelemites, *Set* represents The Dark Lord.

To clarify, Horus was not exactly, as many suppose, the sun god. *Ra* was the sun god, except at those twice daily events when the sun touches the horizon, then Ra and Horus were seen as one—as Ra-Herakhty, "Ra-Horus on the Horizon." Horus is defined as the god who comprises the point *where earth and sky meet*. In fact, the word *horizon* derives from *Horus*. It is this notion of the meeting of earth and sky, an iconic symbol of the connection between humanity and the ancient beings of the heavens, whom Lovecraft called the *Great Old Ones. The aeon of Horus equals the moment of reconnection—* it consists of the "coming" or *return of the aliens to the earth*.[7] Hence, the religion of Crowley (Thelema), focuses on the return of the *ancient aliens*. Again, to be clear, the fact that Horus is the Egyp-tian name for Mars provides a *symbolic* connection between Mars and the return of these beings. However, much more to the point, Crowley's religion at its core *constitutes a credo of ancient aliens.*

The Dark Lord of Kenneth Grant

The title of Levenda's book, *The Dark Lord,* as the reader might infer, refers to the god Set, not to Horus. Set is also known as Seth, Shaitan, but most commonly known as *Satan*. Set was considered by the Egyptians as the god of rage, the desert, and the God of

---

[7] It is in this sense that we should understand the return of Quetzalcoatl, Kukul-kan, and the Feathered Serpent, predicted by the Maya, the Hopi, and the Cherokee.

...s. According to Levenda, in the time of Herodotus, the Greeks ...ntified Set with *Typhon*, their sea monster. Supposedly Set re...sided in the Great Bear constellation and aided the souls of the dead, by assisting them as they climbed Set's "stairway to heaven."[8] Kenneth Grant in the 1950s, asserted leadership of *Thelema* taking over for Crowley (Crowley died in the most magical of years, 1947).[9] Grant's Order employs Typhon as its moniker, connecting his version of Thelema with Set/Satan.

Figure 83 - Kenneth Grant

As Levenda notes, it is no coincidence that when Lovecraft created the fictional *Necronomicon*, he determined it to be written in the eighth century CE by a *"Mad Arab"*. Tying his fictional cult with Middle East religions was no accident. Likewise, the source of dark magic begins with the Kabbala, its Tree of Life, and the mystical path. As this author has noted before, even the Nazis who hated the Jews studied the Hebrew Kabbala to discover its secrets of magic.

Kenneth Grant argued that "all religions and especially all antinomian[10]

---

[8] Rock music buffs might have wondered where Robert Plant and Jimmy Page came up with the name for their hit song by that title—now you know. Nor is it a coincidental fact they wrote the song in the house once owned by Aleister Crowley—Jimmy Page had purchased the house in part because he it was a devotee of Crowley. The property, *Boleskine House*, is located on the shores of that enchanted lake, Loch Ness in Scotland. Perhaps "Nessie" and the "Beast" Crowley felt at home together.

[9] Grant declared yet another change of aeon—the Aeon of Set. Perhaps for Grant, like Dr. Evil's son in the Austin Powers' movies, *Horus*, the analogue to Dr. Evil's son, was the "Diet Coke of Evil... not quite evil enough."

[10] *Antinomian* means anti-law. Antinomian religions do not believe that keeping any specific set of laws supplies salvation. An antinomian is against *legalism*. But an antinomian may believe only that imposing law causes laws to be broken. This appears to be the meaning of the stories of *Rebelaisa*.

cults have their origin in a single cult, a single magical order that has its origin not on earth but in the stars." [11] [Emphasis in original]

Levenda clarifies, "It is this belief—this discovery—that finds itself in line with the most cynical of Lovecraft's horror stories concerning a race of alien beings that once colonized our planet and which will come again to reclaim it, a race whose religion is the mother of all cults."[12] Reiterating, the Ancient Aliens mythos lies at the heart of Crowley's "Thelema" and Grant's "Typhonian Cult."

As discussed at the outset of this book, since the middle of the twentieth century, Lovecraft's writings inspired Ancient Alien Theory. The fact that Grant determined certain fiction—Lovecraft's horror stories in particular—could bring initiates into contact with extraterrestrial entities, taught that our imagination stands as an indispensable element *in conjuring evil.* Evil is not, however, purely an abstract or imagined concept. It is tangible. To be a successful initiate, a Thelemite must conjure the presence of a spirit *to visibility*—others must witness it. Furthermore, "contact" should not just be casual *but intimate.* Levenda states: "Contact with non-human entities is one of the inescapable requirements of magic. There is no magic without this type of supramundane[13] communication. And the most intense form of this contact is sexual."[14] Victims of Satanic Ritual Abuse (SRA) know this contention to be absolutely true.

The linkage between Thelema and alien beings is at the heart of the *Ordo Templi Orientis* (OTO). From a Typhonian Order newsletter published out of Miami, Florida, Levenda documents this key idea: "The central concern of Magick is communion with discarnate or extraterrestrial Intelligences."[15] As Levenda colorfully conveys regarding the "occult policy of the OTO": "There is no insistence on

---

[11] Ibid., p. 21.
[12] Ibid., p. 21.
[13] *Supramundane* means a being who is above the normal world, i.e., *celestial.*
[14] Ibid., p. 285.
[15] Ibid., quoting Kenneth Grant, *Beyond the Mauve Zone,* p. 274.

lofty spiritual goals or an Asian-inspired quest for non-duality or nirvana. While these are present in Grant's works they are there almost as after-thoughts."[16] In other words, it is about contact with ET. What alien abductees unwittingly learn, Themelites openly seek!

> Those who have been inadvertently or unwillingly involved in this type of encounter speak of it in sexual terms. The UFO abductee experience seems to include various types of (often uncomfortable) sexual encounter with alien beings. In the Middle Ages average men and women complained about incubi and succubi. The Witches' Sabbat is portrayed as a kind of orgy. Lovecraft's aversion to sexuality may be a reflection of this unconscious understanding [on his part] that, somehow, sexuality and contact with alien forces are linked.[17]

Levenda emphasizes the impact of the *Necronomicon* on modern occultism. Despite being a purely fictional work of H.P. Lovecraft, it was taken most seriously by Kenneth Grant.[18] The cult of Cthulhu became a serious and global occult religion although based on fiction horror stories. In that sense, it is not altogether different from *Star Wars* in our day. Although "the Force" and the mythos of *Star Wars* meant only to entertain, it brought millions into contact with ideas owing to Hinduism and the occult. "The power of the Dark Side" was Darth Vader's mantra and mirrored the strength one can obtain from the "darkness" of magic. In much the same way, searching for The Dark Lord in real-world occult religion hearkens more to the power *behind the concepts* and *not* whether there is actually *any historical truth behind the mythos*. Myth is about the existential value of the story, not whether or not the account is true. As liberal theologians have consistently argued about faith, "don't ask if the Bible is true historically—only ask if the story rings true for you." If the story teaches life lessons well, then the myth has served its purpose.

Levenda's book investigates the connection between Crowley, Lovecraft, and Kenneth Grants' "Cult of the Dark Lord." Studying

---

[16] Ibid.

[17] Ibid.

[18] A modern version is now available, edited by "Simon", a modern occultist.

the occult does not constitute this author's idea of a good time. Consequently, our interest in Levenda's study relates to the descriptive connection between modern occultism, the "doctrine" of Ancient Aliens, and the goal of occultists. That this modern mythos connects to Gnosticism betokens its ultimate origin. It underscores that there is, as Ecclesiastes said, "nothing new under the sun." This is especially so when it comes to religions composed by the Spirit of Antichrist. It is *not* remarkable that the Apostle John designates Gnosticism as the essence of the Antichrist spirit, and that Aleister Crowley would see that connection as a complement. Simply put, *Ancient Alien Theory constitutes the Gnosticism of our day.* When Crowley claims he is *the Beast* and that Antichrist is the essence of his religious spirit, his assertion is biblically correct—in fact, he is.

Lovecraft and the Cult of Cthulhu

Levenda points out that it was hardly uncommon for a European to head to the Middle East in order to gain spiritual insight. We could mention the Crusades and Christians who made the revered pilgrimage to Jerusalem. However, both before and after the Crusades (and even *during* if one studies the history of the Knights Templar), Egypt held a strong allure for Europeans.

> The theme of European mystics going to the Middle East to obtain secret knowledge is an old one and can be seen in the origin legend of the Rosicrucians (Christian Rosenkreutz, their putative founder, went to the Middle East in search of wisdom). The German founders of the Ordo Templi Orientis itself also claimed to have visited Muslim lands where they obtained secret initiations. It has been shown by historians that Helena Blavatsky herself—the founder of the Theosophical Society—had links to the Brotherhood of Luxor, an Egyptian-based secret society. Thus, this is a tradition among European occultists that has a long pedigree.[19]

The connection between Blavatsky, Crowley, Lovecraft, Grant, and modern occultism *constitutes the essence of why Ancient Alien*

---

[19] Peter Levenda, *The Dark Lord*, Lake Worth, FL, IBIS Press, p. 18.

Theory demands an articulate response from the Church of Jesus Christ. We are not just dealing with over-hyped science fiction.

It is especially intriguing to discover that the connection between Crowley and Lovecraft, between alien visitation sought by Thelema (occult) devotees and ancient religion as practiced in the Middle East, begins with a stunning synchronicity, a synchronicity that bespeaks Someone evil was operating behind the curtains.

The tie between the two relates Lovecraft's most famous story, "The Call of Cthulhu," written in 1926, to Crowley's short-story (or poem) *Liber Liberi vel Lapidus Lazuli* written on or about November 1, 1907. Lovecraft placed the story in New Orleans in 1907 and Providence in 1925. In New Orleans, on Halloween, 1907, an orgiastic ritual is conducted in honor of the "high priest of the Great Old Ones, Cthulhu (where also the police there find a seven to eight inch statue of this figure). At the same moment, back in the real world of 1907 (19 years to the day), Crowley first coined the word "Tutulu" not knowing where the word came from nor exactly what it meant (according to Crowley's story, it was contained in an enchantment meant to be said backwards for effect). Levenda offers that the name *Cthulhu* could be pronounced "Kutulu." Levenda suggests these odd words, *Tutulu* and *Kutulu*, likely originated from the same source—and

Figure 84 - Lovecraft's Cthulhu Mythos

that source must be supernatural. In Lovecraft's story, Cthulhu invaded the dreams of his worshippers. Were Crowley and Lovecraft connected by a malfeasant intermediary—the spirit of Antichrist?

To prove his point, Levenda methodically walks us through the lines from several of Crowley's and Lovecraft's fictional stories to demonstrate the parallels, most notably the traits of resemblance between the evil "anti-heroes"—that of an octopus, a being with tentacles, and the wings of a dragon, "A buried god awakened from a stone, in a coffin, in a sepulcher, and mysterious words written in an ancient book, including Tutulu. And 'of pure black marble is the sorry statute' resonates with the black stone on which the statue of Cthulhu squats."[20]

To summarize H.P. Lovecraft's mythos in a few words: Cthulhu is no "ordinary god", he is the high priest of *The Great Old Ones*, and *these beings from the stars will return to earth when the followers of Cthulhu (or Thelema) are powerful enough or numerous enough.* That is what the phrase, "When the stars are right" means. Or in the vernacular of the pop rocker, Sly Stone, "Everybody is a star." Levenda relates that there is no evidence the two men, Crowley and Lovecraft, knew each other. And it would be conspiratorial to the point of incredulity to suppose they were working together at this early date *in any conscious way.* Consequently, Levenda suggests:

> It may actually be more logical to suggest—as an explanation for some of these coincidences—that darker forces were at work. In fact, it is possible that the same forces of which Lovecraft himself writes— the telepathic communication between followers of Cthulhu and the Great Old Ones—was what prompted him to write these fictional accounts of real events. Either Lovecraft was in some kind of telepathic communication with Crowley, or both men were in telepathic communication with... Something Else. [21]

---

[20] Ibid., p. 101.
[21] Ibid., p. 102.

Lovecraft and Crowley, probably unbeknownst to one another, were contemplating in their respective fictions how the culmination of this new aeon (for Crowley *the Aeon of Horus*) would be realized, in which humans would cavort with the Great Old Ones once again.

Conclusion: Apollyon and Cthulhu

Like Apollyon rising from the bottomless pit, Cthulhu was ready to arise from deep slumber within the darkest ravine of the ocean, to invoke the Old Ones to return to earth. All of this was set to occur once "the stars were right." The parallel to Ancient Alien Theory, and to the prophecy of the Bible, is impossible to ignore. *"And they had a king over them, which is the angel of the bottomless pit, whose name in the Hebrew tongue is Abaddon, but in the Greek tongue hath his name Apollyon."* (Revelation 9:11) The names *Abaddon* and *Apollyon* are usually translated "the Destroyer." The fact that the Beast also rises from the turbulent sea (Revelation 13), implies another interesting parallel between Revelation's Beast and Cthulhu.

Jason Colavito rightly points out that Lovecraft was a self-proclaimed "scientific atheist." His stories were not intended to create a real cult. However, for someone who was neither a true believer nor a practicing occultist, Lovecraft derived pleasure from creating a mythos that included many other authors in its development. Given Kenneth Grant's use of this mythos to advance an occult religion, enlivened today with archeological mysteries interpreted as ancient alien visitation, it suggests that there may have been more behind Lovecraft's imagination than what Lovecraft himself realized. Levenda comments, "Lovecraft was a scientist and an atheist. The concept of sex with aliens frightened and disgusted him. Grant was a magician, and the possibilities of sex with aliens was like something out of *Star Trek*: weird, maybe, but not necessarily a bad thing."[22]

---

[22] Ibid. p 298.

The Typhonian Order focuses on the Lovecraftian entities, especially those of the Cthulhu Mythos. The standard demons and evil spirits of the Judeo-Christian tradition are unequal to the task of representing the deeper archetypes that are encountered in this high-intensity approach to the magic.

More than that, however, is the stated goal of the Order which is to make contact with discarnate and extraterrestrial Intelligences. This is perfectly in accord with the Lovecraftian tales which are concerned almost exclusively with this type of contact. In fact, by using terms like "discarnate" and "extraterrestrial" the Order is changing the parameters within which traditional ceremonial magic functions.[23]

So just how malevolent should we conclude that this *über*-Thelema, aka Typhonian cult is? Could it be a threat? Granted the masses will never seek initiation into this arcane and tiny cult. Like Lovecraft's fictional Cult of Cthulhu, its rituals maybe held in dark and dank places far from public scrutiny. But like all secret societies, it appeals to the well-to-do, those with time on their hands, the elite who believe it is their right and destiny to lead. As the victims of SRA testify, those who perform such rituals do so to acquire power and master their circumstances. Additionally, only a bit of leaven leavens the loaf. Only time will tell if the deeper magick of Crowley and Grant will influence those who have already pledged themselves to follow this path. These beliefs are held in secret. Only "when the stars are right" will the infection present itself.

Thelema is, however, coming of age. It has grown up with technology, UFO sightings, alien abduction, and weapons of mass destruction. It is a brave new world in which Thelema now operates.

Levenda assesses this cultic upgrade: "As early as the 1950s, Kenneth Grant and his circle realized that the only thing separating magic from science was the ultimate ambition: contact with the Otherworldly."[24] In a twisted way, Lovecraft was essential to make the Typhon cult a reality. Levenda summarizes: "There can be no

---

[23] Ibid., p. 295.
[24] Ibid., p. 296.

Typhonian Tradition without Lovecraft, and I will tell you why. The stories of H.P. Lovecraft provide the narrative for this form of Thelema. The protagonists and antagonists one finds in his stories can be identified among the initiates of the Orders and their bewildering experiences... Lovecraft is all about Darkness, and so is the Typhonian Tradition."[25]

The final nightmare of the cult celebrated by Aleister Crowley, Kenneth Grant, and even Jack Parsons, (the founder of JPL and Grand Master of the *Ordo Templi Orientis* in Pasadena), may best be summarized by Lovecraft himself. Says Lovecraft in his fiction:

> That cult would never die till the stars came right again, and the secret priests would take the great Cthulhu from His tomb and revive His subjects and resume His rule of earth. The time would be easy to know, for then mankind would have become as the Great Old Ones; free and wild and beyond good and evil, with laws and morals thrown aside and all men shouting and killing and reveling in joy. Then the liberated Old Ones would teach them new ways to shout and kill and revel and enjoy themselves, and all he earth would flame with a holocaust of ecstasy and freedom. Meanwhile the cult, by appropriate rites, must keep alive the memory of those ancient ways and shadow forth the prophecy of their return.

—H. P. Lovecraft, "The Call of Cthulhu"[26]

It takes little insight to see the parallel with the Bible's description of the last days underscoring the diabolical plan belonging and awaiting expression by Set/Satan and his antichrist. For the spirit of Antichrist has already gone out into the world deceiving many, just as John the Apostle said 1,900 years ago. *"For many deceivers are entered into the world, who confess not that Jesus Christ is come in the flesh. This is a deceiver and an antichrist."* (2 John 1:7).

---

[25] Ibid., p. 301.
[26] Cited from Levenda, op. cit., p. 308.

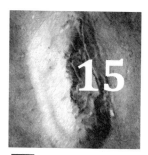

Aliens in Inner Space—
Pyramid Rituals, DMT,
and DNA

The Contrarian in Their Midst

I N HIS FINAL WORKS BEFORE SUCCUMBING TO A RARE DISEASE AND
PASSING AWAY AT THE END OF 2012, THE LATE PHILIP COPPENS PRE-
SENTED AN ARTICULATE, BUT CONTRARIAN TAKE ON ANCIENT ALIEN
Theory. Coppens, born in Belgium, began his slow ascent to minor
celebrity status when he performed research for Lynn Picknett and
Clive Prince, made manifest in perhaps their best book, *The Stargate Conspiracy* (1999). Thereafter, Coppens would gain some no-
toriety at UFO conferences as an eloquent speaker, albeit with a
strange sounding accent to American ears. The television show *Ancient Aliens*, however,
made his star shine much
brighter. He appeared on
virtually every episode
and came across as an au-
thority who knew his
stuff. In his book, *The Ancient Alien Question*
(2012), Philip Coppens
challenged the Martian
hoopla hatched by Rich-

Figure 85 - Philip Coppens, 1971-2012

ard C. Hoagland and Mike Bara. Like the other writers, the so-called
Pyramidiots, which link the "monuments of Mars" with those of
Egypt, Coppens relished the religion of the Pharaohs, seeing *the true
function of the pyramids as one of the real stories behind Ancient
Aliens*. However, before arguing on behalf of Egyptian religion, he
dissed the assumption of many alien theorists by trash talking the
Egyptian-Martian link that so many have advanced.

When it comes to seeing the [Mars'] pyramids, many observe that, unlike the Face, these structures do not seem to have withstood the test of time. Those claiming that there is clear evidence of a pyramid on the Martian surface argue that the pyramids are partially destroyed—which make them, in my opinion, extremely difficult to maintain as "clear evidence," for a heap of rubble or a natural hill are difficult enough to distinguish when you are in front of them, let alone when seeing them from miles up in the sky.[1]

While this author has offered limited support for the photographic evidence provided by NASA and as interpreted by Ancient Alien theorists, although Coppens was numbered among their fold, he was not all that impressed:

These photographs, whether taken on the moon or Mars, are all interesting, and *could* point out evidence of extraterrestrial structures, and they *should* be analyzed and discussed. However, extraordinarily complex theories have been proposed that so far remain unsupported by evidence. These photos are not proof of anything. They cannot prove that we were not alone, but it *is* clear that in recent decades, an enormous amount of discoveries have been made that show that life is a cosmic imperative.[2] [Emphasis in original]

Thus, Coppens opted for a safer, less controversial theory (although this theory to life's start on Earth is NOT one I find compelling). That theory, *Panspermia,* amounts to the only *physical* contact with aliens. Moreover, Coppens made his contrarian opinion clear with these words: "Mars definitely once had microorganisms some of which have been found on earth. And all indications are that life on Earth itself was alien in origin. We *are* the aliens."[3] [Emphasis in original] Of course, allowing the existence of microbes on Mars does not fluff anyone's skirt. And to find out *we* are the aliens we have been searching for, sounds forth with the same fanfare as a single taxicab horn in Times Square. Talk about anticlimactic.

---

[1] Philip Coppens, *The Ancient Alien Question, A New Inquiry Into the Existence, Evidence, and Influence of Ancient Visitors,* Pompton Plains, NJ, Career Press, 2012, p. 238.

[2] Ibid., p. 241.

[3] Ibid., p. 242.

As we have discussed before, *Panspermia* amounts to a semi-scientific "hunch" even Richard Dawkins, that most antagonistic of atheists, affirms. By itself, Coppens was not saying all that much. Wherever the origin of intelligence life, if God is not the creator of that intelligence, then one must assume that *non-intelligence creates intelligence* with no extra help. It pushes the question of "the first mover" back to another planet, another galaxy, another aeon, ad infinitum. As such, it amounts to an *infinite regress*. Thus, Panspermia cheats. By saying intelligent life did not originate here on Earth, but somewhere else first, only begs the question "Then where did life *there* originate?"

The Pyramid as the Primordial Meeting Place

Coppens mounts a somewhat more traditional argument for Ancient Aliens with a mystical, spiritual explanation. In pursuing this pathway, Coppens—like Crowley, Grant, and the Thelemites—proclaims that contact with ET was the goal of Egyptian religion. Furthermore, thousands of years ago Egyptians perfected this contact through their religious rituals. In contrast to other Ancient Alien theorists like Joseph P. Farrell who speculates the Egyptian pyramids might have been weapons in an interplanetary star war, Coppens believes the pyramids were little more than a sophisticated apparatus necessary, or at least useful, in establishing and maintaining contact with inter-dimensional "gods" while simultaneously validating the Pharaoh's prerogative to rule. Giza's monuments were little more than massive geometric temples. How mundane! Coppens does have more to say, however, than clarifying the value of 5,000 year-old pyramids was for the living and not for the dead.

To commence his argument, Coppens discusses the mysterious Andrija Puharich and his research into THE NINE, aka the Egyptian *Ennead* (which means "nine"). As this author has documented elsewhere in his *Power Quest* books, Puharich became fascinated with THE NINE as part of his research into ESP and channeling on behalf of the US Government during the 1950s. This investigation continued as Puharich expanded his work working with several re-nowned (and some less renowned) mediums. Years later, 1971 to be exact, Puharich discovered Uri Geller at a Tel Aviv nightclub, where Geller was performing his "magic" (telekinetic spoon bend-ing and the like). For over a year they hung out in Israel and the pair became friends. Then Puharich brought Geller to the US and put him in front of the physicists (Russell Targ and Hal Puthoff) at Stanford Research Institute, scientists who studied the highly strange (as in *remote viewing*, ESP, and *alternative* physics).

Eventually Puharich created a *Committee of Nine* (including Star Trek's Gene Rodenberry and singer John Denver), who were hosts to séances with a special group of chatty otherworldly entities. "Descendants" of these celestial explorers would eventually sponsor an important book in the history of channeled "gods from outer space", *The Only Planet of Choice: Essential Briefings from Deep Space* (1993), recording the channelings of medium Phyllis Schlemmer. The foreword was written by James Hurtak, the Egyp-tologist who claimed to first see THE FACE. The subject of the book was "Tom" who revealed he was the leader of the *nine gods* of the Egyptian *Ennead* – undoubtedly a name chosen to play on the orig-inal name of the head honcho, *Atum*. Like most channeled mate-rial, the dribble dished out by the disembodied voices speaking through Schlemmer, predicted "the Aliens are coming" and would soon set the world right when they arrived. As you may have noted, their debut remains delayed. Their predicted revealing was to be on the auspicious dates of the year 2000, then later 2012. However, the year 2000 came and went. And so did the year 2012. We await with bated breath their arrival still. Maybe the stars are not right.

So Puharich would wane while Geller would become a guest on talk shows. However, THE NINE continued growing their influence. They even became staff members of *the Institute of the Study of Con-sciousness* in Berkeley, California! The Founder of the Institute was Arthur M. Young, one of Puharich's original Committee of Nine. It seems celestial wisdom never runs short in California.

Moving on, Coppens proposed that the Egyptian NINE constitutes the oligarchy of deities behind much of the Ancient Aliens commotion. He linked the relevance of the NINE (aka Nine Principles) to the role of the Pharaoh and the purpose of the pyramids. In a brief examination of the ancient Pyramid Texts (the predecessor document to the *Corpus Hermeticum*, written in the third century BC to explain the Egyptian religion to its Greek audience), Coppens summarized the verdict of several scholars who determined there was no "wisdom" per se buried within these texts. Egyptian religion was about ritual—about making contact with the gods—not just describing or explaining them. The texts were records of the rituals; they were "how to" instruction manuals. And the pyramids were not funeral monuments. They were intended as chambers within which the Pharaoh could establish contact with the Ennead thereby proving his worthiness to rule. After connecting with THE NINE, the coronation could be occur.[4] Moreover, the Pyramid was considered the

Figure 86 - The Pyramids of Giza

---

[4] Ibid., pp. 259-261.

"mound" of creation,[5] where sky met earth, where the Pharaoh could ascend to meet the gods, or where they could descend to meet him.

Therefore, the pyramid was the exalted place of meeting between the Intelligences and humanity's representative. Coppens argued, as seems to be the belief of many other scholars: whether the pyramids were in Mexico or Egypt—their purpose remained the same. Despite the distance betwixt, the ancient paths were identical worldwide.

The Psychotropic Ascent to God

Again, for Coppens, the Ancient Alien religion was about *contact.* Coppens *confused* his own argument, however, because contact with the gods did not always require a mega structure like a pyramid. As

time went by, meeting with ET became much more pedestrian.

Coppens speaks highly of the late author/ writer/ speaker Terrence McKenna whose books and lectures were instrumental in germinating the 2012

Figure 87 - Author Terrence McKenna

"movement." McKenna advocated the use of very special drugs to contact higher Intelligences. The drug *dimethyltryptamine* (DMT), produced naturally in small quantities by human beings, was of particular interest. A book and documentary movie entitled *DMT: The Spirit Molecule*, explores its mesmerizing impact.

At a conference where Coppens met McKenna, Coppens heard Terrence extol the virtues of DMT—and knock the investigation of

---

[5] The "mound builders" in America were no doubt doing the best to build their version of pyramids, elevated mounds of dirt, as they were without stone quarries nearby. Oh, and the mounds were also good lookouts too.

UFOs from the typical "physical" angle. Coppens summarized what he heard with these words:

> At the conference, McKenna proclaimed his famous slogan that UFOs were not nuts and bolts, as most ufologists believed, and he implied that the methodology used by UFO researchers in trying to prove the existence of extraterrestrial beings visiting the Earth was never going to be successful, pointing to 50 years of documented UFO reports that had led to no solid conclusions. McKenna believed that UFOs were real, but were not physical machines. Instead, McKenna proposed that we had to use our minds to explore and answer the alien question.[6]

Coppens also explained how McKenna would grow more emphatic in his view, that the real contact with aliens was through DMT,

Figure 88 - *The Cosmic Serpent*

even asserting that the alien abduction experience was essentially the same thing as a drug-induced encounter. "Where it's at" so to speak, was meeting ET in "hyperspace" (the name McKenna gave the primordial meeting place). ET was merely the latest physical form through which these beings chose to represent themselves. Former manifestations included fairies, elves, and angels.[7] *Hyperspace*, induced by DMT and other mind-bending drugs, not outer space, comprises the location where we hook up. Given most alien "abductees" consider themselves victims, this comparison presents an obvious contradiction that those who follow McKenna do not resolve.

In the same regard, Coppens also discussed the work of Jeremy Narby and his book *DNA: The Cosmic Serpent and the Origins of*

---

[6] Ibid., p. 267.
[7] Ibid., p. 268.

Knowledge. According to Coppens, Narby contends we encounter aliens *through our DNA*—that is, the thesis asserts DNA possesses the *ability to communicate with us.* In trances, such as produced by *ayahuasca*, a potion derived from plants by shamans in the Amazon. This concoction contains DMT and another drug that inhibits its "take up" by the bloodstream, lengthening its effect. Awhile after drinking it, the subject sees some extremely odd visions (out of respect to McKenna and Coppens, we will not characterize them as hallucinations). In these visions the experiencer often meets talking snakes and humans with bird heads (think *Horus*—the Egyptian god of Mars—whose hieroglyph is familiar to most of us—see figure).

Figure 89 - Horus, Egypt's Mars

According to McKenna (as related by Coppens), under the influence of DMT, our DNA speaks to us, revealing secrets of chemistry, technology, and the meaning of life.[8] Coppens therefore pondered these implications:

Is it indeed just a coincidence that the ancient Egyptians depicted their deities as bird-headed people? Or have we come to the core of the problem—and the answer, which is that these otherworldly denizens were indeed seen as the Egyptian deities and that it was these otherworldly intelligences that

---

[8] Author Graham Hancock comes to the same conclusions in his 2007 book, *Supernatural*, in which he describes his own trips to the Amazon, taking LSD, ayahuasca, and mescaline to experience "the divine." He calls the entities he encountered through taking drugs, "the teachers of mankind." He agrees that the "Greys" and other alien (ET) forms are self-chosen representations of these beings.

provided the extraordinary knowledge that went into the Egyptian monuments?

Then Coppens shared the additional witness of anthropologist Michael Harner. Coppens discussed his experiences with DMT and LSD to contact "the aliens inside our DNA." The following quote by Harner (via Coppens) sounds mysteriously similar to Farrell's "cosmic war" and the story told in the 1958 comic, *The Face of Mars*. Could these stories be coming from the same source? Harner relates his vision of creatures with small, black pterodactyl-like wings and white whale-like bodies (an image reminiscent of Cthulhu—the cephalopod with little dragon wings). Taken from Harner's 1961 book, *The Way of the Shaman,* Coppens cites Harner's inner chat:

> They explained to me in a kind of thought language that they were fleeing from something out in space. They had come to planet Earth to escape their enemy. The creatures then showed me how they had created life on the planet in order to hide in multitudinous forms and thus disguise their presence. Before me, the magnificence of plant and animal creation and speciation—hundreds of millions of years of activity—took place on a scale and with a vividness impossible to describe. I learned that the *dragon-like* creatures were thus inside all forms of life, including man. [Emphasis added] [9]

Coppens comes to the conclusion that in every culture, the aliens were like stars—literally, well almost literally. Whether we are considering the Hopi of North America or the Egyptians of Africa, despite being "worlds apart," the angelic song remained the same.

Is it a coincidence that the Bible infers a connection between angels, songs, and stars? *"When the morning stars sang together, and all the sons of God shouted for joy."* (Job 38:7) Is it intriguing that even in the mythos of Cthulhu "the stars have to be right" for aliens and humans to come together at the end of days? Was Kenneth Grant correct that all religions stem from the same "star cult"? [10]

---

[9] Ibid., p. 273.

[10] And as Crosby, Stills, Nash and Young once sang, "We are stardust, we are golden, we are billion-year old carbon. And we've got to get back to the Garden."

281

What Constitutes Definitive Evidence?

So Coppens suggested that Ancient Aliens live within us, beings inherent within our DNA (and all living forms). We don't have to jump on a spaceship to pay them a visit and they don't have to come to call on us via UFO. So why conduct a ritual in a pyramid? The only trip one need take is a "day-trip" using drugs *not* flying saucers.

Whether we are examining the pyramids in Teotihuacan or Giza, these magnificent structures express our desire to connect with the "star ancestors" or the "star messengers." Practically in the same breath, however, Coppens mixes the two different methods to encounter otherworldly entities. Concludes Coppens: "Whether you call this intelligence, *they* [it is not clear if they refers to the *visions* or perhaps the *visionary entities* described by McKenna, Narby, and Harner et al] *are the Ancient Aliens*. They are *not* evidence of physical contact with an ancient alien, which is the quest most proponents are in search of, but *they* are *definitive evidence* that our ancestors were in contact—repeatedly—with a non-human, alien, extraterrestrial intelligence."[11] [Emphasis added]

Of course, we might ask whether visions induced by psychotropic drugs constitute *definitive evidence* of anything, even if those experiences are common across distant borders and great spans of time. It supplies evidence that people experience the same things in similar ways. But the skeptic might ask, "Does that prove these beings really exist? And even if they are truly present within the experiences of those that take these drugs, given that this is completely subjective, does that imply—let alone prove—you can trust the self-proclaimed mission of talking serpents or advice-giving dragons?" The Christian might go further, "Given that the images are of real snakes or other reptiles—imaginary ones in the form of dragons—maybe we should not listen to snakes since that one in the Garden of

---

No doubt composer Joni Mitchell thought meeting a million strong in Woodstock, New York, could bring out the best in people and maybe find God in the process.
   [11] Ibid., p. 280.

Eden gave such poor counsel. Moreover, since John the Revelator equated the dragon of Revelation with our old adversary, Satan, any religion based on reptilian entities might be extremely dangerous."

Conclusion: The Problems with Coppens' View

We have pointed out, Coppens proposed two methods for connecting with non-human Intelligences. Logically these methods are incompatible. Since shamans learned to connect with aliens via drugs, why build the pyramids? Building those amazing geometric temples was a lot of work to go to, if a special brew from the local medicine man could produce the same effect—connecting humans with alien deities. It stands to reason that stirring a cauldron is much more efficient than quarrying and moving at least one million 2-ton to 50-ton stones to erect a pyramid. If creating an plant concoction and merely imbibing a foul tasting substance like ayahuasca could send you higher than say, a great pyramid is tall (enabling you to reach the stars no less), the pyramids must have had a better reason to exist—a bigger reason for being there—than just contacting ET.

The evidence is certain that many smart (but maybe not so wise) individuals agreed psychotropic drugs provide vivid and life-changing experiences. Their consensus assures us such encounters produce uncommon knowledge. Specifically, all interpret their inner visions as a means to meet the gods. Supplementing the late Messrs. Philip Coppens and Terrence McKenna, we can add the colorful stories of Graham Hancock and author Daniel Pinchbeck[12]. Going back further in time, we could adduce Aldus Huxley of *Brave New World;* Dr. Timothy Leary, who helped father the counter-culture of the 1960s; even Jim Morrison of *The Doors* who chimed in concerning the use of drugs to contact "the other side." There is no doubt something happens when you drop acid or drink ayahuasca. But what?

---

[12] Pinchbeck's *Breaking Open the Head* (2002) and *2012: The Return of Quetzalcoatl* (2006) provide additional confirming experiences in our present day.

Is a "magic bus" the best way to transport humanity to the gods or to bring down the gods to us? Or is that too risky to get you where you are going? Witnesses line up on both sides of the issue. Certainly any form of "mysticism"—of directly connecting with the divine—begets controversy. And yet, there are virtually no orthodox teachers of Christianity who would argue in favor of a drug-induced means to encounter God. Traditional Christian teaching warns us against contacting God within our "inner space." Even the Lord's Prayer begins by asserting that God is a being outside of ourselves: "Our Father Who Art in Heaven." Christianity teaches that God comes to live within the believer when they invite Jesus Christ to come into his or her heart, into their inner being. The Holy Spirit is that person within the Godhead who achieves that connection with our spirit. However, only Gnosticism and numerous cults derived from that ancient point of view (*Thelema* discussed in the prior chapter is a prime example), assert *we are God* and that God and humanity are one and the same. In the final analysis, Philip Coppens argued the same view as Crowley and Grant. He might not have suggested we seek the evil god *Set*—Coppens would have seen either *Atum* (the head divinity of the Egyptian Ennead) or *Horus* (the son of Osiris) as a better fit. Conceptually, however, all of these Egyptian deities remain categorically distinct from the Judeo-Christian conception of God.

Coming back to the Ancient Aliens issue, a few questions persist: "Are UFOs really *not* "nuts and bolts"? Are there no physical attributes to flying saucers? Why do thousands see them every year? When alien abduction victims disappear from their bedrooms, where do they go? Why are there physical "implants" in some abduction victims? Why do the rooms and beds of victims give off detectable radiation? The idea of Aliens "within" arguably tidies up some things, but unfortunately, there are too many physical factors left out. Coppens correctly underscored that contact with ET constitutes a key aspect of Ancient Alien Theory. In the final analysis, however, his thesis is self-contradictory, avoids crucial circumstantial issues, neglects most empirical facts, and dismisses key physical characteristics.

The Children of Prometheus

The Persistent Myth of Our Link with Mars

A
S WE HAVE DEMONSTRATED THROUGHOUT THIS BOOK, HUMAN-
ITY IS INFATUATED WITH THE IDEA THAT OUR PAST LINKS WITH
AN OTHERWORLDLY CIVILIZATION—PERHAPS EVEN ON MARS.

A mountain of material avails itself to any author who wishes to examine the unofficial "credo" that before we were Earthlings, we were Martians. As with most topics, writing a book requires carefully selecting source material. With a subject as vast as this one is, it becomes even harder to make good choices. For the "truth is not only out there," it is all over the place.

Figure 90 - The 1953 TV Series
Tom Corbett Space Cadet

The truth is, we seem relentless in pursuit of this mythos. It finds its way into the most seemingly out of the way places, the most peculiarly stated hypotheses, the farthest far-fetched myths, even the most outrageous stories. The belief persists that humanity hails from another time and another place. That does not necessarily prove the notion to be true. It infers, however, the concept exists as an archetype of human consciousness that continues to bubble to the surface in odd, far flung places. Why does this archetype exist if it is entirely a figment of our subconscious? Why are there so many proponents, many of them highly sophisticated, if there is nothing to it?

Nick Redfern makes this point for me by citing a 1950s TV show which illustrates the Egypt-Martian connection. *Tom Corbett Space Cadet* was based on Robert Heinlein's 1948 novel *Space Cadet* and Joseph Greene's *Tom Ranger and the Space Cadets.* Of particular interest was the Tom Corbett 3D View-Master Photoshow telling three stories: *The Moon Pyramid, The Red Planet,* and *The Mystery of the Asteroid.* Redfern describes the interplanetary plotline:

> While at work on one particular asteroid, the miner stumbles upon what looks like some sort of archeological relic. Pyramid-like in shape, and coated in hieroglyphics that resemble the work of the Egyptians, an ancient artifact is exactly what has been found. Speculation abounds that the Asteroid Belt is the remains of a world home to intelligent aliens that once existed between Mars and Jupiter, a theory not at all unlike the exploding planet theory of Tom Van Flandern, as noted by Mac Tonnies [and Joseph P. Farrell].
>
> From the dark depths of the Asteroid Belt, the Tom Corbett story then takes us to our very own Moon, where a similar pyramid-type structure has been found. But it's more than just that. When placed together, the two creations comprise a singular object that allows for a holographic viewing of Mars and that reveals some astounding image on the surface of the Red Planet. Anxious to capitalize on this astounding discovery, a team of astronauts heads to Mars, where the find nothing less than a massive, 1,000-fott high pyramid, a number of obelisks, and even a small, carved face displaying feline attributes. A closer comparison to what was uncovered by Face on Mars researchers, decades later, one would be extremely hard-pressed to ever find.[1]

Redfern informs us that Willy Ley was a consultant to this series. Ley was the German rocket scientist who, in 1957, published a book that greatly influenced the U.S. space program: *Rockets, Missiles, and Space Travel.* How did Ley get to the U.S.? Ley took a vacation to London in 1935 and fled to the United States, where after the war, he eventually joined up with Wernher von Braun. Ley authored many books on astronomy and space travel. Additionally, Ley teamed with von Braun and Disney on the Tomorrowland adventure,

---

[1] Redfern, *The Pyramids and the Pentagon*, op. cit., p. 158.

Mars and Beyond. Clearly, Wernher was not the only German rocket scientist who showed an interest in traveling to Mars. Willy was right there with him.

As the collection of book covers below illustrates, the Egypt-Mars connection was a favorite of other authors too. Otto Binder (using a pseudonym, Eando Binder), wrote a 1971 science fiction novel, *Puzzle of the Space Pyramids.* Binder wrote about such subjects because he too was fascinated by the idea that intelligent life could be found beyond our world. Redfern affirms that Binder believed in UFOs. In Binder's vision, the pyramids on Mars were gravity generators that could manipulate space and time. He also wrote a 1976 book with Max Flindt, entitled *Mankind Child of the Stars* with a foreword penned by no less an Ancient Alien hunter than Erich Von Däniken.

Figure 91 - Pyramids in Other Places

Redfern points out that Willy Ley also supplied a foreword for another Binder work: *Victory in Space.* Obviously, these authors and scientists had an affinity for one another. Furthermore, as has been aptly demonstrated by the many facts brought forward in this book, the line that separates science and science fiction may be a very thin one. No question this line has been crossed many, many times.

Transforming Humanity into Gods

What would become of humanity if we believed our distant ancestors were not "Earthlings" but Martians—if suddenly we were told that once we were "star children" who came to Earth to realize a new and greater potential—to conquer a different world, a blue one as its surface was over 75% covered with water? What would we think if in the days ahead, visitors from another world appeared and demonstrated we shared a common genetic heritage? What if these humanoids—we will call them *Homo universalis* for want of a better name—showed how accepting a small bit of their DNA would solve our most difficult physiological and social issues? Might our government, even our religious leaders, entreat us to join the party with promises of greater health once we alter our physical attributes, our DNA, with the supposed advanced genetic material of the OTHERS? Why, they come in the name of evolution—to elevate us to the next phase of humanity. What if our leaders *demanded our compliance* for the good of society, to stamp out the inferior genetics of the "old" human race?

Of course, this vision comprises only one scenario of what could be in the offing for humanity in the last days. It stands out, however, as a possibility we should contemplate, even guard against to the extent that that is possible, since so many well-regarded eschatological writer/researchers propose it to be the most likely manner in which the "Mark of the Beast" (Revelation 13) will be made manifest.[2] But please note: this author chooses not to be dogmatic on this point, insisting this scenario will come to pass. Nor do I advocate that the Mark of the Beast necessarily requires some sort of genetic splice supplied by ET—perhaps constituting the DNA "fix" that will wean us away from war, eradicate disease, cure a future plague, or even offer immortality. And yet, while I do not assert this scenario constitutes how the Antichrist will reveal his "Mark," I confess, for the most

---

[2] These authors include Tom Horn, Steve Quayle, L.A. Marzulli, Douglas Hamp, and myself with the caveats I mention here.

part, I consider myself aligned with those who affirm that this ultimatum could await us. I judge it is at least a real possibility.

On the other hand, I contend without equivocation that Mars and the Ancient Alien debate are prelude to the *coming great deception*, a deception hundreds of years in the making, a deception already partially in place but especially threatening as we rush into the "singularity" engendered by massive, unrelenting change. The pace of knowledge acquisition is itself mind-boggling. Only the smartest among our race can begin to keep up with those changes, and then only if they specialize in well-bounded areas. Stephen Hawking says as much in his book, *An Illustrated Brief History of Time.* He goes on to state, "The rest of the population has little idea of the advances being made or the excitement they are generating."[3] Despite Hawking's confidence, caution best prevail over such optimism. For more is at stake than just advancing technological knowledge of human physiology, and implementing the so-called mind-machine interface. We are edging closer to irreversible decisions on engineered heredity. Ultimately, at stake is nothing less than our identity as humans—indeed, it is our human genome that stands to be contaminated by "fixes" whose implications remain impossible to foresee. The promise of *transhumanism* will not likely exceed the pitfalls. This is true whether engineered by human science or engrafted from extraterrestrial DNA. Dystopian rather than utopian outcomes could result demanding remedies beyond our ability to invent.

There are any number of possible "futures" that might transpire, likely predetermined by what we believe about our "past." Noted alternative historian (and conspiracy theorist) Jim Marrs in his recent book, *Our Occulted History,* argues an elite leadership exists in our world that knows the truth about Ancient Aliens. From his vantage point, the evidence compels him to believe these aliens have hostile intentions. Affirming the same premise implicit in Corso's *The Day*

---

[3] Cited by Marrs. Jim Marrs, *Our Occulted History: Do the Global Elite Conceal Ancient Aliens?* New York: HarperCollins. Kindle Edition, (2012), location 3626.

after Roswell, these ETs seek a planetary takeover. Marrs says, "There is another narrative growing in public consciousness, that can no longer be written off as mere fable: the idea that aliens from outer space or another dimension may have—or may be trying to— take control of the world." Marrs claims that history, our history, is "occulted" or hidden from us. The elite know the truth—but they keep it to themselves. "It would appear that something nonhuman seeks to control the planet Earth and may have even contributed to the advent of modern humankind."[4] Given our findings in this study, it seems noteworthy that Marrs begins his book's introduction with an extended quotation from Lovecraft's, *The Call of Cthulhu*. He also cites a lengthy passage from William Bramley's 1990 book, *The Gods of Eden* which more or less confirms the convictions of Ancient Alien theorist Zecharia Sitchin:

> [Bramley] said he began studying the causes of war but came to the conclusion that "Human beings appear to be a slave race languishing on an isolated planet in a small galaxy." He added that "the human race was once a source of labor for an extraterrestrial civilization and still remains a possession today. To keep control over its possession and to maintain Earth as something of a prison, that other civilization (Bramley called them Custodians) has bred never-ending conflict between human beings, has promoted human spiritual decay, and has erected on Earth conditions of unremitting physical hardship. This situation has lasted for thousands of years and it continues today." [5]

This extravagant theory of humanity's condition, its origin, and the reason for our "being born this way," hardly squares on all points with the biblical record. Nevertheless, it coincides in some regards: humanity is a slave to the landowner; Earth constitutes a prison for the commoner; most generally experience great hardship; we often serve the purposes of a kingdom of darkness; and our compromised condition has been ongoing nonstop for thousands of years.

---

[4] Marrs, Jim (2013-02-12). *Our Occulted History: Do the Global Elite Conceal Ancient Aliens?* New York: HarperCollins. Kindle Edition. Location 122.

[5] Ibid., Kindle Location 171.

To advance this line of thought in biblical motif: there is an alternative proposal from a much more trustworthy source. His method to redeem our property and to save us from endless slavery mandates we forsake today's landowner and renounce his rule. For when we originally sold our deed to the property in exchange for a mind-bending upgrade, the current landowner promised we would be "as the gods, knowing good and evil." Today, he still dangles a similar promise before us. If we will but follow his guidance, so he says, he will transform us into deities. In this respect, those who look to solutions from advances in genetic science (in the form of transhumanism) or ET (with his soon return), fail to detect the most sinister possibility that *the final planetary takeover may transpire when society goes "all in" to force transformation—a mandated DNA makeover for all.*

Prometheus—Making a Man out of Clay

Classical mythology proposed that a Titan, *Prometheus*, teamed with Aphrodite to take a lump of clay out of the riverbed and fashion Adam. Adam literally means "red clay" or "of the earth." The Greeks

Figure 92 - A Statue of the Classical God Prometheus

saw Prometheus as our creator and champion. According to their mythology, Prometheus gave "fire" to humanity which represented intelligence, but more precisely, the development of civilization.

291

From the Greek, the name Prometheus comprises two words—*pro* and *manthano*—literally meaning "before intelligence." Prometheus also symbolized, however, a god of "unintended consequences"—a tragic figure symbolizing humanity's questing for knowledge and striving to improve its circumstances.

The image of Prometheus has been employed in many different media to teach lessons about humanity, its origins, and its limits. Mary Shelly subtitled *Frankenstein*, "The Modern Prometheus"—and spun a tale forever forewarning us about the dangers of "overreaching." Goethe wrote his poem *Prometheus*, comparing his character Prometheus to the Son of God in the New Testament with Zeus as the New Testament Father, thus altering Prometheus from a Titan to an Olympian (by casting him as the son of Zeus). Fast-forward to modern day: in his 2012 movie prequel to the highly successful horror series of *Alien* films, Ridley Scott brought to the silver screen the mythos of an ET demi-god creating humanity through his movie *Prometheus*. What also stands out in Scott's film: the creator of humankind (*Alien* fans called him "the space jockey") awakens at the prompting of a descendant of his creation, a mechanical masterpiece—the human-looking android (played by Michael Fassbender), also created in the image of his maker. But the now alerted creator, the "Prometheus" of the human race, becomes the crew's nightmare. We learn that the financier of the outer space voyage has secreted himself away on the spaceship, seeking out "Prometheus" on this distant planet that he might learn the secret of eternal life and be made immortal. Instead, the creator dispatches the decrepit old man (from a Judeo-Christian perspective) to *where he will meet his real maker*.

With "Prometheus" awaking from aeons of sleep in "suspended animation" on a planet far, far away, we recall Lovecraft's Cthulhu, asleep in the darkest, deepest recesses of the ocean. Perhaps Kenneth Grant was right in this one respect—all "cults" are derived from one and the same story. Coincidentally, Scott's originator of humankind in the movie, "Prometheus," *happened to be a giant*.

Hollywood and the Remaking of Mankind

The barrage of alien movies continues unabated today. The movie *Cowboys and Aliens* (2011) by highly successful filmmaker Jon Favreau brought portions of Zecharia Sitchin's Sumerian "Anunnaki" myth to audiences. The aliens are here to mine gold to save their world. Only the combined efforts of mega movie stars Daniel Craig and Harrison Ford can thwart their interplanetary gold heist.

The *Transformers* franchise has continued to thrill audiences with some of cinema's best-ever special effects. The last chapter of the story, *Transformers: Dark of the Moon* (2011), links many of the ideas put forth by Mike Bara and Richard C. Hoagland to these "now-you-see-them, now-you-don't" mechanical wonders. Even the so-called "Secret Space Race" takes a bow with the less-successful-than-expected, *Apollo 18* (2011). Likewise, another franchise, *Star Trek* has been rebooted—again—with popular actors Chris Pine and Zachary Quinto in the roles of Kirk and Spock. The 2013 *Star Trek* film, *Into Darkness,* was a huge success demonstrating that audiences have not lost interest in achieving all-out victory in space. Humanity rules—Klingons beware.

We could go on. Movie after movie propogate aliens, flying saucers, good extraterrestrials, bad extraterrestrials, and humankind's destiny in space. As a culture, we could hardly be more smitten. Indeed, the impact of film on the human psyche goes beyond these explicitly "spaced-out" stories. The superhero genre almost always includes extraterrestrials in the plot. We certainly recall Superman battling his father's archenemies from Krypton, Zod and Company.

Given that this constant bombardment surrounds us, do we suppose our Children are immune to the dreams implanted in their minds by these most awesome tales? After all, what child doesn't want to run faster than a speeding bullet? Or be able to leap tall buildings in a single bound? Surely you get the idea. The *transformation of humanity into gods* is something that we live, sleep, and breathe in pop culture. Soon not one, but two generations will have grown up

293

believing in the viability of various ET scenarios and the desirability of becoming gods.

Now, taking a step back: I judge the most likely reason for the reader to reject the thesis of this book would be to assume that we simply have our minds on other more mundane matters. However, this conjectured counter-point falls short of a bona fide challenge given the prowess of the unrelenting, overwhelming message of movies, television, and a few Ancient Alien "fact books" thrown in "to set the record straight." Furthermore, assuming that someday the mainstream media will pick up on the story (when the plutocrats give the signal), we will be inundated with the idea our destiny does reside "in the stars." We will no longer be restrained and earthbound. We will soar to new heights—the sky will no longer be the limit. With that outcome, reshaping the collective mind will then be complete. No longer will ET need to set the mother ship on the White House lawn to impress. All we will require to set a celestial destination will be little more than a nudge. Should we stumble upon an artifact or two demonstrably evincing ET (the implications of the discovery will be drawn out to prove Ancient Alien theory), we surely will be more than captivated, we will be permanently marooned in the alien mythos.

But will that occur? Will alien archeology (aliens long gone) send civilization off in a new direction? Or will an intervening incident alter what appears to be the inevitable galactic fate of humanity? In any event, it appears that the old worldview of the common man and woman stands ready to be forever altered by a supramundane occurrence.

Disclosure—Will It Ever Happen?

Finally, we come to the matter of UFO disclosure. UFO researchers (and Ancient Alien theorists) ask earnestly: "Will the governments of the world, most notably, the United States of America, ever admit that ET exists—that we have incontrovertible proof, and that (possibly) we already have a pact with alien beings?"

Richard M. Dolan and Bryce Zabel, in their 2012 book, *AD: After Disclosure,* describe the world AFTER the government tells us the truth about extraterrestrials. As is customary, the publisher provided numerous approbations to market the book. The contributors comprise a *Who's Who* in the UFO world. Jim Marrs (who also wrote the foreword), Nick Pope (the former Director of the U.K.'s research into UFOs), Stanton Friedman (perhaps the most scientifically competent and well-spoken advocate for telling the truth about ET), and Stephen Bassett (the most highly respected activist for disclosure), all shower praise on Dolan and Zabel's book, *A.D.*

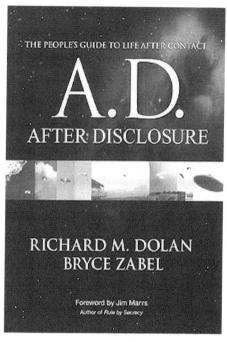

Figure 93 – A. D. After Disclosure

Friedman comments, "Considering the overwhelming evidence that Earth is being visited by alien spacecraft and that many intelligence agencies and military groups have known this to be true for some time, we certainly need to consider the serious question of what happens when Disclosure actually occurs." Likewise, Stephen Bassett shares a similar conviction: "Disclosure, the formal acknowledgment by the world's governments of an extraterrestrial presence engaging the human race, is inevitable. So was this how-to book on what to do when a new world begins."

Just recently, Bassett achieved a true high-water mark for the whole topic of UFOs and government secrecy when he gathered all the experts together for five days of public testimony in early spring, 2013. *The Citizen's Hearing on Disclosure* obtained a level of credibility for the topic that surpassed anything before its conduct.

From the official website, we read this summary of the event:

> From April 29 to May 3, 2013 researchers, activists, and military/agency/political witnesses representing ten countries gave testimony in Washington, DC to six former members of the United States Congress about events and evidence indicating an extraterrestrial presence engaging the human race.

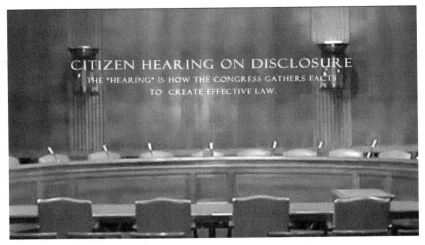

Figure 94 - The Citizen Hearing on Disclosure, 2013

> The Citizen Hearing on Disclosure was an unprecedented event in terms of size, scope and the involvement of former members of the U.S. Congress. With over 30 hours of testimony from 40 witnesses over five days. The event was the most concentrated body of evidence regarding the extraterrestrial subject ever presented to the press and the general public at one time.[6]

And yet, despite the noteworthy progress made by Bassett and Company, this author remains skeptical that the subject of DIS-CLOSURE will be broached by the U.S. government anytime soon. As we saw with NASA, when our leaders evaluate the pros and the cons of earthshaking announcements they move at a snail's pace. Admitting intelligent life exists beyond our world becomes something of a "business decision." Is there more to be gained or to be lost by announcing ET to the Planet? Will higher-up government

---

[6] See http://www.citizenhearing.org/.

officials follow the lead of NASA Scientists and avoid declaring for or against the reality of UFOs? We have assumed these scientists suspend judgment publicly for self-serving reasons. Maybe it has been a ploy to keep the dollars flowing from Congress. Maybe the majority remain silent for career reasons. Then again, perhaps their rationale rests only in holding the majority view to present a conservative demeanor. Who can say? But political leaders will be no less "political" in determining what to say and when to say it. Of that fact, we can be highly confident.

Several governments in our hemisphere (e.g., Mexico and Brazil to name two), seem eager to disclose what they know. In contrast, just a few years ago our British friends took a passive approach when they released their UFO files to the public without any definitive conclusion. Their action amounted to a calculated decision that whatever the UFO phenomenon was, it no longer merited national funding and dedicated resources. ET was no longer a threat. Still, the U.S. government holds its peace. Will this ever change?

Perhaps a key principle of our government, the separation of Church and State, weighs on the minds of certain leaders. Maybe confirming the existence of aliens so threatens religious views and our societal self-image, our leaders suppose it is "not for them to say" whether ET should be "outed." Regardless of the conviction belonging to most UFOlogists (that is, that our government knows far more than it chooses to tell us), our leadership's reluctance to inform the public may only be fueled by a failure to know enough details concerning ET's status. Would our leaders want to broadcast what it knows about ET when it still does not know enough to assure the population that aliens constitute nothing of a threat? After all, it is normal human behavior to avoid a subject about which you know too little. In the government's defense, if it cannot claim to have "all the answers," better not to raise the subject at all. Otherwise it would invite public ridicule for failing to have mastered the details. It might only encourage anger and even panic if *Disclosure* occurs and the citizenry determines its leaders performed incompetently in the face of this potential danger. We know it is one thing to be caught off-guard. It is quite another to perform inadequate "due diligence."

On the other hand, if Jim Marrs is right and the elite of the world wish to continue holding all the cards, disclosing the truth about aliens (or at least *what they believe is true* about ET), represents information threatening the status quo. What will the long-term effects be of disclosure? Dolan and Zabel try to answer this question, but the reality is that the effects could be anybody's guess. Francis Bacon said, "Knowledge is power." Therefore, telling the truth might be seen as weakness—it could be judged that the elite were forced to spill the beans. Egos at the top would never acquiesce to such plebian pressure.

Conclusion: Disclosure Bit-by-bit

In the final analysis, disclosure seems to be happening, slowly, methodically, without fanfare. Step-by-step, an awareness of alien existence, perhaps by the release of information about artifacts on Mars, will suggest that intelligent life does exist elsewhere because we have proven it existed in the past on another world. Artifacts uncovered 200 million miles from home, dated from a million years ago are a lot less threatening than ET in your face at the front door.

Stephen Bassett, in an interview conducted by L.A. Marzulli included in Marzulli's video (DVD) *Watchers 7*, supposes that disclosure is bound to happen very soon. Once it does, Bassett concludes all that we will hear about 7 by 24, will be ET. Our media will be consumed with the subject. It will change everything.

To my way of thinking, however, that sort of "shock and awe" encompasses the strongest reason why it will not happen with a mighty splash. Disclosure will not be all at once. Too much change implies a disruption of public politics, social institutions of all kinds, and most especially, the economy. The elite may be many things, but they are not stupid. They have vested interests to protect. Making money remains their number one priority.

Differing with the views espoused by many conspiracy theorists and certain eschatological experts, I do not believe that the hidden leadership of the world seeks chaos so that martial law can be invoked. This implies that, at present, the elite lack sufficient control over the affairs of society. But is that really what they believe? Granted, avarice assumes "one can never have enough." But how much control is enough control? No doubt our civil leadership sees to it that the government stands ready to deal with all sorts of catastrophes that could undoubtedly disrupt the normal ebb and flow of life. That does not mean, however, they are actively engineering chaos. The transition they seek, if I may speculate unreservedly for a moment, seems much more likely to be a peaceful transition. Why seek to gain greater control by compromising the control you already have? Inviting chaos is a risky game in which no one, not even the most capable of leaders, can guarantee the outcome.

There is little doubt that the U.S. government has been whittling away at our national sovereignty in order to advance global governance. The U.S. led the League of Nations initiative. The U.S. funded the creation of the United Nations. The U.S. is the catalyst to bring about a functional (but not necessarily "official") one-world system. As this author has argued (with co-authors Douglas W. Krieger and Dene McGriff) in *The Final Babylon*, the United States has become the Babylon of the last days. Our policies are the de facto agenda for most of the world. Even China no longer lurks on the sidelines. By encouraging China's investment in the U.S.A., we have effectively made China complicit in our global program. By encouraging its financial bets be placed here, China has been co-opted. Why would China want the U.S. to default on its China-financed loans? It stands to lose too much. The remaining outliers like Cuba and North Korea are little more than a nuisance. Defeating ideology is not worth crashing the world economy. The only remaining obstacle is the Middle East. Once defused, no more big political bombs exist. Indeed, global leadership intends that wars occur only as a matter of choice and not of necessity, primarily to assure that the world

economy stays in good working order and the rich continue to ac-
cumulate wealth. Any debate about whether this transfer of power
endures today remains an unresolved discussion only for the unin-
formed, those so mired in daily affairs they are unable to raise their
heads to look about, or those intentionally oblivious to reality.
Those are the hard cold facts about the world we live in.

The subject of origins, the acknowledgement of the truth, the possibility that the masters of the human species may return to Earth (or
the disclosure that they have been among us already), is clearly not
the priority of human governments, especially the most powerful
government in the world. Wanting to know where we come from remains a preoccupation of those *not* in power. It constitutes no more
than a "people's imperative." We should not expect any favors from
those who, at the highest level, reign over us. Whether we are talking
about the U.S. government or the so-called shadow government that
exists behind it, such information is available only on a "need to
know" basis—and in their judgment, we do not need to know.

In conclusion, the truth we require remains a truth that does not
come from any human government. Our real hope lies elsewhere.
As Christianity has maintained for 3,000 years, we are not citizens of
this world but of another altogether. We are only passing through.
The faithful are like Abraham the father of all monotheistic faiths.
*"For he looked for a city which hath foundations, whose builder and
maker is God."* (Hebrews 11:10) To look for an origin or destination
on any world other than the place which Christ has prepared for us
stands as the greatest deception to which we can fall prey.

Jesus comforts His disciples with these eternal words: *"Let not
your heart be troubled: ye believe in God, believe also in me. In my
Father's house are many mansions: if it were not so, I would have
told you. I go to prepare a place for you. And if I go and prepare a
place for you, I will come again, and receive you unto myself; that
where I am, there ye may be also."* (John 14:1-3)

Even so, come Lord Jesus!

300

Bibliography

Alec, Wendy. *A Pale Horse*. Dublin, Ireland: Warboys Publishing, 2012.

Bara, Michael. *Ancient Aliens on the Moon*. Kempton, IL: Adventures Unlimited, 2012. Print.

Bara, Michael. *Ancient Aliens on Mars*. Kempton, IL: Adventures Unlimited, 2013. Print.

Bauval, Robert and Gilbert, Adrian, *The Orion Mystery: Unlocking the Secrets of the Pyramids,* New York, Three Rivers Press, 1994, 325 pages.

Bosley, Walter. *Lattitude 33: Key to the Kingdom*. 2nd ed. Highland, CA: Corvos Books, 2011. Print.

Braden, Russell, Pinchbeck, Jenkins, et al., *The Mystery of 2012*, Sounds True, Boulder, CO., 2009, 465 pages.

Brandenburg, John. *Life and Death on Mars: The New Mars Synthesis*. Kempton, IL: Adventures Unlimited Press, 2011. Print.

Burroughs, Edgar Rice. *The Warlord of Mars*. Charlottesville, Va.: University of Virginia Library, 1993. Print.

Butler, Alan and Dafoe, Stephen, *The Knights Templar Revealed*, Barnes & Noble, New York 1999, 233 pages.

Carey, Thomas J., Donald R. Schmitt, and Tracy Torme. *Inside the Real Area 51: The Secret History of Wright-Patterson*. Pompton Plains, NJ: New Page Books, 2013. Print.

Colavito, Jason. *The Cult of Alien Gods: H.P. Lovecraft and Extraterrestrial Pop Culture*. Amherst, N.Y.: Prometheus Books, 2005. Print.

Colavito, Jason. *Faking History: Essays on Aliens, Atlantis, Monsters, and More*. Albany, N.Y.: Jason Colavito.com. Books, 2013. Print.

Collins, Andrew, *Beneath the Pyramids: Egypt's Greatest Secret Uncovered*, Virginia Beach, VA, A.R.E. Press, 2009, 262 Pages.

Coppens, Philip. *The Ancient Alien Question*: A New Inquiry Into the Existence, Evidence, and Influence of Ancient Visitors, Pompton Plains, NJ: New Page Books, 2012. 321 pages.

Coppens, Philip. *The Lost Civilization Enigma: A New Inquiry into the Existence of Ancient Cities, Cultures, and Peoples Who Pre-date Recorded History*. Pompton Plains, NJ: New Page Books, 2013. Print.

Corso, Philip J., and William J. Birnes. *The Day After Roswell.* New York: Pocket Books, 1997. Print.

Crossley, Robert. *Imagining Mars: A Literary History.* Middletown, Conn.: Wesleyan Univ. Press, 2010. Print.

Dolan, Richard M., *UFOs and the National Security State: The Cover-Up Exposed, 1973-1981,* Rochester, NY: Keyhole Publishing Company, 2009, *781 pages.*

Dolan, Richard M., and Zabel, Bryce, *A.D. After Disclosure: When the Government Finally Reveals the Truth about Alien Contact,* Pompton Plains, NJ: New Page Books, 2012, 327 pages.

DiGregorio, Barry E.. *The Microbes of Mars.* Middleport, NY: Barry E. Di-Gregorio, 2010. Print.

Farrell, Joseph P., *The SS Brotherhood of the Bell: The Nazis' Incredible Secret Technology,* Kempton, IL, 2006, 459 pages.

Farrell, Joseph P., *Genes, Giants, Monsters and Men: The Surviving Elites of the Cosmic War and their Hidden Agenda,* Port Townsend, WA., Feral House, 2011, 239 pages.

Farrell, Joseph P., *The Philosophers' Stone: Alchemy and the Secret Research for Exotic Matter, Port Townsend,* WA., Feral House, 2009, 350 pages.

Farrell, Joseph P. *The Cosmic War: Interplanetary Warfare, Modern Physics, and Ancient Texts : a Study in Non-Catastrophist Interpretations of Ancient Legends.* Kempton, IL: Adventures Unlimited Press, 2007. Print.

Farrell, Joseph P. *Covert Wars and the Clash of Civilizations.* Kempton, IL: Adventures Unlimited, 2012. Print.

Farrell, Joseph P., and Scott D. Hart. *Grid of the Gods: The Aftermath of the Cosmic War and the Physics of the Pyramid Peoples.* Kempton, IL: Adventures Unlimited Press, 2011. Print.

Farrell, Joseph P. *Covert Wars and Breakaway Civilizations: The Secret Space Program,* Celestial Psyops and Hidden Conflicts. Kempton, IL: Adventures Unlimited, 2012. Print.

Flowers, Stephen E. and Michael Moynihan. *The Secret King: The Myth and Reality of Nazi Occultism.* Waterbury Center, VT: Dominion Press, 2007. Print.

Flynn, David E., *Cydonia: The Secret Chronicles of Mars.* Bozeman, MT: End Time Thunder, 2002. Print.

Flynn, David, *Temple at the Center of Time: Newton's Bible Codex Deciphered and the Year 2012,* Official Disclosure, A Division of Anomalous Publishing House, (Crane, Mo.), 2008, 296 pages.

Hale, Christopher, *Himmler's Crusade,* Edison, NJ, Castle Books, 2006, 422 pages.

Hamp, Douglas, *Corrupting the Image: Angels, Aliens, and the Antichrist Revealed,* Crane, MO., Defender Books, 348 pages.

Hancock, Graham, *Supernatural: Meetings with the Ancient Teachers of Mankind,* New York, The Disinformation Company, 2007, 468 pages.

Hancock, Graham and Bauval, Robert, *The Master Game: Unmasking the Secret Rulers of the World,* The Disinformation Company, 2007, 636 pages.

Hoagland, Richard C. and Bara, Mike, *Dark Mission: The Secret History of NASA,* Feral House, Port Townsend, WA., 2009, 616 pages.

Heron, Patrick, *The Nephilim and the Pyramid of the Apocalypse,* Citadel Press, Kensington Publishing, New York, 2004, 241 pages.

Horn, Thomas R., *Nephilim Stargates: The Year 2012 and the Return of the Watchers,* Anomalous Publishing House, (Crane, MO.), 2007, 232 pages.

Horn, Thomas R, *Apollyon Rising: 2012,* Anomalous Publishing, Crane, MO., 2009, 352 pages.

Horn, Dr. Thomas, Editor, *Pandemonium's Engine, Satan's Imminent and Final Assault on the Creation of God,* Defender Books, Crane, MO., 2011, 372 pages.

Howarth, Stephen, *The Knights Templar,* Barnes & Noble, New York, 1982, 321 pages.

Jacobs, David Michael. *The Threat.* New York, NY: Simon & Schuster, 1998. Print.

Jenkins, John Major, *Maya Cosmogenesis 2012,* Bear & Company Publishing, Rochester, Vermont, 1998, 425 pages.

Joseph, Frank, *Atlantis and 2012,* Rochester, VT., Bear & Company Books, 2010, 246 pages.

Jung, C.G., *Flying Saucers: A Modern Myth of Things Seen in the Skies,* MJF Books, New York, 1978, 138 pages.

Knight, Christopher, and Butler, Alan, *Before the Pyramids: Cracking Archeology's Greatest Mystery*, Watkins Publishing, London, 2009, 271 pages.

Kreisberg, Glenn, Editor, *Lost Knowledge of the Ancients: A Graham Hancock Reader*, Bear and Company, Rochester, Vermont, 2010, 241 pages.

Lawrence, Joseph E., *Apocalypse 2012: An Investigation into Civilization's End*, Broadway Books (New York), 2007, 2008, 262 pages.

Levenda, Peter. *The Dark Lord: H.P. Lovecraft, Kenneth Grant and the Typhonian Tradition in Magic.* Lake Worth, FL: Ibis Press, 2013. Print.

Levenda, Peter, *Sinister Forces: A Grimoire of American Political Witchcraft, Book One: The Nine,* Walterville, OR., Trineday, 2005, 371 pages.

Lovecraft, H.P. *H.P. Lovecraft, The Complete Collection.* Springfield Gardens, NY: Palmera Publishing, 2012. Print.

Marrs, Jim, *Rule by Secrecy,* Harper Collins, New York, 2000, 467 pages.

Marrs, Jim, *PSI Spies: The True Story of America's Psychic Warfare Program,* New Page Books, Franklin Lakes, NJ., 2007, 319 pages.

Marrs, Jim *The Rise of the Fourth Reich: The Secret Societies that Threaten to Take Over America,* HarperCollins Publishers, New York, 2008, 435 pages.

Marrs, Jim. *Our Occulted History: Do the Global Elite Conceal Ancient Aliens?* New York: William Morrow, 2013. Print.

Marzulli, L.A., *Politics, Prophecy, and the Supernatural: The Coming Great Deception and the Luciferian Endgame,* Anomalous Publishing, Crane, Mo., 2007, 248 pages.

Marzulli, L.A *The Cosmic Chess Match*, Malibu, CA., Spiral of Life, 2011, 336 pages.

Marzulli, L.A. *On the Trail of the Nephilim.* Malibu, CA. Spiral of Life Publishing, 2013.

Nietzsche, Friedrich, *The Antichrist: A Criticism of Christianity*, New York, Barnes and Noble Publishing, 2006, Originally Published in 1896, 77 pages.

Nietzsche, Friedrich *Thus Spoke Zarathustra*, Barnes and Nobles Classics, New York, NY., 2005 (First published in 1883), 315 pages.

Newton, Sir Isaac, *Revised History of Ancient Kingdoms: A Complete Chronology,* Larry and Marion Pierce, Editors, Master Books, Green Forest, AR., Revised Edition, 2009, 205 pages.

Pauwels, Louis and Bergier, Jacques, *The Morning of the Magicians: Secret Societies, Conspiracies, and Vanished Civilizations*, Destiny Books, Rochester, Vermont, 1960, 414 pages.

Picknett, Lynn and Prince, Clive, *The Stargate Conspiracy: Revealing the Truth behind Extraterrestrial Contact, Military Intelligence and the Mysteries of Ancient Egypt*, Berkley Books, New York, 1999, 425 pages.

Pinchbeck, Daniel, *2012: The Return of Quetzalcoatl*, New York, Penguin Group, 2007, 411 pages.

Pinchbeck, Daniel *Breaking Open the Head: A Psychedelic Journey into the Heart of Contemporary Shamanism*, Broadway Books, New York, 2002, 322 pages.

Pyle, Rod. *Destination Mars: New Explorations of the Red Planet.* Amherst, N.Y.: Prometheus Books, 2012. Print.

Quayle, Stephen. *True Legends: Tales of Giants and the Plumed Serpents.* Bozeman, MT: End Time Thunder, 2013. Print.

Quayle, Stephen. *Genesis 6 Giants: The Master Builders of the Prehistoric and Ancient Civilizations.* Bozeman, MT: End Time Thunder Publishers, 2002. Print.

Quayle, Stephen. *Angel Wars.* Bozeman, MT: End Time Thunder Publishers, 2011. Print.

Ravenscroft, Trevor, *The Spear of Destiny*, Samuel Weiser Inc., York Beach, Maine, 1st American Edition, 1973, 362 pages.

Redfern, Nick, *The NASA Conspiracies: The Truth Behind the Moon Landings, Censored Photos, and the Face on Mars,* New Page Books, Pompton Plains, NJ., 2011, 237 pages.

Redfern, Nicholas. *Final Events and the Government Group on Demonic UFOs and the Afterlife.* San Antonio: Anomalist Books, 2010. Print.

Redfern, Nicholas. *The Pyramids and the Pentagon: the Government's Top Secret Pursuit of Mystical Relics, Ancient Astronauts, and Lost Civilizations.* Pompton Plains, NJ: New Page Books, 2012. Print.

Roland, Paul. *The Nazis and The Occult: The Dark Forces Unleashed By the Third Reich.* Edison, N.J.: Chartwell Books, 2007. Print.

Sagan, Carl. *Cosmos.* Ballantine Books, December 10, 2013. Print.

Schoch, Robert M., *Forgotten Civilization: The Role of Solar Outbursts in Our Past and Future.* Rochester, VT: Inner Traditions, 2012. Print.

Sellers, Michael D., *John Carter and the Gods of Hollywood: The True Story of What Went Wrong With Disney's John Carter and Why Edgar Rice Burroughs' Original Superhero Isn't Dead Yet*. Los Angeles, Calif.: Universal Media, 2012. Print.

Sheehan, William, and Stephen James Meara. *Mars: The Lure of the Red Planet*. Amherst, N.Y.: Prometheus Books, 2001. Print.

Stevens, Henry, *Dark Star: The Hidden History of German Secret Bases, Flying Disks and U-Boats,* Adventures Unlimited, Kempton, IL. 366 pages.

Thomas, I.D.E., *The Omega Conspiracy: Satan's Last Assault on God's Kingdom,* Anomalous Publishing, Crane, MO., 2008, 195 pages.

von Däniken, Erich, *Chariots of the Gods,* Berkeley Books (Penguin Putnam), New York, 1999, 200 pages.

Wilcock, David, *The Source Field Investigations: The Hidden Science and Lost Civilizations behind the 2012 Prophecies,* Dutton / Penguin Group, New York, 2011, 536 pages.

Woodward, S. Douglas, *Decoding Doomsday: The 2012 Prophecies, the Apocalypse and the Perilous Days Ahead,* Crane, Mo., 2010, 380 pages.

Woodward, S. Douglas. *Power Quest--Book One: America's Obsession with the Paranormal*. Woodinville, WA: Faith Happens, 2011. Print.

Woodward, S. Douglas. *Power Quest—Book Two: The Ascendancy of Antichrist in America*. Woodinville, WA: Faith Happens, 2012. Print.

About the Author

S. Douglas Woodward is the author six other books including *Power Quest*, Books One and Two, as well as co-authoring *The Final Babylon* with co-writers Douglas W. Krieger and Dene McGriff. Over the past five years, he has appeared frequently on radio and television shows, and speaks at major seminars and conferences on the topics of eschatology, alternative history, and the intersection of science and theology.

For many years, Mr. Woodward served as executive for Microsoft, Oracle, Honeywell, and Burroughs (Unisys). He was also a Partner-in-Charge of a Microsoft Center of Excellence on behalf of Ernst & Young LLP. For the past fourteen years, he has managed his own consultancy focused on start-up companies, venture finance, and operational management of several high-growth, high-impact emerging companies in software technology, new media, distanced learning, and the Internet. During this period, he also took on numerous roles as CEO, CFO, and President/COO of several high tech and medical device companies.

Mr. Woodward has been married to wife Donna for 38 years, has two adult children, and now lives in Oklahoma City, after previously working in Seattle and Boston for over 27 years. Throughout his professional life, he has studied and taught on theological and biblical topics. He has served as Elder on the Consistory of the Reformed Church and Board of the Presbyterian Church. Early in his career, he served as Youth Minister and Associate Pastor in the Reformed and United Methodist Churches.

"Woodward provides a serenade of stories that spellbinds the reader."
Author, Douglas Hamp, *Corrupting the Image*

POWER QUEST

BOOK ONE:
AMERICA'S OBSESSION WITH THE PARANORMAL

WITH A FOREWORD BY GARY STEARMAN

S. Douglas Woodward

Newly Revised for eBook Formats

POWER QUEST, BOOK ONE

Now in eBook Format. See Kindle, iBook, Lulu and Barnes and Noble.

POWER QUEST, BOOK TWO

Now in eBook Format. See Kindle, iBook, Lulu and Barnes and Noble.

Made in the USA
San Bernardino, CA
18 January 2014